Michel Desma

THIAOOUBA PROPHECY: THE GOLDEN PLANET

Formerly Known as "Abduction to the 9th Planet"

A true report by the Author who was PHYSICALLY
ABDUCTED
to another planet

Believing is not enough...
You need to KNOW

Publisher: Arafura Publishing 1993

Translated from French manuscript (now lost) by Kay Smith

Report from the journey undertaken in June 1987
Manuscript completed in January 1989
Postscript written in April 1993

Previous editions:
"Abduction to the 9th Planet" 1993, paperback ISBN 0-646-15996-8
Reprinted 1993,1994,1999 (Australia), 1995 (USA)

Author's Note:
The original title of this book is "Abduction to the 9th Planet."

Foreword

There are ways of receiving information from a higher level of consciousness and therewith knowledge about the laws of all existence and the way we would live a better and easier life: through intuition, through astral travelling, and through actual physical experience.

Michel Desmarquet was chosen to do the latter, and that in connection with a mission of the people of a planet of a higher, more advanced and enlightened existence, to bring to us messages and knowledge so much needed at this critical stage of development on our planet in order to construct a bridge to the next higher step in our ladder of evolution.

As it appears, Michel had been taken to a planet, spiritually and technologically so far advanced that is in a position to take on the role of a mentor for those planets still on a lower evolutionary stage in this galaxy, a role that is naturally foreseen for a more advanced planet in the hierarchy of our universe.

It is important to realise that Michel has confirmed what we have always known, and what we have recognised as our unique Free Will to reflect upon situations, assess them and make decisions for the way we want to act.

It is still up to our Free Will whether we ignore the tidings brought to us and cling to the self-made concept that man is different from nature and can afford to live outside of it or to use our mental and emotional capabilities to reach the insight of our Free Will is nothing but the limitations to think, feel and act within the realms of the laws of this nature as these apply to every other, non-human system.

After having read Michel's report of his journey, four conditions have become very apparent to me:

1.   Everywhere in this universe (the galaxy) there exists a material/physical world.

2.   Likewise there exists everywhere a non-material/non-physical world, that is the one to which we have given the name spiritual world;

3.   Both worlds are only the two antipodes of form-manifestations which make the entire universe, that is all existence possible: namely

energy;

4.   It is the understanding and subsequent mastery of the behaviour of this energy – the so-called metaphysical laws which enable us to come to terms with and to the proper handling of the physical world – not vice-versa.

Michel Desmarquet's book is not only a straight forward report of his awesome experiences, but also the many doubts he (and others of us) expresses as he goes through a world so paradisiacally different from ours and yet so familiar to us, for intuitively we feel and know that the real difference between them lies only in the maturity applied to handle the abundance the universe provides for us.

The "proof" for the truth of Michel's report does not lie in the "forgotten" pieces of metal or "not taken" photographs of what he has seen: it lies in the *common sense* that his news expresses and the verifiability of the principles that he conveys, many of which he has not the scientific and metaphysical education to confirm.

Will Michel Desmarquet's role as a messenger, and more important, his information be acknowledged?

Our daily experience tells us that we humans have taken a destructive path on this planet and in fact in our whole development. Whether we will stubbornly and childishly adhere to steer against the flow of the river we swim in or be part of it for the harmonious and enjoyable experience of it, is up to the wisdom in the conclusions we draw. The big institutions we have set up will not (because they cannot) help change direction, nor will the custodians of the universe, as they abide strictly by the law of non-interference with others' endeavours to come to wisdom and thus evolution.

The quantum leap in consciousness we hear so much about these days, cannot be organised or institutionalised: it is bound to take place in the heart and in the head of every individual for this is so by the very laws of nature.

Howard Hencke
August 1993
Author of: *Involution/Evolution and the Development of Consciousness*.

Contents

Special note to the reader

I, the author, Michel Desmarquet, wish to thank publicly, Janet Henderson who has edited this book. She has done an excellent job, respecting absolutely, word-for-word the true report I had to write.

Many editors want to turn the words and sentences as they wish, to "look good", as they say. That may be permissible for a fictional novel, but here, Janet has respected my will and the will of the Thaori and she has done well – believe me.

Preface

I have written this book as the result of orders received and which I have obeyed. Further, it is an account of events that happened to me *personally* - this I affirm.

I imagine that, to some extent, this extraordinary story will appear to some readers as science fiction - a story entirely invented - but I do not have the imagination that such a fabrication would require. This is *not* science fiction.

The reader of good faith will be able to recognise the *truth* in the message I transmit from my new friends to the people of the planet Earth.

This message, in spite of numerous references to races and religions, reflects *neither* racial *nor* religious bias on behalf of the author.

Michel Desmarquet,

January, 1989

They have eyes but they do not see - ears, and they do not hear...

The Bible

Abduction

I awoke suddenly, not knowing how long I had slept. I was completely awake - fresh and alert - but good God, what time could it be? Lina was sleeping beside me, her fists closed, but then Lina always sleeps...

I had no desire at all to go back to sleep and besides, it was possibly already five in the morning. I got up, made my way to the kitchen and checked the clock. Only 12.30am! It was unusual for me to wake up at such an hour.

I took off my pyjamas and dressed in trousers and a shirt, why, I had no idea. Neither can I explain why I went to my desk, took a sheet of paper and a biro and *watched* myself write, as if my hand had a mind of its own.

'My dear, I'll be away for about ten days. Absolutely no need to worry.'

Leaving the note by the telephone, I headed through the door and on to the verandah. I avoided the table on which last night's chess game remained, with the white King still in checkmate, and silently opened the door leading on to the garden.

The night seemed to be suffused with a strange brightness, which had nothing to do with the stars. Instinctively, I tried to recall what phase the moon was currently in, thinking that perhaps it was about to rise. Here, in the north-east of Australia where I live, the nights are generally quite clear.

I descended the outside stairs and headed towards the pandanus. Usually, at this time of night, we would have a veritable concert from the frogs and crickets whose chirring sounds fill the night. Now however, there was a heavy silence and I wondered why.

I had only walked a few steps when, quite suddenly, the colour of the philodendrons changed. The wall of the house too, and the pandanus - all were bathed in a kind of bluish light. The lawn seemed to undulate beneath my feet and the ground beneath the pandanus waved also. The philodendrons distorted and the wall of the house resembled a sheet floating in the wind.

Beginning to believe that I was not well, I decided to return to the house when, at that precise moment, I felt myself lifted quite gently from the ground. I rose, slowly at first, above the philodendrons, and then quicker, until I saw the house becoming smaller and smaller below me.

'What is happening?' I exclaimed in utter bewilderment.

'All is well now, Michel.'

By then, I believed I was dreaming. Before me, a human being of impressive size, dressed in a one-piece suit and wearing a completely transparent helmet on 'her' head, was looking at me - friendly and smiling.

'No, you are not dreaming,' she said, answering the question in my mind.

'Yes,' I replied, 'but it always happens this way in a dream and in the end you find you've fallen out of bed and have a lump on your forehead!' She smiled. 'Further', I continued, 'you are speaking to me in French, my native tongue, and yet we are in Australia. I do speak English, you know!'

'So do I'.

'It *has* to be a dream - one of those stupid dreams, moreover. If not though, what are you doing on my property?'

'We are not *on* your property, but above it.'

'Ah! It *is* a nightmare. You see I was right. I'll pinch myself!' I accompanied the words with the action. Ouch!

She smiled again. 'Now are you satisfied, Michel?'

'But if it's not a dream, why am I here sitting on this rock? Who are those people over there, dressed in the fashion of the last century?'

I was beginning to distinguish, in a milky light, people talking and at a slight distance, others moving around.

'And you, who are you? Why aren't you normal sized?'

'I am a normal size, Michel. On my planet we are all this size. But everything in good time, my dear friend. I hope you don't mind me calling you that? If we aren't good friends already, I am sure that we will be soon.'

She stood there in front of me, intelligence reflected in her smiling face and goodness emanating from her entire being. It would not be possible to meet anyone with whom I could feel more at ease.

'Of course, you may call me what you wish. And what is your name?'

'My name is Thao, but first, I would like you to know, once and for all, that this is *not* a dream. Indeed, it is something quite different. For certain reasons which will be explained to you later, you have been chosen to undertake a journey which very few Earthlings have made - particularly in recent times.

'We are, you and I, at this moment, in a universe which is parallel to that of Earth. In order to admit you, as well as ourselves, we have made use of an 'airlock'.

'At this instant, time has stopped for you, and you could remain here twenty or fifty of your Earthly years and then return as if you hadn't left. Your physical body would remain absolutely unchanged.'

'But what are these people doing?'

'They exist as well as can be expected and, as you will learn later, the population density is very low. Death only occurs by suicide or accident. Time is suspended. There are men and women, as well as some animals who are 30 000, 50 000 or even many more Earth years old.'

'But why are they here and how did they come to be here? Where were they born?'

'On Earth. . . they are all here by accident.'

2

'By accident? What do you mean?'

'It's very simple. You have heard of the Bermuda Triangle?' I nodded. 'Well, quite simply, in this spot and in others less well known, this parallel universe becomes confused with your universe so that there exists between them a natural warp.

'People, animals or even objects finding themselves in the immediate vicinity of a warp are literally sucked into it. Thus, you can have, for example, an entire fleet of boats disappear in several seconds. Sometimes a person, or persons, can pass back into your universe after several hours, several days or several years. More often, however, they never return.

'When a man does return and relates his experience, the vast majority of people don't believe him - and if he persists, he is assumed 'crazy'. Most of the time, such a person recounts nothing at all, realising how he will appear in the eyes of his peers. Sometimes too, he returns amnesic, and if he recovers some memory, it is not of what happened in the parallel universe, and therefore sheds no light on the subject.

'There was,' Thao continued, 'a typical case of this passage into a parallel universe in North America, where a young man literally vanished while going to fetch water from a well which was situated several hundred metres from his house. About an hour later, family and friends set out in search of him and, as there had been a fresh snowfall of about 20 centimetres, it should have been quite simple - they had only to follow the footprints left by the young man. But, right in the middle of the field - the footprints stopped.

'There were no trees around, no rocks on to which he could have jumped - nothing strange or unusual - the footprints just stopped. Some people believed that he had been taken by a spacecraft, but that could not have been, as you will see later. This poor man had quite simply been sucked into the parallel universe.'

'I remember', I said, 'I did hear of that particular case, but how do *you* know all about it?'

'You will find out later how I know,' she replied enigmatically.

We were interrupted by the sudden appearance of a group of people so bizarre that again, I wondered if this was all a dream. About a dozen men, accompanied by what seemed to be a woman, emerged from behind a pile of rocks a hundred metres from where we were. The sight was even stranger, since these human beings appeared to have stepped out of the pages of prehistoric records. With the gait of gorillas, they brandished enormous clubs which modern man would not have been able to lift from the ground. These hideous creatures were coming straight for us, howling like wild beasts. I made a move to retreat, but my companion told me there was nothing to fear and that I should stay still. She put her hand on the buckle of her belt and turned so that she faced them.

I heard a series of small clicks and five of the strongest looking men fell to the ground, motionless. The rest of the group stopped cleanly and began moaning. They prostrated themselves before us.

I looked again at Thao. She stood like a statue, her face set. Her eyes were fixed on those people as though she was trying to hypnotise them. I later learned that she was giving orders by telepathy to the female of the group. Suddenly, this woman got up and began, it seemed to me, to issue orders in a guttural voice to the others. They then helped remove the bodies, carrying them on their backs to the pile of rocks mentioned earlier.

'What are they doing?' I asked.

'They will cover their dead with stones.'

'Did you kill them?'

'I had to.'

'What do you mean? Were we really in danger?'

'Of course we were. These are people who have been here for ten or fifteen thousand years - who knows? We don't have time to establish that and besides, it is of no importance. Nevertheless, it illustrates well what I was explaining to you a few moments ago. These people passed into this universe at a certain time, and they have lived in that time ever since.'

'It's frightful!'

'I agree. However it is part of natural, and therefore universal, law. Furthermore, they are dangerous because they behave more like wild beasts than human beings. Dialogue would not have been possible between them and us, just as it is not possible between them and most of the others living in this parallel universe. For one thing, they are unable to communicate; and for another, they, less than anyone, understand what has happened to them. We were in real danger and, if I do say so, I have done them a favour just now, of liberating them.'

'Liberating?'

'Don't look so shocked, Michel. You know quite well what I mean by that. They are liberated from their physical bodies and are now able to continue their cycle, like every living being, according to the normal process.'

'So if I understand correctly, this parallel universe is a curse - a kind of hell or purgatory?'

'I didn't realise you were religious!'

'I just make this comparison to show you that I am trying to understand,' I replied, wondering how she could know whether or not I was religious.

'I know, Michel, I was only teasing. You were right in explaining it as a kind of purgatory but, of course, this is quite accidental. In fact, this is one of several accidents of nature. An *albino* is an accident, and a four-leafed clover can also be considered as an accident. Your appendix is just as much an accident. Your doctors still wonder what use it could possibly have in your body. The answer - no use whatsoever. Now usually, in nature, everything has a precise reason for existing - that's why I list the appendix among the natural 'accidents'.

'People living in this universe suffer neither physically or morally.

For example, if I hit you, you would feel no pain, but if the blows were strong enough, although without pain, you could still die from them. This might be difficult to comprehend, but it is so. Those existing here know nothing of what I have just explained to you, and it is fortunate because they would be tempted to commit suicide - which, even here, is not a solution.'

'What do they eat?'

'They don't eat, nor do they drink, because they don't feel the need to. Here, remember, time has stopped - those dead won't even rot.'

'But that's terrible! In all, the greatest service that one can render these people would be to kill them!'

'You raise an important point there. Effectively it would be one of two solutions.'

'What is the other?'

'To send them back where they came from - but that would pose great problems. Because we are able to make use of the warp, we could return many of them to your universe, and thus deliver them, but I'm sure you are aware of the enormous problems that would create for the majority of these people. Here, as I have already said, you have people, who have been here for thousands of years. What would happen if they found themselves back in the universe they left so long ago?'

'They might go insane. In all, there is nothing to do.' She smiled gently at my affirmation.

'You are certainly the man of action we require, Michel, but beware of jumping to conclusions - you have much more to see.'

She put her hand on my shoulder, having to incline forward slightly to do so. Although I didn't know it at the time, Thao measured 290 centimetres, exceptionally tall for a human being.

'I see with my own eyes that we made the right choice in selecting you - you have an astute mind, but I cannot explain everything to you now, for two reasons.'

'Namely?'

'First, it is still too soon for such an explanation. By this, I mean that you must be instructed further on certain points before proceeding beyond.'

'I understand - and second?'

'The second reason is that they are waiting for us. We must leave.'

With a light touch, she turned me around. I followed her gaze and stared wide-eyed with surprise. About 100 metres from us was an enormous sphere, from which emanated a bluish Aura. I later learned that it measured 70 metres in diameter. The light was not steady, but shimmered, resembling a heat haze when one looks from a distance at sand heated by the summer sun.

This enormous sphere 'shimmered' about ten metres from the ground. With no windows, no openings, no ladder, it appeared as smooth as the shell of an egg.

5

Thao signalled for me to follow her and we set out towards the machine. I remember that moment very well. During the short time we took in approaching the sphere, I was so excited that I lost control of my thoughts. A constant stream of images flashed through my mind, resembling a film in the 'fast-forward' mode. I saw myself relating this adventure to my family, and I saw again newspaper articles I had read on the subject of UFOs.

I remember a feeling of sadness sweep over me when I thought of my family whom I loved so much; I saw myself caught, as though in a trap, and it occurred to me that I might never see them again...

'You have absolutely nothing to fear, Michel,' said Thao. 'Trust me. You will be reunited with your family very soon, and in good health.'

I believe my mouth fell open in surprise, triggering in Thao a melodious laugh, such as is rarely heard among us Earthlings. That was the second time she had read my thoughts; the first time I thought might have been a coincidence, but this time there could be no doubt.

When we arrived in close proximity to the sphere, Thao placed me in a position opposite her and about a metre's distance away.

'Do not touch me under any pretext, Michel, whatever happens. *Under any pretext* - do you understand?'

I was quite taken aback by this formal order, but I nodded.

She placed her hand on a type of 'medallion' I had noticed earlier 'attached' at the height of her left breast, and with the other hand, she held what resembled a large biro which she unclasped from her belt.

She pointed the 'biro' above our heads and in the direction of the sphere. I thought I saw a green beam of light flash from it but I couldn't be sure. She then pointed the 'biro' at me, her other hand still on the 'medallion' and quite simply, we rose, simultaneously, towards the wall of the machine. Just when I was sure we were going to collide with it, a portion of the hull retracted like an enormous piston in the core of a cylinder, revealing an opening, oval in shape, of about three metres in height.

We regained our feet, Thao and I, on a type of landing inside the craft. She let go of her 'medallion' and with a dexterity that suggested she had done it often, she refastened her 'biro'.

'Come. We can touch each other now,' she said.

Taking me by the shoulder, she guided me towards a small blue light, so intense that I had almost to half close my eyes. I had never seen a colour like it on Earth. When we were almost below the light, the wall on which it was located 'let us pass'. That is the only way to describe it. From the way in which my mentor was leading me, I could have sworn I was going to have a handsome lump on my forehead, *but we passed through the walls* - like *ghosts!* Thao laughed heartily at the shocked expression on my face. That did me good. I remember that laugh - like a refreshing breeze and reassuring at a time when I was not feeling at ease.

I had often spoken with friends of 'flying saucers' and was persuaded that they did, in fact, exist - but when you are actually faced with the reality, so many questions cloud your brain that you think it will burst. Of course, deep down I was delighted. From Thao's manner towards me, I sensed that I had nothing to fear. However, she was not alone: I wondered what the others were going to be like. In spite of my fascination with this adventure, I still doubted if I would see my family again. Already, they seemed so far away, when only several minutes earlier I was in my own garden.

We were now 'gliding' at ground level along a tunnel-shaped corridor that led to a small room, the walls of which were of a yellow so intense that I had to close my eyes. The walls formed a vault - exactly as if we were inside an upturned bowl.

Thao covered my head with a helmet made from a transparent material and I found, by opening one eye, that this enabled me to tolerate the light.

'How do you feel?' she asked.

'Better, thank you, but that light - how can you stand it?'

'It is not a light. It is just the present colour of the walls in this room.'

'Why 'present'? Have you brought me here to repaint them?' I joked.

'There is no paint. There are only vibrations, Michel. You still believe that you are in your Earthly universe, when you are *not.* You are now in one of our super long-range spacecraft, capable of travelling at several times the speed of light. We will be leaving soon, if you will lie down on this bunk..?'

There, in the centre of the room were two boxes - rather like coffins without lids. I stretched out in one of them and Thao in the other. I heard her speak in a language unfamiliar to me, but very harmonious. I wanted to lift myself up a little but couldn't, being held by an unknown and invisible force. The yellow colour progressively disappeared from the walls, to be replaced by a blue that was certainly no less intense. The 'paintwork' had been redone...

One third of the room suddenly became dark and I noticed minute lights sparkling like stars.

Thao's voice was clear in the darkness. 'These are stars, Michel. We have left Earth's parallel universe and will be leaving your planet further and further behind, to take you to visit ours. We know you are going to be greatly interested in the journey, but also in our departure that will be quite slow, for your benefit.

'We can watch on the screen you see in front of you.'

'Where is Earth?'

'We still can't see it, being almost directly above it, at approximately 10 000 metres altitude...'

Suddenly, a voice could be heard, speaking what seemed to be the same language Thao had used moments earlier. Thao answered briefly and then the voice spoke to me in *French* - excellent French (although the tone was more melodic than is typical) welcoming me aboard. It was very much the 'welcome aboard' of our airline companies, and I recall being quite amused by that - in spite of the unique situation in which I found myself.

At the same instant, I felt a very light movement of the air and it became cool, as though air-conditioned. Things began to happen quickly. On the screen, appeared what could only have been the sun. At first, it seemed to touch the edge of the Earth or, more precisely, South America, as I later learned. Again, I wondered if I could be dreaming. Second by second America was shrinking. Australia couldn't be seen, as the sun's rays had not yet reached it. Now the contours of the planet could be distinguished, and we seemed to move around the globe, to a position above the North Pole. There, we changed direction, drawing away from Earth at an incredible speed.

Our poor Earth became a basketball, then a billiard ball until it finally disappeared - or almost - from the screen. Instead, my vision was filled with the sombre blue of space. I turned my head in Thao's direction hoping for further explanation.

'Did you like that?'

'It was wonderful, but so fast - is it possible to travel at such a high speed?'

'That was nothing, my dear friend. We 'took off very gently. Only now are we travelling at full speed.'

'How fast?' I interrupted.

'Several times the speed of light.'

'Of *light*? But how many times? It's incredible! What about the light barrier?'

'I can well understand that it appears incredible to you. Not even your experts would believe it - it is, however, the *truth.* '

'You say several times the speed of light, but how many times?'

'Michel, during this journey many things will be intentionally revealed to you - many things, but there will also be details to which you will not have access. The precise speed of our spacecraft is one such detail. I'm sorry, for I know it will disappoint you not to have your great curiosity for all things satisfied, but there will be so many new and interesting things for you to see and learn, that you must not mind too much when information is withheld from you.'

Her manner indicated that the matter was closed and I didn't insist further, sensing that to do so would have been rude.

'Look' she said to me. On the screen a coloured dot had appeared and was growing rapidly.

'What is it?'

'Saturn.'

The reader must forgive me if the descriptions I give are not as detailed as he/she might wish, but it must be understood that I had not yet recovered all my senses. I had seen so much in so short a time, and was somewhat 'disoriented.'

As we approached, the famous Saturn grew rapidly larger on the screen. Its colours were wonderful - incomparable to anything I had ever seen on Earth. There were yellows, reds, greens, blues, oranges - within each colour, an infinite range of nuances mingled, separated, grew stronger then weaker, creating the famous rings and confined within them...

It was an amazing spectacle, which filled more and more of our screen.

Realising I was no longer restrained by the force field, I wanted to remove my mask so as to see the colours better, but Thao signalled that I should do nothing. 'Where are the satellites?' I asked.

'You can see two, almost side by side towards the right of the screen.'

'How far away are we?'

'We must be approximately 6 000 000 kilometres or perhaps more. They know exactly on the flight deck of course, but to give you a more precise estimate, I'd have to know whether our 'camera' is on full zoom or not.'

Saturn suddenly disappeared from the left side of the screen, which filled again with the 'colour' of space.

I believe it was at that moment I felt exalted, as I never had before. It hit me that I was in the process of living an extraordinary adventure - and why? I had asked for nothing and had never contemplated the possibility (who would have dared?) of experiencing such an adventure.

Thao got up. 'You can do the same now, Michel.' I obeyed and we found ourselves again, side by side in the centre of the cabin. It was only then, I noticed Thao no longer wore her helmet.

'Can you explain to me,' I asked, 'why just now, you were still wearing a helmet while I was able to accompany you without one, and yet now I have one while you don't?'

'It is very simple. We come from a planet bacteriologically different from Earth, which, for us, is a veritable culture medium. Thus, in order to contact you, I was obliged to take this basic precaution. You, yourself, were a danger to me but you are no longer.'

'I don't follow you.'

'When you entered this cabin, the colour was too intense for you and I gave you the helmet you are now wearing, which was specially designed for you. Indeed, we were able to anticipate your reaction.

'During the very short time the cabin was yellow and then blue, eighty per cent of the dangerous bacteria in you was destroyed. Then perhaps you felt a coolness in the air, similar to when an air conditioner is working; this was another form of disinfection by...let's call it radiation, although that is not the correct word - it cannot be translated into any Earth language. In this way, I have been disinfected one hundred per cent, but you still have enough bacteria to harm us considerably. I am going to give you these two pills, and in three hours you will be able to consider yourself as 'pure' as one of us.' As she spoke, she took a little box from beside her bunk, removed the pills and held them out to me, along with a test tube containing a liquid that I supposed to be water. I swallowed them both, lifting the base of my helmet to do so. Next ... well, everything happened very quickly and it was all *very* strange.

Thao took me in her arms, put me on the bunk and removed my mask. I *saw that happen from two or three metres from my body!* I imagine that certain things in this book will seem incomprehensible to the unwarned reader, but I saw my body from a distance and I was able to move about in the room just by thought.

Thao spoke. 'Michel, I know that you see me and hear me, but I am not able to see you myself, therefore I cannot look at you when I speak to you. Your Astral being has left your body. There is no danger in this - you needn't worry. I know that this is the first time this has happened to you, and there are people who panic...

'I have given you a special drug in order to cleanse your body of all bacteria that is dangerous to us. I have also given you another drug that has caused your Astral being to leave your body - this will last three hours, the time it will take to purify you. In this way, you will be able to visit our spacecraft, without danger of contamination to us and without wasting time.'

As strange as it seems, I found this quite natural - and I followed her. It was fascinating. She arrived in front of a panel that slid open to let us pass into one chamber after another. I was following at some distance and each time, *if* the panel had already closed by the time I reached it - I quite simply passed *through* it.

Finally, we reached a circular room, about 20 metres in diameter, in which there were at least a dozen 'astronauts' - all women and all about Thao's size. Thao approached a group of four who were seated in enormous, comfortable-looking armchairs, arranged in a circle. When she sat down in a vacant seat, the four heads turned towards her questioningly. She almost seemed to take delight in making them wait: finally she spoke.

I was again charmed to hear that language - the assonance was quite new to me, and the intonations so harmonious one would have thought they were singing. They all seemed to be greatly interested in Thao's report. I supposed they were speaking of me, believing correctly that I was the main purpose of their mission.

When Thao stopped, the questions streamed forth, and two other astronauts joined the group. The discussion swelled and developed a tone of increased excitement.

Not understanding a word of what was being said, and having noticed on entering three people positioned in front of screens displaying 3-dimensional images, more or less vividly coloured, I approached to discover that this must certainly be the control room of the spacecraft. Being invisible made it even much more interesting since each person was performing her duties without being disturbed, or even distracted, by my presence.

On a screen bigger than the rest, I was able to discern dots - some larger than others and some brighter, which moved steadily and without interruption in their prescribed directions, several towards the left of the screen and others towards the right.

Their speed increased as they grew on the screen and finally exited from it. Their colours were often brilliant and extraordinarily beautiful, ranging from subtle tones to a blinding yellow, like the light from our sun.

I soon realised that these were the planets and suns among which we were navigating, and I was absolutely fascinated by their silent progression across the screen. I can't say how long I had been watching them, when suddenly a strange sound filled the cabin - a sound which was soft and at the same time, insistent, and which was accompanied by many flashing lights.

The effect was immediate. The astronauts that had been talking with Thao now approached the control post and each took a seat that seemed to be personally assigned to her. Everyone's eyes were fixed attentively on the screens.

Right in the middle of these large monitors, I began to distinguish an enormous mass that is difficult to describe. Let me say only that it was round in form and blue-grey in colour. It remained immobile in the centre of each screen.

In the room, all was silent. The general attention was focused on three astronauts in command of oblong-shaped pieces of equipment resembling in some ways, our computers.

Suddenly, covering a huge area of what I believed was a wall of the cabin I was stupefied to see an image of New York - no! That's Sydney, I said to myself, and yet the bridge is different...was it even a bridge?

My surprise was such I had to ask Thao, at whose side I was standing. I had forgotten however, that I was no longer *in my physical body* and no one could hear me. I was able to hear Thao and others commenting on what they were seeing but, not understanding their language, it didn't get me far. I was convinced though, that Thao had not lied to me and therefore we had well and truly left Earth behind. My mentor had explained we were travelling at several times the speed of light...and I had seen Saturn pass by and later, what I took to be planets and suns - so had we come back, and why?

Thao spoke aloud and in French, which caused all heads to turn in her direction.

'Michel, we are stationed above the planet Aremo X3 which is almost twice the size of planet Earth, and as you can see on the screen, quite similar to your world.

'I can't explain at any length our current mission as I am required to participate in the operation, but I will do so later. To put you on the right track, I will tell you that our mission concerns atomic radiation such as you know on Earth'.

Everyone seemed preoccupied: each knew exactly what to do and when to do it. We were stationary. The large panel projected an image of the centre of a town. The reader should understand that this large panel was in fact, no more than an immense television screen, projecting an image in relief so real, we could have been looking out the window of a tall building.

My attention turned to another smaller screen being monitored by two of my 'hostesses'. On this panel I could see our spacecraft, as I had already seen it in our parallel universe. As I watched, I was surprised to see, slightly below the middle of our vessel, a small sphere ejected, like an egg from a hen. Once outside, this sphere accelerated rapidly towards the planet below. As it disappeared from view, another sphere emerged in the same manner, and then a third. I noticed each sphere was being monitored on separate screens by different groups of astronauts.

The descent of the spheres could now be easily followed on the large panel. The distance should have made them invisible in quite a short time but they remained in sight and I deduced that the camera had to have an extraordinarily powerful 'zoom'. Indeed, the effect of the zoom was so strong that the first sphere disappeared from the right of the panel and the second from the left. We could now only see the middle one and followed its descent to the ground quite clearly. It stopped in the centre of an immense square, situated among apartment buildings. There it hovered, as though suspended several metres from the ground. The other spheres were monitored in the same detail. One was above a river that flowed through the town, and the other hovered above a hill, near the city.

Unexpectedly, the panel projected a new image. I could now distinctly see the doors of the apartment buildings, or rather, the doorways, for where doors should have been, were gaping openings.

I remember clearly that, until then, I had not realised how odd this town was...

Nothing had moved...

Atomic destruction

A single word can impart what was being reflected from the panel: 'Desolation'. The street we were observing, piece by piece, was cluttered with 'mounds' generally arranged one behind the other. Some stood apart while others lay right in the middle of the openings to the buildings. Imperceptibly, the camera zoomed closer and I soon understood that these 'mounds' had to be vehicles - vehicles that were somewhat similar in shape to flat-bottomed boats.

Around me, the astronauts were attending to their desks. From each sphere emerged a long tube that descended slowly towards the surface. When the end of the tube touched the ground, a little cloud of dust rose, and I realised that the vehicles too were covered in a thick blanket of dust, rendering them formless and unrecognisable. Of course, the sphere that hovered above the river had its tube in the water. My attention was now riveted on the panel, for the scene was quite fascinating - one had the exact impression of being in the street.

My attention was especially drawn to a darkened place in the entrance of a huge building. I could have sworn something moved...

I also felt there was a certain agitation among the astronauts. Abruptly, and with a series of jerks, the 'thing' emerged into the light. I was horrified by what I saw. As for my 'hostesses', apart from some utterances spoken more quickly, and a few exclamations in which emotion could be discerned, I must say that they didn't really seem surprised. However, what we were seeing so clearly on the panel was a horrible cockroach, about two metres long and 80 centimetres high.

The reader will certainly have seen, at one time or another, these nasty little insects we have on Earth, particularly in hot climates, living in cupboards and damp places.

You will agree that they are loathsome, but the biggest would be no more than five centimetres in length. Imagine then, one with the dimensions I have just described. It was truly an abomination.

The tube from the sphere began to retract, yet was still a metre from the ground when suddenly, the creature hurried forward to attack this thing which moved. Untrustingly, it stopped again, when from under the building, a veritable swarm of the creatures emerged, spilling one over the other. Just then, a ray of intense blue light beamed from the sphere and swept over the group, reducing it instantly to carbonised dust. A cloud of black smoke hid the entrance to the building from view.

My curiosity further aroused, I watched the other screens, but they indicated no problems. The sphere from the river was returning towards us, and the sphere on the hill retracted its tube, moved a little higher and lowered the tube again, along with a second cylinder above the sphere. I had guessed, of course, that the astronauts were collecting samples of soil, water and air. Being in Astral body, I couldn't ask Thao any questions; in any case, she seemed quite busy conferring with two of the 'hostesses. The spheres began climbing towards us and were soon ready to be 'reabsorbed' by our spacecraft.

When the operation was complete, Thao and the two astronauts mentioned took their places opposite their respective desks. Instantly, the images we received on the panel and screens changed completely.

I understood we were leaving when each one took her place. I observed that all the astronauts had a similar posture in their seats that intrigued me. I later learned that a force field restrained them exactly as a security harness would have restrained a stuntman on Earth.

The suns illuminated the planet through a reddish fog. We had left by then, and I assumed we were following the contour of the planet, at the same altitude. In fact, we could see a desert-like area passing by, dissected by dry riverbeds that sometimes crossed each other at right angles. It occurred to me they might be canals, or at least had been manmade.

The panel revealed images of a town apparently intact, then it disappeared and the screen went blank. The vessel had obviously gained speed in flying over the planet, as the images on the smaller screens, showing a lake or inland sea, flashed by quickly. Suddenly, several exclamations were heard and we immediately slowed down. The panel was turned on and presented a close-up of the lake. We stopped.

We could clearly see a portion of the coast and, beyond some large rocks by the lake, we could make out cube-like structures which I imagined to be habitations. As soon as we had stopped, the spheres began their operations again, just as they had earlier.

We received some excellent shots taken from one of the spheres that hovered above the beach at a height I judged to be 40 to 60 metres from the ground. Its tube extended right to the shore. Very clearly, it transmitted a scene of a group of *human beings...* Indeed, at first sight, they were identical to people found on Earth.

We had a very close view. In the middle of the panel appeared the face of a woman of uncertain age. She had brown skin, with long black hair that fell to her breasts. As we could see on another screen, she was quite naked. Only her face appeared to be deformed - she was Mongoloid.

When I saw her, I didn't realise she was deformed, I simply assumed we had to contend with a race of humans only slightly different from our own - as science fiction writers like to describe them - all twisted, with big ears or such like. Still, we had other shots and, in this group, the men and women seemed to resemble the Polynesian race. It was, however, obvious that more than half of these people were either deformed or eaten away by what appeared to be *leprosy.*

They were looking towards the sphere and gesticulating, appearing to be greatly agitated. Many more were emerging from the cubic constructions which proved to be their habitations, and on which I will elaborate a little.

These structures closely resembled the 'blockhaus' of the Second World War, to which had been added very thick chimneys (installed, I supposed, for the ventilation of the buildings) which only seemed to rise about one metre above the ground. These blockhaus were all built with the same orientation and the people emerging from them, did so by openings on the sides which were in shadow...

Without warning, I felt myself drawn backwards away from the panel. Rapidly, I passed through several partitions until I found myself once again, in the cabin where my physical being lay stretched out on the bunk, just as I had left it.

Instantly, everything was completely black. How well I remember the unpleasant sensation that followed! My limbs felt like lead and when I tried to move them, it was as if I was paralysed. I could not understand what prevented me from moving. I must confess I panicked a little and wished with all my heart that I might leave my physical body again, but I couldn't do that either.

I don't know how much time elapsed before the cabin gradually became suffused with the most restful blue-green light. Finally Thao entered, wearing a different suit.

'I am sorry to have made you wait, Michel, but just as your physical body recalled you, it was impossible for me to come and help you.'

'Don't apologise, I understand perfectly,' I interrupted, 'but I believe I have a problem - I can't move. I'm sure something in me is disconnected.'

She smiled and put her hand just beside mine, undoubtedly operating a control mechanism, and immediately I was freed.

'Again, a thousand apologies, Michel. I should have pointed out to you the spot where the control cell for the security harness is found. All the seats, beds or bunks are equipped with them, and they are automatically activated if occupied, as soon as there is the least possibility of danger.

'When the vessel arrives in a dangerous area, the three security computers cause the closing of the force fields, to use their proper name. When the danger has passed they automatically release them.

'At the same time, if we do want to be released in a zone deemed dangerous, or even if we simply want to change position, we have only to pass a hand or just a finger in front of the cell and the force field is immediately neutralised. When we return to our seats, we will be automatically restrained again.

'Now, I'm going to ask you to go and change - I'll show you where. In the room, you will see an open trunk where you can put your clothes -in fact, all that you are wearing apart from the glasses. You'll find a suit there, which you are to put on before meeting me back here.'

Thao bent down and taking my hand, she helped me up. I was really quite stiff. I went into the small room she had pointed out, undressed completely and put on the suit, which fitted me perfectly. This was surprising, given that, in spite of my 178 centimetres in height, I was a dwarf compared with my hostesses.

A short time later, back in the cabin, Thao handed me something in the form of a bracelet, which was actually a pair of enormous glasses.

A little like motorcycle goggles, they were strongly tinted. At her request, I put them on, but to do so, I was obliged to remove my own glasses, as they would have been crushed by this larger pair. They fitted exactly into the shape of my eye sockets.

'A last precaution,' she said.

Lifting her hand towards the partition, she in some way released a certain mechanism, for the intense light reappeared and I felt the intensity in spite of the strong glasses. I was again aware of the current of cool air.

The lights went out. The air current could no longer be felt, but Thao did not move, appearing to be waiting for something. Eventually a voice was heard and she removed my large tinted glasses. I replaced them with my own and she asked that I follow her. We took the same route as when I followed her in Astral body, and we found ourselves again, in the command room.

One of the older astronauts (I say older but perhaps I should instead say 'more serious' as they all appeared to be about the same age) signalled briefly to Thao who took me to a seat in front of the panel and asked that I stay there. She quickly rejoined her colleague and I realised they were very busy.

As for me, I began checking whether I could in fact free myself from the force field. As soon as I sat down, I was effectively plastered to my seat - a feeling I did not like at all.

Moving my hand slightly, I found I was immediately liberated for as long as my hand remained in front of the cell.

The panel relayed an image of about 500 people standing on the shore and quite near the 'blockhaus'. Thanks to the close-ups possible with our cameras, we had an excellent view of these people, who were quite naked, from the oldest down to the youngest. Again, I could see many of them were either deformed or sporting ugly wounds. They were all gesturing towards the spheres taking sand and soil samples, but no one approached. The strongest looking men were holding what appeared to be machetes or sabres. They seemed to be watching something.

I felt pressure on my shoulder and turned round, surprised. It was Thao. She smiled at me and I clearly remember appreciating, for the first time, the beauty and nobility of her face.

I have already mentioned her hair, which was long and silky, golden-blond in colour, which fell to her shoulders and framed a face that was perfectly oval in shape. She had a large, slightly protruding forehead.

Her blue-mauve eyes and long curled lashes would have been the envy of many women on our planet. Her eyebrows curved upwards, similar to the wings of a seagull, adding a unique charm. Under her eyes, which sparkled and sometimes teased, was her nose, well-proportioned and slightly flat at the bottom, which accentuated a sensual mouth. When she smiled, she revealed perfect teeth - so perfect, one could believe they were false. (This would have surprised me.) The chin, well-shaped but slightly angular, suggested a wilful determination that was somewhat masculine, but this did not detract from its charm. A faint shadow of hair above her upper lip could have spoiled this perfect face, were it not blond.

'I see you already know how to free yourself from the force field, Michel.'

I was about to reply, when an almost general exclamation made us turn our eyes to the panel.

The people on the beach were surging back en masse towards the habitations and dived inside in one big rush, while a line of men had been formed armed with sabres or picks, facing the most incredible 'thing' I could ever have imagined.

A group of red ants, *each the size of a cow,* were rushing from behind the rocks onto the beach. They moved quicker than horses in gallop.

The armed men kept glancing behind, as if to compare the speed at which the people scrambled to safety, with the advance of the ants. Already, the latter were near - too near...

The men faced them bravely as, with only a second's hesitation, the first beast attacked. We could distinguish the mandibles clearly - each the size of a man's arm. At first, the creature feigned, enabling the man to strike with his sabre, but he slashed only air. Immediately, the mandibles encircled his waist, severing him cleanly in two. Another pair of ants helped the first to shred him, while the rest launched their assault on the fleeing combatants, gaining rapidly on them - too rapidly...

From the sphere, an electric-blue beam of unbearable intensity shot out, just as the ants were upon the men. The creatures were struck dead, one after the other, with amazing precision and effectiveness. Curls of smoke rose from the burnt flesh of the animals strewn over the ground, their enormous legs convulsing in a last spasm.

The beam continued its devastation among the ants, instantly and systematically annihilating the giant insects. They must have known instinctively that they could not match this almost supernatural force and fled in retreat.

Everything had happened so quickly. Thao was still at my side, her face reflecting disgust and sadness, rather than anger.

Another glance at the panel revealed a new scene - of the sphere pursuing the ants in their hasty retreat, not only with the camera, but also with the deadly beam. The rest of the swarm, which I estimated to comprise six or seven hundred, were being decimated. Not one was left alive.

The sphere returned to its earlier position above the beach and produced a special tool with which it combed through the carcasses. I could see one of the astronauts seated at her desk, talking into her computer. This prompted me to ask Thao if she was supervising the work being carried out.

'At the moment, yes, for this work was not originally scheduled. We are taking samples of these creatures, pieces of lung in particular, in order to analyse them. We think that certain types of radiation have produced this mutant form of creature. In fact, ants do not have lungs but the only logical explanation for their sudden gigantism is...'

Thao stopped short. The camera was relaying a picture of the men now reemerging form their shelters, gesticulating wildly at the sphere. They were holding their arms open-wide and prostrating themselves on the ground. They repeated this pattern.

'Can they see this vessel?' I asked.

'No. We are at an altitude of 40 000 metres, and, further, there are presently three layers of cloud between the planet and us. On the other hand, they can see our satellite and I think it is to that they are addressing these gestures of gratitude.'

'Perhaps they take the sphere to be a God which has saved them from ruin?'

'It's quite possible.'

'Can you tell me what is happening? Who are these people?'

'It would take too long to explain to you, Michel, especially now with so much activity in the vessel, but I can satisfy your curiosity by explaining briefly.

'These people are, in a way, the descendants of certain ancestors of people existing still on your planet. In fact, a group of their ancestors peopled a continent on the planet Earth about 250 000 of your Earth years ago. Here, they possessed a civilisation which was very advanced but, having raised enormous political barriers between themselves, they finally destroyed themselves, 150 years ago, with the atom.'

'Do you mean - a total nuclear war?'

'Yes, brought about by chain reaction. We come, from time to time, to take samples in order to study the degree of radiation still existing in various regions. Sometimes too, just as a few moments ago, we help them.'

'But they must take you to be God himself after what you did just now!'

Thao smiled and nodded her head. 'Ah yes, that's certainly true, Michel. They take us to be gods, exactly as, on your planet, certain of your ancestors also took us to be gods. Still, they talk of us...

I must have shown complete surprise, as Thao threw me a look of amusement.

'I told you a moment ago that my explanation is somewhat premature. We'll have plenty of time to talk of this again. Besides, that's why you are with us.'

With that, she excused herself and resumed her place in front of a 'screen-desk'. The images were changing rapidly on the panel. The sphere was on its way up and we had a view of a whole section of the continent, on which, I noticed in places, patches of green and brown. The sphere took its place again within the vessel and we departed.

We flew over the planet at a breathtaking speed and I allowed myself to be imprisoned in my armchair by the force field.

On the screen were images of the waters of an immense ocean. We could distinguish an island, which 'grew' rapidly.

It seemed to be a very low island although, for me, the problems of estimating dimensions were very real.

The entire procedure, already described, was repeated. We stopped above the coast and, this time, four spheres left the spacecraft and descended to the island. On the panel I could see a beach which the camera was scanning.

On the water's edge lay what looked like thick slabs, around which were gathered naked men - the same kind we had seen earlier. They didn't appear to have noticed the sphere and I assumed that this time, it was at a much higher altitude, in spite of the ever-closing images we were receiving.

On the panel, we could now see the men carrying one of the slabs into the waves. It floated, as if made of cork. The men hoisted themselves up on to it, grabbed large oars that they handled skilfully and the boat took to the open sea. When they were a good distance from the shore, they threw out fishing lines and, to my surprise, almost immediately, pulled up fish of what seemed a respectable size.

It was quite fascinating to see how these men were surviving, and to be capable of helping them, as if we were gods.

I had released myself from the force field, wanting to go and study the other screens that were receiving different images. Just as I was about to venture from my seat, I received an order, *without hearing a sound:* 'Stay where you are, Michel.' I was stupefied. It was as if the voice was inside my head. I turned my head in Thao's direction and she was smiling at me. I decided to try something, and thought as hard as I could, 'Telepathy is great, isn't it Thao?'

'Of course,' she replied in the same manner.

'It's wonderful! Can you tell me what the temperature is down there at the moment?'

She checked the data at her desk. 'Twenty-eight of your degrees Celsius. By day, the average temperature is thirty-eight degrees.'

I said to myself if I was deaf and mute, I could communicate with Thao quite as easily as I can with the spoken word.

'Exactly, my dear.'

I looked at Thao with some surprise. I had been making a personal reflection and yet she had intercepted my thoughts. I was a little put out by this.

She gave me a wide smile. 'Don't worry, Michel. I was merely being playful and I ask that you forgive me.

'Normally, I only read your thoughts when you ask me a question. I just wanted to demonstrate what is possible in this domain; I won't do it again.'

I returned her smile and redirected my attention to the panel. There I could see a sphere on the beach, very close to a group of men who didn't seem to notice it. This sphere was removing sand samples from a spot about ten metres from the group. By telepathy, I asked Thao why these people were unable to see the machine.

'It's night,' she answered.

'Night? But how is it that we can see things so clearly?'

'Special cameras, Michel - something like your infra-reds.'

Now I better understood why the images received were less 'luminous' than on our preceding stops. However, the close-ups were excellent. Just then, on the panel, we had a shot of a face apparently that of a female. It was really horrible. The poor creature had an enormous gash where her left eye should have been. Her mouth was positioned to the right of her face and appeared as a tiny little opening in the middle of her jaw, around which were lips that seemed fused together. On the top of her head, a single tuft of hair hung pitifully.

We could now see her breasts, and very pretty they would have been, if one of them hadn't had a purulent wound on the side.

'With breasts like that she must be young?' I asked.

'The computer puts the age at 19 years.'

'Radiation?'

'Of course.'

Other people appeared, some of whom were perfectly normal looking. There were males among them, with an athletic build, who looked to be in their twenties.

'What is the age of the oldest? Do you know?'

'At present, we have no record of anyone older than 38 years, and a year on this planet is 295 days of 27 hours. Now, if you look at the screen, you can see a close-up of the genital area of that handsome and athletic young man. As you will note, the genitals are totally atrophied. We've already worked out, from previous expeditions, that there are very few men actually capable of procreation - and yet, there are great numbers of children. It's the survival instinct of all races to reproduce as soon as possible. Thus, the obvious solution would be that the males capable of reproduction are 'studs'. This man must be one of them, I think.'

Indeed, the camera was showing a man of about 30 years perhaps, possessing physical attributes certainly capable of producing offspring.

We were also able to see many children coming and going around small fires on which food was cooking.

The men and women seated around the fireplaces were taking cooked pieces and sharing them with the children. The fires seemed like wood fires, but I couldn't be sure. They were fuelled by something shaped rather like stones.

Behind the fires, slabs similar to the boats seen earlier, were piled and assembled so as to form shelters that looked quite comfortable.

In the camera's field of vision, no trees could be seen - perhaps they did exist, because I had noticed green patches earlier as we flew over the continent.

From between two huts, some little black pigs appeared, pursued by three furious yellow dogs, only to disappear rapidly behind another hut. I was dumbfounded and couldn't help but wonder if I really was looking down on another planet. These humans looked like me - or rather, like Polynesians - and here were dogs and pigs. It was all more and more surprising...

The sphere began to return, as did the other spheres no doubt, that were being monitored by screens I couldn't easily see from my position. The operation 'return to ship' was initiated, and all the spheres 'reabsorbed' without incident, the same as before.

I assumed we were about to leave again and so installed myself comfortably in my seat, allowing the force field to restrain me thus.

Some moments later, the suns of the planet appeared, two in number, then everything dwindled rapidly, just as it had done when we left Earth. After a time, which seemed quite short, the force field was neutralised and I understood that I was free to get out of my seat. This was a good feeling. I noticed Thao heading towards me accompanied by two of the 'oldest', if I can say so, of her companions. I remained standing beside my seat before the three astronauts.

In order to look at Thao, I was already obliged to raise my head, but when she introduced me, in French, to the 'elder' of them, I felt even smaller. The latter was easily a head taller than Thao.

I was completely astonished when she, Biastra, spoke to me correctly, although slowly, in French. She placed her right hand on my shoulder, saying,

'I am delighted to have you on board, Michel. I hope that all is well with you and that it continues to be so. May I present Latoli, the second-in-charge of our spacecraft, myself being what you would call 'Commander-in-Chief of the *Alatora*.'

Turning to Latoli, she spoke a few words in her own language and Latoli too, placed her hand on my shoulder. With a warm smile, she repeated my name several times slowly, as would someone who had difficulty pronouncing a new language.

Her hand remained on my shoulder and a feeling of well-being, a definite fluid sensation, passed through my body. [1]

I was so obviously overcome by this, that the three of them began to

---

1 *Alatora,* in their language, is the name given to their super long-distance spacecraft. (Author's comment)

laugh. Reading my thoughts, Thao reassured me.

'Michel, Latoli possesses a special gift, although not rare among our people. What you have been able to experience, is a fluid which is magnetic and beneficial, and which emanated from her.'

'It's wonderful!' I exclaimed. 'Please compliment her on my behalf.' I then addressed the two astronauts. 'Thank you for your welcome, but I must confess I am absolutely astounded by what is happening to me. It really is the most incredible adventure for an Earthling such as me. Although I have always believed in the possibility that other planets might be inhabited by human-like beings, I'm still having a hard time convincing myself that this is not a fantastic dream.

'I had often discussed things such as telepathy, extra-terrestrials and what we call 'flying saucers' with friends on Earth, but they were just words and grand phrases uttered in ignorance. Now I have the proof of what I had suspected for so long regarding the existence of parallel universes, the duality of our beings, and other unexplained occurrences. To experience all that I have in these last few hours is so exciting it takes my breath away.

Latoli, admiring my monologue, uttered an exclamation, in words I didn't understand but which Thao immediately translated for me.

'Latoli understands your state of mind perfectly well, Michel.' 'As do I,' added Biastra.

'How could she have understood what I said?'

'She has 'dipped' telepathically into your mind while you were speaking. As you must realise, telepathy is not hindered by language barriers.'

My astonishment amused them and perpetual smiles played on their lips. Biastra addressed me.

'Michel, I am going to introduce you to the rest of the crew, if you will kindly follow me.' She guided me, by the shoulder, to the furthest desk, where three astronauts were monitoring the instruments. I hadn't yet approached these desks and, even in Astral body, I had not paid any attention to the read-out of these computers. The glance I now gave them immobilised me completely. The numerals before my eyes were in *Arabic!* I know the reader will be as surprised as I was, but it was fact. The 1s, 2s, 3s 4s etc. appearing on the monitors, were the same numerals that occur on Earth.

Biastra noticed my astonishment. 'It is true, isn't it Michel, for you there is one surprise after another. Don't think we are having fun at your expense, as we totally understand your wonder. All will fall into place in good time. For the moment please allow me to introduce Naola.'

The first of the astronauts rose and turned towards me. She placed her hand on my shoulder, as Biastra and Latoli had done. It occurred to me that this gesture must correspond to our handshake. Naola addressed me in her own language and then she, too, repeated my name three times, as if she wanted to commit it to memory forever. She was about the same size as Thao.

The same ceremony followed each time I was introduced, and thus I officially made the acquaintance of all the members of the crew. There was a striking resemblance between them. Their hair, for example, varied only in length and shade, which ranged from a dark copper to a light golden-blond. Some had longer or broader noses than others, but all had eyes of a colour which tended towards light rather than dark, and all had very neat, well-shaped ears.

Latoli, Biastra and Thao invited me to sit down in one of the comfortable seats.

When we were all comfortably installed, Biastra moved her hand in a particular way near the armrest of her seat and-I saw coming towards us, *floating* in the air - four round trays. Each carried a container of yellowish liquid and a bowl of something whitish with a consistency similar to fairy-floss but in granulated form. Flat 'tongs' served as forks. The trays came to rest on the arms of our seats.

I was quite intrigued. Thao suggested, if I wished to partake of this refreshment, I might like to follow her lead. She sipped from her 'glass' and I did likewise, finding it quite a pleasant-tasting drink, similar to a water-honey mixture. My companions used the 'tongs' to eat the mixture in the bowls. Following their example, I tasted for the first time what we, on Earth, called 'manna'. Similar to bread, it is however, extremely light and without any particular flavour. I had eaten only half the amount in my bowl when already, I felt satisfied, which surprised me considering the consistency of this food. I finished my drink and, although I couldn't say I'd dined in fine style, I experienced a sense of well-being and was neither hungry nor thirsty.

'Perhaps you would have preferred a French dish, Michel?' asked Thao, a smile twitching on her lips.

I merely smiled, but Biastra snorted.

Just then, a signal drew our attention to the panel. In the centre, and in close-up, appeared the head of a woman, resembling my hostesses. She spoke rapidly. My companions turned slightly in their seats to better attend to what was being said. Naola, at her desk, entered into a dialogue with the figure on the screen, just as our television interviewers do on Earth. Imperceptibly, the shot changed from the close-up to a wide angle, revealing a dozen women each in front of a desk.

Thao took me by the shoulder and guided me over to Naola, installing me in a seat in front of one of the screens. She took a seat next to me and addressed the people on the monitor. She spoke for some time, rapidly, in her melodious voice, turning frequently towards me. From all evidence, I was the main topic of conversation.

When she had finished, the woman re-appeared in close-up, responding in several brief sentences. To my great surprise, her eyes fixed on me and she smiled. 'Hello Michel, we wish you a safe arrival on Thiaoouba.'

She waited for my reply. When I had overcome my surprise, I expressed warm thanks. This, in turn, elicited exclamations and numerous comments from her companions, appearing again in a wide-angle shot on the screen.

'Did they understand?' I asked Thao.

'Telepathically yes, but they are delighted to hear someone from another planet speak his own language. For most of them, this is quite a rare experience.'

Excusing herself, Thao re-addressed the screen and, what I assumed was a technical conversation, ensued, including Biastra. Eventually, after a smile in my direction and a 'see you soon', the picture was cut.

I say 'cut' because the screen did not simply become blank; rather, the image was replaced by a beautiful, soft colour - a mixture of green and indigo blue - which produced a sense of contentment. It gradually faded after a minute or so.

Turning to Thao, I asked what it had all meant - had we rendezvoused with another spacecraft and what was this Thiaba or Thiaoula..?

'Thiaoouba, Michel, is the name we have given to our planet, just as you call yours 'Earth'. Our intergalactic base has been in touch with us, as we will be arriving in Thiaoouba in 16 of your Earth hours and 35 minutes.' This she had checked with a glance at the nearest computer.

'Those people then, are technicians on your planet?'

'Yes, as I just said, at our intergalactic base.'

'This base monitors our spacecraft continually and if we were in trouble for technical or human reasons, in eighty one per cent of cases, they would be able to control our safe return to port.'

This did not particularly surprise me as I had realised I was dealing with a superior race, whose technological possibilities were beyond my comprehension. What did occur to me was that, not only this spacecraft, but also the intergalactic base appeared to be manned by only women. An all female team such as this would be quite exceptional on Earth.

I wondered if Thiaoouba was populated only by women...like space Amazons. I smiled at the image. I have always preferred the company of women rather than men: it was quite a pleasant thought..!

My question to Thao was direct. 'Are you from a planet solely populated by women?'

She looked at me with apparent surprise, then her face lit up with amusement. I was a little concerned. Had I said something stupid? She took me by the shoulder and asked that I follow her. We left the control room and immediately entered a smaller room (called the *Haalis)* which had quite a relaxing ambience. Thao explained that we would not be interrupted in the room, since the occupants acquired, by their presence, the right to absolute privacy. She invited me to choose one of the many seats that furnished the room.

Some were like beds, some like armchairs, others resembled hammocks, while others again, were like high stools with adjustable backs. I would have been difficult to please if one of them did not suit my requirements.

Once settled comfortably in a kind of armchair with Thao facing me, I watched, as her face became serious again. She started to speak.

'Michel, there are no *women* aboard this spacecraft...'

If she had told me that I wasn't on a spaceship but rather, in the Australian desert, I would have more readily believed her. Seeing the expression of disbelief on my face, she added, 'neither are there any *men.* ' At this, my confusion was absolute.

'But,' I faltered, 'you are - what? Just robots?'

'No, I think you misunderstand. In a word, Michel, we are hermaphrodites. You know, of course, what an hermaphrodite is?'

I nodded, quite dumbfounded, and then asked, 'Is your whole planet inhabited only by hermaphrodites?'

'Yes.'

'And yet your face and mannerisms are more feminine than masculine.'

'Indeed, it might appear so, but believe me when I tell you that we are not women, but hermaphrodites. Our race has always been this way.'

'I must confess, this is all very confusing. I'm going to find it difficult to think of you as 'he' rather than the 'she' I have done since I've been among you.'

'You have nothing to imagine, my dear. We are simply what we are: human beings from another planet living in a world different from yours. I can understand you would like to define us as one sex or the other, for you think as an Earthling and a Frenchman. Perhaps, for once, you could make use of the neuter gender of English and think of us as 'it'.'

I smiled at this suggestion but continued to feel disoriented. Only moments ago, I had believed myself to be among Amazons.

'But how can reproduction of your race occur?' I asked. 'Can an hermaphrodite reproduce?'

'Of course we can, exactly as you do on Earth; the only difference being that we genuinely control the births - but that is another story. In good time, you will understand, but now we should rejoin the others.'

We returned to the control post, and I found myself looking at these astronauts with new eyes. Looking at the chin of one, I found it to be more masculine than it had seemed earlier. Another's nose was decidedly masculine, and the hairstyles of some were now more manly. It occurred to me that we really do see people as we *think* they are and not as they are.

In order to feel less embarrassed among them, I created a rule for myself: I had taken them to be women, as to me they were more like females than males: thus I would continue to think of them as women and we'd see how that worked.

From where I was, I could follow, on the central panel, the movement of stars as we proceeded on our way. Sometimes they appeared enormous and blinding as we passed by a little too closely - a few million kilometres from them. At times too, we noticed planets of strange colours. I remember one was of an emerald green, so pure I was stunned. It resembled an enormous jewel.

Thao approached and I took advantage of the opportunity to ask her about a band of light that had appeared at the base of the screen. This light was composed of what looked like millions of tiny explosions.

'These are caused by our anti-matter guns, as you would call them on Earth, and are, in fact, explosions. At the speed at which we travel, the most minuscule of meteorites would shatter this spacecraft were we to hit it. So, we make use of specific rooms to store certain forms of dust under enormous pressure, and this is fed into our anti-matter guns. Our vessel could be considered to be a cosmotron, firing streams of accelerated particles that disintegrate the most microscopic of errant bodies in space, for great distances ahead and to the sides of our spacecraft. This is what allows us to attain speeds that we can. Around our vessel, we create our own magnetic field...'

'Oh please, not so fast. As you know Thao, I have no scientific background and if you speak of cosmotrons and accelerated particles, you are going to lose me. I understand the principle, which is certainly very interesting, but I'm not good on technical terms. Can you tell me instead, why the planets on the screen are coloured the way they are?'

'Sometimes because of their atmospheres and sometimes because of the gases which surround them. Do you see a multicoloured point with a tail, at the right of the screen?' The 'thing' was approaching at high speed. Second by second we were better able to admire it.

It seemed to explode constantly and change form, its colours indescribably rich. I looked at Thao.

'It's a comet,' she said. 'It completes a revolution around its sun in approximately 55 of your Earth years.'

'How far are we from it?'

She glanced at the computer: '4 150 000 kilometres.'

'Thao,' I said, 'How is it you use the numerals of Arabic? And when you speak of "kilometres", are you translating for me, or do you actually use this measure?'

'No. We count in Kato and Taki. We use the numerals that you recognise as Arabic, for the simple reason that it is our own system - one which we took to Earth.'

'What? Please explain further.'

'Michel, we have several hours before arriving at Thiaoouba. This is probably the best time to start 'educating' you seriously on certain matters. If you don't mind, we'll go back to the Haalis, where we were before.'

I followed Thao, my curiosity stronger than ever.

The first man on Earth

Once comfortably re-established in the Haalis, the relaxation room previously described, Thao began her strange recital.

'Michel, 1 350 000 years ago precisely, on the planet Bakaratini of the constellation Centaur, a decision was made by the leaders of that planet, following numerous conferences and reconnaissance expeditions, to send inhabited vessels to the planets Mars and Earth.

'There was a very simple reason for this: their planet was cooling down internally and would become uninhabitable within 500 years. They thought, with good reason, that it was preferable to evacuate their people to a younger planet of the same category...'

'What do you mean by 'the same category'?'

'I will explain later, to do so now would be premature. Going back to these people, I must tell you that these beings were human - very intelligent and highly evolved. A black race, they had thick lips, flattened noses and frizzy hair - resembling, in these ways, the blacks now living on Earth.

'These people had inhabited the planet Bakaratini for 8 000 000 years, in cohabitation with a yellow-coloured race.

'To be precise, this was what you call on Earth, the Chinese race and they had inhabited Bakaratini for about 400 years prior to the blacks. The two races witnessed numerous revolutions during their time on the planet. We tried to provide relief, assistance and guidance but, in spite of our intervention, wars broke out periodically. These, along with the natural disasters occurring on the planet, served to thin the ranks in both races.

'Finally, a nuclear war broke out on such a grand scale that the entire planet was plunged into darkness and temperatures fell to minus 40 of your degrees Celsius. Not only did atomic radiation destroy the population, but cold and lack of food accomplished the rest.

'It is a recorded fact that a mere 150 black people and 85 yellow people survived the catastrophe, from a population of seven billion black and four billion yellow humans. A register of survivors was taken just before they began to reproduce and when they had stopped killing each other.'

'What do you mean 'killing each other'?'

'Let me explain the whole situation to you and you'll be able to understand better.

'First of all, it is important to explain that those who remained were not, as you might expect, the leaders, well protected in specially equipped shelters.

'The survivors, comprising three groups of blacks and five groups of yellows, had come, some from private shelters and others from large public shelters. Of course, at the time of the war, there were many more than 235 people in shelters: indeed it is believed there were over 800 000 in all. Following months of confinement in the darkness and intense cold, they were eventually able to risk going outside.

'The blacks ventured out first, finding almost no trees, no plants and no animals to speak of, on their continent. It was a group, isolated from their shelter in the mountains, who first knew cannibalism. Because of the lack of food, when the weakest died, they were eaten; then, in order to eat, they had to kill each other - and that was the worst catastrophe on their planet.

'Another group, near the ocean, managed to survive by eating the only living things left on the planet, which were not too contaminated, that is, the molluscs, some fish and crustaceans. They still had unpolluted drinking water thanks to very ingenious installations enabling them to obtain water from incredible depths.

'Of course, many of these people still died, as a result of lethal radiation on the planet and from eating fish which were filled with radioactivity.

'Much the same course of events occurred in the yellows' territory; so that, as I have said, 150 blacks and 85 yellows remained, then finally, deaths resulting from the war ceased and reproduction began again.

'All of this occurred, in spite of all the warnings they had received. It should be said that before this almost total decimation, both the black race and the yellow race had attained a very high level of technological advance. The people lived in great comfort. They worked in factories, private and government enterprises, offices - just as happens now on your planet.

'They had a strong devotion to money which, to some, meant power and to others, wiser, it meant well-being. They worked on average 12 hours per week.

'On Bakaratini a week comprises six days of 21 hours each. They tended to the material rather than the spiritual side of their existence. At the same time, they allowed themselves to be duped and led in circles by a structure of politicians and bureaucrats, exactly as is happening now on Earth. Leaders fool the masses with empty words and, motivated by greed or pride, they 'lead' entire nations towards their downfall.

'Gradually, these two great races began to envy each other and, as there is only one step from envy to hate, eventually they hated each other so much and so completely that the catastrophe occurred. Both possessing very sophisticated arms, they achieved their mutual destruction.

'Our historical records show, then, that 235 survived the disaster, six of them being children. These statistics were recorded five years afterwards, and their survival is attributed to cannibalism and certain marine life.

'They reproduced - not always 'successfully' as it was not

uncommon for babies to be born with horribly misshapen heads or ugly weeping sores. They had to endure all the effects of atomic radiation on human beings.

'One hundred and fifty years later, there were 190 000 blacks - men, women and children, and 85 000 yellows. I speak to you of this 150-year period because this was when both races began to re-establish and when we were able to help them materially.'

'What do you mean?'

'Just a few hours ago, you saw our spacecraft stop above the planet Aremo X3 and take samples of soil, water and air, did you not?' I nodded. 'Then,' Thao resumed, 'you watched as we quite easily annihilated a mass of giant ants as they attacked the inhabitants of a village.'

'Indeed.'

'In that particular case, we helped those people by intervening directly. You saw that they were living in a semi-wild state?'

'Yes, but what happened on that planet?'

'Atomic war, my friend. Always and eternally the same story.

'Don't forget Michel that the universe is a gigantic atom and everything is affected by that. Your body is composed of atoms. My point is, in all galaxies, each time a planet is inhabited, at a certain stage in its evolution, the atom is discovered or rediscovered.

'Of course, the scientists who discover it are very soon aware that the disintegration of the atom can be a formidable weapon, and, at one moment or another, the leaders want to use it; just as a child with a box of matches is driven to set fire to a bale of straw in order to see what will happen.

'But, coming back to the planet Bakaratini, 150 years after the nuclear holocaust, we wanted to help these people.

'Their immediate need was food. Still they were subsisting essentially from products of the sea, resorting occasionally to cannibalism to satisfy their omnivorous yearnings. They needed vegetables and a source of meat. Vegetables, fruit trees, grains, animals - all that was edible had disappeared from the planet.

'There remained just enough inedible plants and bushes to replenish the oxygen in the atmosphere.

'At the same time, an insect, resembling in some ways your praying mantis, had survived and, as a result of spontaneous mutation caused by the atomic radiation, had evolved to gigantic proportions. It grew to about eight metres in height and had become extremely dangerous to the people. In addition, this insect, having no natural predator, reproduced rapidly.

'We flew over the planet locating the whereabouts of these insects. This was a relatively easy task thanks to technology that has been at our disposal since time immemorial. When we detected the insects, we destroyed them so that, in a short time, we had exterminated them.

'Next, we had to re-introduce livestock, plants and trees on the planet according to the species known to have adapted climatically in specific regions before the catastrophe. This too, was relatively easy...'

'It must have taken years for such a task!'

A large smile lit up Thao's face. 'It took just two days - two 21-hour days.'

Faced with my incredulity, Thao burst into laughter. She, or he, laughed so heartily that I joined in, still wondering however, if the truth was being stretched somewhat.

How could I know? What I was hearing was so fantastic! Perhaps I was hallucinating; perhaps I had been drugged; perhaps I would soon 'wake up' in my very own bed? 'No, Michel,' interrupted Thao, reading my thoughts. 'I wish you would stop doubting in this way. Telepathy itself should be enough to convince you.'

As she uttered this sentence, it struck me that, even in the best-planned hoax, it would hardly be possible to bring together so many *supernatural* elements. Thao was able to read my mind like an open book, and proved it over and over again. Latoli, simply by placing her hand on me, had produced such an extraordinary feeling of well-being, I must acknowledge the evidence. I was well and truly experiencing an extra-extraordinary adventure.

'Perfect,' Thao agreed aloud. 'May I continue?'

'Please do,' I encouraged.

'So, we helped these people materially; but, as so often when we intervene, we did not allow our presence to be known and there are several reasons for that.

'The first is security. The second reason is a psychological one; if we had made these people aware of our existence and if they had realised we were there in order to help them, they would passively have allowed themselves to be helped and would have felt sorry for themselves. This would adversely affect their will to survive. As you say on Earth: 'God helps those who help themselves.'

'The third and last reason is the main one. Universal Law is well-established and is as strictly enforced as that which controls the planets revolutions around their suns. If you make a mistake, you pay the penalty - immediately, in ten years time, or in ten centuries time, but errors must be paid for. Thus, from time to time we are permitted, or even advised, to offer a helping hand but we are formally forbidden to 'serve the meal on a plate'.

'Thus, in two days, we repopulated their planet with several pairs of animals and re-established numerous plants so that eventually the people could raise the animals and cultivate the plants and trees. They had to start from scratch and we guided their progress, either by dream or telepathy. At times we did it by means of 'a voice coming from the heavens'; that is to say, the 'voice' came from our spacecraft but, to them, it came from 'heaven'.'

'They must have taken you to be gods!'

'Exactly so, and it is in this way that legends and religions are established; but, in cases as urgent as that one was, the end justified the means.

'Finally, after several centuries, the planet was almost as it had been before the nuclear holocaust. All the same, in some places, deserts had been definitely established. In other spots less affected, the flora and fauna were easily developed.

'One hundred and fifty thousand years later, the civilisation was highly successful but, this time, not only technologically: happily the people had learned their lesson and had also evolved to a high psychic and spiritual level. This occurred in both races and the blacks and the yellows had developed strong bonds of friendship.

'Thus, peace reigned on the planet, for the legends remained quite clear; many of them recorded in writing, so that future generations would know exactly what had provoked the nuclear catastrophe and what its consequences had been.

'As I said earlier, the people knew that their planet was going to become uninhabitable within 500 years. Knowing there were other planets, inhabited and inhabitable, in the galaxy, they mounted one of the most serious exploratory expeditions.

'Eventually, they penetrated your solar system, first visiting Mars which was known to be inhabitable and which, at that time in fact *was* inhabited.

'The human beings on Mars had no technology but, by contrast, they were spiritually, highly evolved. They were very small people measuring in height between 120 centimetres and 150 centimetres, and of Mongoloid type. They lived in tribes, in huts of stone.

'The fauna on Mars was scarce. There was a kind of dwarf goat, some very large hare-like creatures, several species of rat, and the largest animal resembled a buffalo but had a head like a tapir. There were also some birds and three species of snakes, one of which was quite venomous. The flora was also poor, trees attaining no more than four metres in height. They had too, an edible grass that you might compare with buckwheat.

'The Bakaratinians conducted their research, realising soon that Mars was also cooling down at a rate which indicated that it would no longer be inhabitable in four to five thousand years. In terms of its flora and fauna, it was barely rich enough to sustain those already living there, let alone cope with an emigrant mass from Bakaratini. Besides, the planet did not appeal to them.

'Thus, the two spacecraft headed for Earth. The first landing took place where Australia is now found. At that time, it should be explained that Australia, New Guinea, Indonesia and Malaysia were all part of the one continent. A strait existed, about 300 kilometres wide, exactly where Thailand is now found.

'In those times, Australia possessed a great inland sea fed by several large rivers, so that diverse and interesting flora and fauna flourished there. All things considered, the astronauts chose this country as their first immigration base.

'I must say, to be more precise, that the black race chose Australia and the yellow people established themselves where Burma is now - here too, was a land rich in wildlife. Bases were quickly set up on the coast, on the Bay of Bengal, while the black people constructed their first base on the shores of the Inland Sea in Australia. Later, further bases were established where New Guinea is presently located.

'Their spacecraft were capable of super-light speeds and took approximately 50 of your Earth years to bring 3 600 000 black people and the same number of the yellow race, to Earth. This bears witness to the perfect understanding and excellent association between two races determined to survive on a new planet and exist in peace. By common agreement, the aged and infirmed remained in Bakaratini.

'The Bakaratinians had explored *all* of the planet Earth before establishing their bases, and were absolutely persuaded that no human life existed before their arrival. Often they thought they had located a humanoid form of life, but on closer inspection, realised they had made contact with a species of large apes.

'Gravity on Earth was stronger than on their planet and it was quite uncomfortable initially, for the two races, but eventually they adapted very well.

'In building their towns and factories, they were fortunate to import from Bakaratini, certain materials which were very light and, at the same time, very strong.

'I have not yet explained that, at that time, Australia was on the equator. Earth rotated on a different axis - taking 30 hours and 12 minutes to complete a rotation, and achieved a revolution around its sun in 280 such days. The equatorial climate was not as you will find it today. It was much more humid than now, for the Earth's atmosphere has changed.

'Herds of huge zebras roamed the country, in company with enormous edible birds, referred to as 'dodos', very large jaguars, and another bird measuring almost four metres in height, which you have called Dinornis. In certain rivers, there were crocodiles up to 15 metres in length and snakes 25 to 30 metres long. They, at times, nourished themselves on the new arrivals.

'Most of the flora and fauna on Earth was totally different from that on Bakaratini - both from a nutritional and ecological point of view. Numerous experimental farms were established in an endeavour to acclimatise plants such as sunflower, maize, wheat, sorghum, tapioca and others.

'These plants either didn't exist on Earth or else existed in such a primitive state that they couldn't be consumed. The goat and the kangaroo were both imported, for the immigrants were quite partial to these, consuming them in great numbers on their planet. They were particularly keen to raise kangaroos on Earth, experiencing enormous difficulties however, in acclimatising them. One of the main problems was food. On Bakaratini, the kangaroo fed on a fine, hardy grass called *arilu,* which was totally unknown on Earth. Each time the Bakaratinians tried to grow it, it died, attacked always by millions of microscopic fungi. So it happened that the kangaroo were hand-fed, so to speak, for several decades, as they gradually adapted to the grasses on Earth.

'The black race persevered in its endeavours and finally succeeded in growing the plant, but it had taken so long that the kangaroos no longer required more than their new pastures. Very much later, some arilu plants took root and, as there were no animals to eat them, they spread throughout Australia. They still exist under the botanical name *Xanthorrhoea* and the popular name "black boys''.

'On Earth, this grass grows much taller and thicker than it did on Bakaratini, but that often happens when species are introduced from other planets. This plant is one of the rare vestiges of those distant times.

'It indicates, by being found only in Australia, along with the kangaroo, that the Bakaratinians remained in that particular part of the planet for a very long time before seeking to colonise other parts. I am about to explain this, but I wanted first, to cite the examples of the kangaroo and the *Xanthorrhoea* so that you might better understand all the problems of adaptation these people had to overcome; of course, it is only one small example among so many others.

'The yellow race had settled, as I said, in the hinterland of the Bay of Bengal. Most were in Burma where they too, had established cities and experimental farms. Principally interested in vegetables, they had imported from Bakaratini cabbages, lettuce, parsley, coriander and some others. For fruit, they brought the cherry tree, the banana and the orange trees. These last two were difficult to establish, for the climate of the time was generally colder than it is now. Thus, they gave some of the trees to the blacks who, by contrast, had enormous success with them.

'In the same way, the yellow people had far greater success in the growing of wheat. In fact, the wheat from Bakaratini produced enormous grains, around the size of a coffee bean, with ears measuring up to 40 centimetres in length. Four varieties of wheat were grown and the yellow race wasted no time in establishing a very high production level.'

'Did they also bring rice to the planet?'

'No, not at all. Rice is a plant absolutely native to Earth, although it was greatly improved by the yellow people on its way to becoming what it is now.

'To continue, immense silos were constructed and soon, commercial exchanges began between the two races. The black race exported kangaroo meat, dodos (which were prolific at the time) and zebra meat. In domesticating the latter, the blacks in fact, produced breeds that were equal in taste, to kangaroo meat and more nutritious. Trade was carried out using Bakaratini spacecraft, bases for these vessels having been set up all over the land...'

'What you are saying, Thao, is that the first men on Earth were black and yellow. How is it then, that I come to be white?'

'Not so fast, Michel, not so fast. The first men on Earth were, indeed, the blacks and the yellows, but for the moment I will continue to explain how they organised themselves and how they lived.

'Materially, they were successful, but they were also careful not to neglect the construction of their immense meeting halls, in which they practised their cult.' 'They had a cult?'

'Oh yes, they were all Tackioni, which is to say, they all believed in reincarnation; something in the way present-day Lamaists do on your planet.

'There was much travel between the two countries and they even combined efforts to explore deeper into certain regions of Earth. A mixed group of blacks and yellows landed one day, on the tip of South Africa, now called the Cape of Good Hope. Africa has changed very little since those times - apart from the Sahara, the north-eastern area and the Red Sea, which didn't exist then. But that is another story we will get to later.

'At the time of the exploration, they had already been established on Earth for three centuries.

'In Africa, they discovered new animals such as the elephant, the giraffe and the buffalo, and a new fruit that they had never before encountered - the tomato. Don't imagine Michel, that this was the tomato as you know it today. When discovered, it was the size of a very small currant and very acidic. The yellow people, having developed great expertise in such things, undertook to improve the tomato over the succeeding centuries, just as they did with rice, until it became the fruit you are now familiar with. They were equally surprised to find banana trees that, at first sight, resembled those they had imported. They had no reason to regret their efforts however, for the African banana was practically inedible and filled with large seeds.

'This African expedition comprised 50 blacks and 50 yellows, bringing home elephants, tomatoes and many mongeese, for they soon discovered the mongoose to be the mortal enemy of snakes. Unfortunately, they also brought with them without realising it, the terrible virus which is now called 'yellow fever'.

'In a very short time, millions of people had died, without their medical experts even knowing how the sickness had spread.

'Since it is mainly spread by the mosquito, and since there are many more mosquitoes in equatorial climates where there is no winter to reduce their numbers, it was the blacks in Australia who suffered most. In fact, they counted four times more victims than the yellows.

'The yellow race on Bakaratini has always been superior in the field of medicine and pathology; nevertheless, it took many years before they discovered a remedy for this curse, during which time hundreds of thousands died in terrible suffering. Eventually the yellow people produced a vaccine that was immediately made available to the blacks - a gesture that reinforced the bonds of friendship between the two races.'

'What were they physically like, these blacks?'

'When they migrated from Bakaratini, they were about 230 centimetres tall - their women too. They were a beautiful race. The yellow people were smaller in size, the average man measuring 190 centimetres and the women, 180 centimetres.'

'But you said that the present-day blacks are the descendants of those people - why is it they are now so much smaller?'

'Gravitation, Michel. Being stronger on Earth than on Bakaratini, both races gradually became smaller in size.'

'You also said that you are able to help people in trouble - why did you not give any assistance in regard to the yellow fever outbreak. Was it that you weren't able to find the vaccine either?'

'We could have helped; you will realise our potential when you visit our planet - but we didn't intervene because it wasn't in the program that we had to follow. I have already told you, and I can't repeat it often enough, we can help in certain situations but only so far. Beyond a certain point, the law strictly forbids aid of any kind.

'I'll give you a simple example. Imagine a child who goes to school each day in order to learn. Returning home in the evening, this child asks for assistance with his homework. If his parents are smart, they will help him understand the concepts involved so that the child can complete his task himself. If, however, his parents did his work for him, he wouldn't learn much, would he? He'd have to repeat each year and his parents would have done him no favours.

'As you will see later, although you know it already, you are on your planet in order to learn how to live, suffer and die, but also to develop spiritually as much as you can. We'll come back to this point later when the Thaori speak to you. For now, I want to tell you more of these people...

'They overcame the curse of the yellow fever and spread their roots deeper on this new planet. Not only was Australia heavily populated, but so was the area now known as Antarctica - of course, in those days, its position meant that its climate was temperate. New Guinea was also densely settled. By the end of the yellow fever scourge, the blacks numbered 795 million.'

'I thought that Antarctica was not really a continent?'

'At that time, it was attached to Australia and very much warmer than now, since Earth rotated on a different axis. The Antarctic climate was more like southern Russia is now.'

'Did they never go back to Bakaratini?'

'No. Once established on Earth, they made strict rules that no one would return.'

'What became of their planet?'

'It cooled down as predicted and became a desert - much like Mars.'

'What was their political structure like?'

'Very simple - election (by raised hands) of the leader of a village or district. These district leaders elected a town leader as well as eight old people chosen from among those most respected for their wisdom, common sense, integrity and intelligence.

'They were never selected on the basis of wealth or family, and all were between 45 and 65 years of age. The town or regional leaders (a region comprised eight villages) had the role of negotiating with the eight old people. The council of eight elected (by a secret ballot requiring that at least seven voted in accord) a delegate to represent them at meetings of State Council.

'In Australia, for example, there were eight states, each of which comprised eight towns or regions. At state council meetings there were thus, eight delegates, each representing a different town or region.

'At a state council meeting, presided over by a great sage, they discussed the type of day-to-day problems that confront any government: water conveyance, hospitals, roads etc. In regards to roads, both the black and the yellow races used very light vehicles, with a hydrogen motor, which travelled above the ground, thanks to a system based on antimagnetic and anti-gravitational force.

'But, to get back to the political system, there was no such thing as a 'party', everything being based solely on reputation for integrity and wisdom. Long experience had taught them that to establish an order that would endure, required two golden ingredients: fairness and discipline.

'I will speak to you some other time of their economic and social organisation, and give you an idea now, of their system of justice. A thief for example, genuinely considered to be guilty, was branded with a red-hot iron on the back of the hand he or she ordinarily used. So, a right-handed thief was branded on the right hand, a subsequent offence resulted in the left hand being cut off. This is a practice that still occurred quite recently among the Arabs - a practice conserved throughout time past. If he or she continued to steal, the right hand would be cut off and the forehead marked with an indelible symbol. Without hands, the thief was at the mercy and pity of his family and passers-by for food, for everything. Because people would recognise the symbol as that of a thief, life became very difficult. Death would have been preferable.

'In this way, the thief became a living example of what happened to a habitual offender. Needless to say, theft was a rare occurrence.

'As for murder, this too was rare, as you will see. Accused murderers were taken to a special room and left alone. Behind a curtain, a 'mind-reader' would be installed. This was a man who not only possessed a special telepathic gift but who also cultivated that gift in a constant endeavour, in one or another of the special universities. He would intercept the thoughts of the supposed murderer.

'You are going to retort that it is possible, with training, to make one's mind blank - but not for six hours at a stretch. Further, at various times when he or she might least expect it, certain predetermined sounds would be heard, obliging the 'subject' to break concentration.

'As a precautionary measure, six different 'mind-readers' were used. The same procedure was applied to witnesses for the prosecution or defence, in another building some distance away. Not a word would be exchanged and, on the two following days, the procedure would be repeated, this time for eight hours.

'On the fourth day, all the 'mind-readers' submitted their notes to a panel of three judges, who interviewed and cross-examined the accused and the witnesses. There were no lawyers or juries to impress. The judges had before them all the particulars of the case, and wanted to be *absolutely* sure of the guilt of the accused.'

'Why?'

'The penalty was death Michel, but a terrible death, the murderer being thrown alive to the crocodiles. As for rape, which was considered worse than murder, the punishment was even more cruel. The offender was coated with honey and buried to the shoulders in the immediate vicinity of an ant colony. Death, at times, would take ten or 12 hours.

'As you will now understand, the crime rate was extremely low among both races and, for this reason, they had no need for prisons.'

'Don't you consider that excessively cruel?'

'Consider the mother of a 16-year-old-girl, for example, who was raped and murdered. Doesn't she endure, in the loss of her child, cruelty of the worst kind? She did not provoke or seek her loss but she must suffer. The criminal, on the other hand, is aware of the consequences of his actions; thus, it is just that he be punished very cruelly. As I have explained however, criminality was almost nonexistent.

'Returning to religion: I said earlier that both races believed in reincarnation, but there were variations on their beliefs that, at times, divided them. Certain priests diverted masses of people to group them, under their leadership, in these variant religions. The divisions that resulted among the blacks had disastrous repercussions.

'Eventually, about 500 000 blacks emigrated in the wake of their priests, to Africa - to the area where the Red Sea is now. At that time, the Red Sea did not exist and the land was African. They began to construct villages and towns, but the political system as I described to you, which was fair and effective in all respects, was abandoned. The priests themselves elected the heads of government, so that these leaders became, more or less, puppets manipulated by the priests. From that time on, the people had to face many of the problems that are so familiar to you on Earth at the present time: corruption, prostitution, drugs and all manner of injustices.

'As for the yellow people they were very well structured and, in spite of some slight religious distortions, their priests had no say in the affairs of state.

'They lived in peace and affluence - quite different from the secessionist black race in Africa.'

'And in regard to arms, what sorts of weapons did they have?'

'It was quite simple and, as simplicity is often superior to complexity, it worked wonderfully well. Both races brought with them what we could call 'laser weapons'. These weapons were under the control of a special group which, in turn, was under the direction of the leaders of each country. By common accord, each race had exchanged 100 'observers' whose presence was permanent in each foreign country. These observers were ambassadors and diplomats for their own countries, at the same time, ensuring that an arms excess did not occur. This system worked perfectly and peace was maintained for 3550 years.

'The blacks who emigrated to Africa however, had not been allowed to take these weapons with them, being, as they were, a secessionist group. Little by little they spread further, settling the area that is now the Sahara desert. In those times, it was a rich land with a temperate climate, providing a well-vegetated habitat for many animals.

'The priests had temples constructed and, to satisfy their desire for wealth and power, they taxed the people heavily.

'Among a people who had never before known poverty, there now formed two distinct classes: the very rich and the very poor. The priests of course, belonged to the former, as did those who helped them to exploit the poor.

'Religion became idolatry and the people worshiped stone or wooden gods, offering sacrifices to them. It was not long before the priests insisted that the sacrifices must be human.

'From the beginning of the secession, the priests took pains to ensure that the people were kept in ignorance to the greatest extent possible. By lowering their intellectual and physical level of development over the course of years, the priests were better able to maintain domination over them. The religion which had 'developed' had absolutely nothing in common with the 'cult' that had originally inspired the secession; so control of the masses was essential.

'Universal Law decrees that man's principal obligation, regardless of which planet he happens to inhabit, is to develop his spirituality. These priests, by degrading an entire 'nation' through keeping them in ignorance and leading them with lies, infringed this fundamental Law.

'We decided at this point, to intervene, but, before doing so, offered the priests a last chance. Using telepathy, as well as a dream, we contacted the Great Priest: 'Human sacrifices must cease and these people must be led back to the Right Path. Man exists physically for the sole purpose of developing spiritually. What you are doing contravenes Universal Law.'

'The Great Priest was terribly shaken and, the next day, called a meeting of his priests, telling them of his dream. A few among them accused him of betrayal; others suggested senility; and some suspected hallucinations. Eventually, following several hours of discussion, 12 of the 15 priests who formed this council, remained determined to preserve the religion as it was, claiming that the ideal was to maintain control and to promote the belief in, and fear of, 'vengeful gods' whose representatives they were on Earth. They didn't believe a word of what the Great Priest had told them regarding his 'dream'.

'Sometimes our position is very delicate, Michel. We could have appeared with our spacecraft and spoken directly to the priests, but they were able to identify vessels from space, having had them too, before the secession.

'They would have attacked us immediately - no questions asked - for they were very suspicious and fearful of losing their pre-eminence within their 'nation'. They had formed an army and possessed quite powerful weapons, to be used to counter possible revolutions. We could also have destroyed them and spoken directly to the people in order to lead them back to the Right Path but, psychologically, this would have been a mistake. These people were accustomed to obeying their priests and would not have understood why we interfered in the affairs of their country - thus all would have been spoiled.

'So it was that one night we flew above the country at an altitude of 10 000 metres in one of our 'tool spheres'. The temple and the Holy City were situated about one kilometre from the town. We woke, by telepathy, the Great Priest and the two acolytes who had followed his advice, making them go, on foot, to a beautiful park, one-and-a-half kilometres from the Holy City. Then, by collective hallucination, we had the guards open the gaols and release the prisoners. Servants, soldiers - in fact, all the inhabitants of the Holy City, with the exception of the 12 evil priests, were evacuated. Inspired by strange 'visions' in the sky, everyone ran for the other end of the town.

'In the sky, winged personages hovered around an enormous incandescent cloud which shone in the night...'

'How is that done?'

'Collective illusion, Michel. Thus, in a very short time, it was arranged that only the 12 evil priests remained in the Holy City. When all was ready, the 'tool sphere' destroyed it all, including the Temple, by means of the same weapon that you have already seen in action. Rocks were shattered and walls crumbled to a height of one metre, that their ruins might bear witness to the consequence of this 'sin'.

'Indeed, if they had been totally effaced, men would soon have forgotten, for men easily forget...

'Further, and for the edification of the people, a voice issuing from the incandescent cloud, warned that the anger of God could be terrible - much worse than they had seen - and that they must obey the Great Priest and follow the new way which he would show them.

'When it was all over, the Great Priest stood before the people and spoke to them. He explained to the poor wretches that he had been wrong, and that it was now, important that everyone strive together to follow the new way.

'He was assisted in his work by the two priests. Of course, times were often hard, but they were aided by the memory and the fear of the event that had destroyed, in a matter of minutes, the Holy City and killed the evil priests. Needless to say, this 'event' was considered by all to be a miracle of the Gods, for it also involved the liberation of more than 200 prisoners who were to face human sacrifice the next day.

'All the details of the incident were noted by the scribes, but they were also distorted in the legends and tales passed on through the centuries. Nevertheless, the immediate consequence was that everything changed. The rich who had previously had a hand in the exploitation of the people, now, in view of what had happened to the evil priests and the Holy City, were fearful of meeting a similar fate. They were considerably humbled and assisted the new leaders in instigating the changes required.

'Gradually, the people became contented again, as they had been in times prior to the secession.

'Inclined towards pastoral rather than industrial or urban pursuits, they spread throughout Africa during the course of the centuries that followed and numbered, eventually, several million. Nevertheless, towns were only established in the area where the Red Sea is now, and along the banks of a large river that flowed through the centre of Africa.

'The people managed to develop their psychic abilities enormously. Many were able to travel short distances by means of levitation, and telepathy resumed its significance in their lives, becoming commonplace. There were also frequent instances of physical ailments being cured by the laying on of hands.

'Amicable relations were re-established with the black people in Australia and New Guinea who came to visit them regularly on 'chariots of fire' as they sometimes called the spaceships still being used by their Australian brothers.

'The yellow race, being closer neighbours, began to immigrate, in small numbers, to northern Africa, and were fascinated by the tales of 'The arrival of God on a Chariot of Fire'. This is how the legends subsequently referred to our intervention.

'The yellow people were the first to mix with the black race physically speaking, I mean. It might be surprising, but never, on Bakaratini, had the race mixed to the extent that they did on Earth. The ethnologists were greatly interested in the results of this union, which produced on Earth, a great new tribe. Indeed, these 'crossbreeds' as I'll call them, being crossed with more yellow blood than black, ended up feeling more at ease among themselves than with either black or yellow. Eventually, they grouped together and settled in the area now called Algeria - Tunisia, North Africa. Thus, a new race was born - the Arab race that you know. Don't think though, they immediately resembled the race they are now. Climate and time, the passing of centuries, had its effect. My story simply gives you the idea of how the race began through inter-breeding.

'And so, all was going well for the inhabitants of the planet Earth, except for one thing...the astronomers and scholars were very worried, for an enormous asteroid was approaching Earth, almost imperceptibly, but unmistakably.

'It was first picked up by the observatory of Ikirito, located in the centre of Australia. After several months, it could be seen by the naked eye, provided one knew where to look, glowing a most sinister, vivid red. In the weeks to follow it became ever more readily visible.

'The governments of Australia, New Guinea and Antarctica made a most important decision, which was soon agreed to by the yellow leaders. Ahead of the inevitable collision with the asteroid, they agreed that all space vessels in a condition to fly, would leave Earth, carrying on board as many specialists and experts as possible - doctors, technicians etc. - of the kind most likely to be of service to the community following the catastrophe.'

'Where were they going? To the Moon?'

'No Michel, at that time Earth didn't have a moon. Their spacecraft were now capable of 12 weeks autonomous flight. For a long time, their capability for super long distance travel had been lost to them. Their plan was to remain in orbit around the earth, ready to land as soon as possible and give assistance where it was most needed.

'Eighty Australian spacecraft were equipped and loaded to carry an elite group, which was chosen as a result of meetings held day and night. The yellow race followed the same procedure, making 98 spacecraft ready. In Africa of course, there had never been any spaceships.

'I ask you to note, in passing, that apart from the supreme leader of each country, none of his 'ministers', as you might call them, was given a place on any vessel. This will probably seem odd to you, for if the same situation were to occur today on Earth, many politicians would be pulling strings to save their own skins.

'All was ready. The people were then warned of the impending collision. The role of the spacecraft was kept secret though, for fear that the people would believe they had been betrayed by their leaders and that a panic would be created, perhaps even an attack on the airports. By the same token, the leaders had played down the impact the collision was likely to have, in order to minimise the collective panic.

'The collision was now as much imminent as it was inevitable, considering the estimated speed of the asteroid. It was only 48 hours away. The experts all agreed with this calculation - well, almost all.

'The spaceships were to take off together - 2 hours before the supposed collision time, their very late departure intended to allow them to remain in space for the full 12 weeks if necessary, following the catastrophe. It had been calculated that the asteroid would hit where South America is now.

'So, all was ready and the signal for take-off to be given on D-day, at 12 noon, Central Australian Time. Whether there had been an error in the calculations, although highly unlikely, or whether there was a sudden, unpredicted acceleration of the asteroid, it appeared in the sky at 11 am, shining like an orange sun. The order for take-off was given immediately and all the spacecraft took to the sky.

'In order to leave Earth's atmosphere and gravitational force quickly, it is necessary to make use of a 'warp', which at that time, was above present day Europe. In spite of the speed these space vessels were capable of, they had not quite made it to the warp, when the asteroid hit Earth. When it entered the Earth's atmosphere it had broken into three huge pieces. The smallest, which measured several kilometres in diameter, hit where the Red Sea is now.

'Another, much bigger, hit where the Timor Sea is now, and the largest of the three landed in the region of the actual Galapagos Islands.

'The simultaneous impacts were terrible. The sun became a dull red and slid towards the horizon like a falling balloon. Soon, it stopped and climbed slowly, but when only to half the distance, it 'fell'. The Earth had suddenly changed the inclination of its axis! Explosions of incredible force occurred, for two larger pieces of asteroid had pierced the Earth's crust. Volcanoes erupted in Australia, New Guinea, Japan, South America - indeed, just about everywhere on the planet. Mountains formed instantly and tidal waves more than 300 metres in height swept over four-fifths of Australia. Tasmania separated from the Australian continent and a huge portion of Antarctica sank in the waters, creating two immense underwater canyons between Antarctica and Australia. An enormous continent rose from the waters in the centre of the South Pacific Ocean. A huge piece of Burma subsided where the Bay of Bengal is now. Another basin of land subsided and the Red Sea was formed.'

'Was there time for the spaceships to get out?'

'Not quite, Michel, for the experts had made one mistake. It could be said in their defence that they could not really have anticipated what would happen. They had predicted the tilting of the Earth on its axis but what they hadn't been able to predict was its oscillation. The spacecraft were literally caught in the anti-gravitation warp and dragged in the 'backwash' caused by the re-entry of the asteroid into the Earth's atmosphere. Further, they were bombarded by millions of particles coming from the asteroid and trailing in its wake.

'Only seven vessels, three with black passengers and four with yellow, struggling with all the power they could manage, succeeded in escaping the horror occurring on Earth.'

'It must have been a frightening sight for them to watch Earth change before their eyes.

'How long did it take for the continent you mentioned in the Pacific Ocean to emerge?'

'Merely a matter of hours. This continent was raised by gaseous belts resulting from upheavals, occurring as deep as the centre of the planet.

'The upheavals on the Earth's surface continued for months. In the three points of impact of the asteroids, thousands of volcanoes were created. Poisonous gases spread over most of the Australian continent, causing painless death within minutes, of millions of blacks. Our statistics indicate an almost total annihilation of humankind and of animals in Australia. A count taken when calm was restored indicated a mere 180 people had survived.

'The poisonous gases were the cause of this frightful toll. In New Guinea, where less gas had drifted, there were fewer deaths.'

'I have been wanting to ask you a question, Thao.'

'Please do.'

'You said that it was the black people from Australia who spread to New Guinea and Africa. How is it then, that now, the Aborigines are so different from the blacks throughout the world?'

'Excellent question, Michel. My account should have included more detail. You see, as a result of the catastrophe, there had been such an upheaval, that deposits of uranium scattered on the surface of the Earth emitted strong radiation. This happened only in Australia, and those who escaped death were badly affected, just as in an atomic explosion.

'They were genetically affected, so that today, the genes of Africans are different from those of Aborigines. Further, the environment totally changed and their diet drastically altered too. With the progress of time, these descendants of Bakaratinians were 'transformed' into the Aboriginal race of today.

'As the upheavals continued, mountains were formed, some suddenly, others within days. Crevasses opened swallowing entire towns, and then closing, removing all traces of existing civilisation.

'On top of all the horror, there was a deluge such as the planet had not known for eons. In fact, the volcanoes spat so many ashes into the sky simultaneously, and to such incredible altitudes, that the sky darkened. The vapour from the oceans, which in places actually boiled over an area of thousands of square kilometres, combined with the clouds of ashes. The thick clouds thus created, burst with rain so torrential you'd find it hard to imagine...'

'And the vessels orbiting in space?'

'After 12 weeks, they were obliged to return to Earth. They chose to descend over the area we now know as Europe, having absolutely no visibility over the rest of the planet. Of the seven vessels, only one managed to land.

'The others were hurled into the ground by gales, which occurred all over the planet - cyclonic winds of 300-400 kilometres per hour. The main cause of these winds was differences in temperature - these in turn, caused by the sudden volcanic eruptions.

'So, the sole remaining spaceship managed to land in what is now called Greenland. There were 95 yellow passengers on board, many of whom were doctors and experts of various kinds. Having landed in extremely adverse conditions, damage was incurred which made it impossible for the vessel to take off again. However, it remained useful for a shelter. They had provisions enough to last a long time and so they organised themselves as best they could.

'About one month later, they were all engulfed in an earthquake - the spacecraft too, and it was with this last catastrophe that all trace of civilisation on Earth was destroyed. The chain of catastrophes that followed the collision with the asteroid had dispersed entire populations - in New Guinea, Burma and China, and in Africa, although the region of the Sahara suffered to a lesser extent than elsewhere. However, all the towns established in the Red Sea area were engulfed by the newly-formed sea. In brief, no city remained on Earth and millions of people and animals had been wiped out. It was, therefore, not long before widespread famine occurred.

'Needless to say, the wonderful cultures of Australia and China were no more than memories that would become legends. And so it was, that the people (suddenly disseminated and separated from each other by newly gouged chasms and newly formed seas) experienced for the first time on the planet Earth, cannibalism. '

The Golden Planet

As Thao was winding up her narrative, my attention was drawn to lights of different colours, which had lit up near her seat. When she had finished talking, she made a gesture. On one of the walls of the room, there appeared a series of letters and numbers, which Thao examined attentively. Then the light went out and the image disappeared.

'Thao,' I said, 'you spoke just now of hallucination or collective illusion. I have trouble understanding how you can delude thousands of people -isn't it charlatanism, just as when an illusionist on stage fools the crowd with a dozen, more or less 'chosen' subjects?'

Thao smiled again. 'You are right in a certain sense, for it is extremely rare these days on your planet and especially on stage to find a true illusionist. I must remind you that we are experts in all manner of psychic phenomena Michel, and for us it is quite easy because...'

At that moment, a shock of extraordinary violence shook the spacecraft. Thao looked at me with horrified eyes - her whole face had completely changed and one could read in it sheer terror. With a dreadful cracking sound, the vessel split into several pieces and I heard screams from astronauts, as we were all hurled into space. Thao had grabbed hold of my arm and we were flung through the sidereal emptiness at a giddying speed. I realised, only because of the speed we were travelling, that we were about to cross paths with a comet - exactly like the one we had passed by several hours earlier.

I felt Thao's hand on my arm but didn't even think to turn my head in her direction - I was literally mesmerised by the comet. We were going to collide with its tail - that was certain - and already I could feel the terrible heat. The skin on my face was ready to burst - it was the end...

'Are you OK, Michel?' asked Thao gently from her seat. I thought I was going mad. I was sitting opposite her in the same seat where I had listened to her account of the first man on Earth.

'Are we dead or mad?' I asked.

'Neither, Michel. There is a saying on your planet that a picture is worth a thousand words. You asked me how we were able to delude crowds of people. I replied immediately by *creating an illusion* for you. I realise I should have chosen a less frightening experience, but the subject is a very important one in this case.'

'It's fantastic! I never would have believed that it could happen like that - and so suddenly. It was so very *real* - the whole scenario. I don't know what to say... The only thing I ask of you is not to frighten me like that again. Besides, I could die of fright...'

'Not at all. Our physical bodies were in our seats and we simply separated our...let's call them 'astropsychic' bodies from our physical ones and from our other bodies...'

'What other bodies?'

'All the others: the physiological, the psychotypical, the astral, and so on. Your astropsychic body was separated from the others by a telepathic system originating in my brain which, acts in this case, like a transmitter. A direct correlation is established between my astropsychic body and yours.

'All that I imagined was projected in your astropsychic body exactly as if it was happening. The only thing is, not having had time to prepare you for the experience, I had to be very cautious.'

'What do you mean?'

'Well, when you create an illusion, the subject, or subjects, should be prepared to see what you want them to see. For example, if you want people to see a spaceship in the sky, it is important that they are expecting to see one. If they expect to see an elephant, they will never see the spaceship. Thus, with the right words and cleverly controlled suggestions, the crowd will unite around you in anticipation of seeing a spaceship, a white elephant, or the Virgin of Fatima - a typical case of the phenomenon on Earth.'

'It would have to be easier with a single subject than with 10 000.'

'Not at all. On the contrary, with several people, a chain reaction is produced. You release the astropsychic bodies of the individuals and when you put the procedure in motion, they telepathise among themselves. It's a bit like the famous domino-lines - when you make the first one fall, all the others must fall right down to the last one.

'So it was a very easy game with you. Since you left Earth, you have remained more or less anxious. You don't know what will *logically* happen next.

'I took advantage of this typical case of conscious or unconscious fear that is always present when one travels in a flying machine - the fear of exploding or crashing. Then, as you had seen the comet on the screen, why not use it too? Rather than cook your face as you approached the comet, I could have made you cross the tail believing it to be frozen.'

'In all, you could have driven me insane!'

'Not in such a short time...'

'But that had to have lasted more than five minutes..?'

'No more than ten seconds - just as in a dream, or should I say a nightmare, which occurs by the way, in approximately the same manner. For example, you are sleeping and you begin to dream... You are in a field with a wonderful white stallion. You approach to catch him, but each time you try, he runs away. After five or six attempts, which take time of course, you leap on the horse's back and begin to gallop and gallop. Faster and faster you go and you are happily intoxicated by the speed... The stallion gallops so fast that he no longer touches the ground. He is airborne and the countryside passes beneath you - river, plains and forests.

'It is truly wonderful. Then a mountain appears on the horizon, looming taller and taller as you approach. You have to rise higher with difficulty. The horse flies up and up - it is almost over the highest peak when his shoe strikes a rock, unbalancing you, so that you fall - down and down - you go into a chasm that seems to have no end...and you find you have fallen out of bed on to the floor.' 'No doubt you are going to tell me this dream lasts only a few minutes.'

'It would have lasted four seconds. The dream started as though, from a certain point you wound back a film on video and then watched it. I know it is difficult to comprehend but in this particular dream, all would have begun at the moment you lost your balance in bed.'

'I confess that I don't understand.'

'I'm not at all surprised, Michel. To understand completely requires much more study in the field and, on Earth at the present time, you don't have anyone capable of instructing you on the subject. Dreams don't really matter for the moment Michel, but without your realising it, during the few hours you have spent with us, you have made great progress in certain areas and this is what matters. Now it is time to explain to you our motives for bringing you to Thiaoouba.

'We are entrusting you with a mission. This mission is to report all that you are going to see, live and hear during your time with us. Report everything in one, or several books that you will write when you return to Earth. We have been observing the behaviour of the people on your planet for thousands and thousands of years, as you now realise.

A *certain percentage of these people are arriving at a very critical point in history and we feel that the time has come to try to assist them. If they will listen, we can ensure that they take the right path. This is why you have been chosen...'*

'But I am not a writer! Why haven't you chosen a good writer - someone well known, or a good journalist?'

Thao smiled at my vehement reaction. 'The only writers who might have done it, as it must be done, are dead - I mean Plato or Victor Hugo - and they still would have reported the facts with too much stylistic embellishment. We require the most precise account possible.'

'Then you need a journalist reporter...'

'Michel, you know yourself, that journalists on your planet are so inclined towards sensationalism, that they often distort the truth.

'How often for example, do you see news reports that differ from channel to channel or paper to paper? Whom do you believe when one gives the death toll in an earthquake as 75, another as 62 and another as 95? Do you really imagine we would trust a journalist?'

'You're absolutely right!' I exclaimed.

'We have observed you and we know all about you as we know about some others on Earth - and you were *selected...*

'But why exactly me? I am not the only one on Earth capable of objectivity.'

'Why not you? In time, you will learn the principal reason behind our choice.'

I didn't know what to say. Moreover, my objections were ridiculous since I had already embarked on this affair and there was no going back. Ultimately, I had to admit I was enjoying this space voyage more and more. Certainly, millions of human beings would have given all they owned to be in my place.

'I will argue no further Thao. If this is your decision, I can only yield to it. I hope I will be equal to the task. Have you considered that ninety nine per cent of people will not believe a word of what I say? For most people it will be too incredible.'

'Michel, almost 2000 years ago, did they believe that Christ was sent by God as he claimed? Certainly not, for they wouldn't have crucified him had they believed. Now however, there are millions who believe what he said...'

'Who believes him? Do they really believe him Thao? And who was he anyway? First of all, who is God? Does he exist?'

'I have been expecting this question and it is important that you ask it. On an ancient stone tablet, which I believe is *Naacal,* it is written: In the beginning there was nothing - all was darkness and silence.

'The Spirit - the Superior Intelligence decided to create the worlds and he commanded to four superior forces...

'It's extremely difficult for the human mind, even when highly developed, to comprehend such a thing. In fact, in a sense, it is impossible. On the other hand, your Astral Spirit assimilates it when it is freed from your physical body. But I'm getting ahead of myself - let's go back to the very beginning.

'In the beginning there was nothing except darkness and a spirit - THE *Spirit.*

'The Spirit was, and is, infinitely powerful - powerful beyond the comprehension of any human mind. The Spirit is so powerful that he was able, by the action of his will alone, to trigger an atomic explosion with chain reactions of unimaginable force. In fact, the Spirit imagined the worlds - he imagined how to create them - from the most enormous to the most minuscule. He imagined the atoms. When he imagined them he created, in his imagination, all that moved and will move: all that lived and will live; all that is motionless, or seems to be - every single thing.

'But it existed only in his imagination. All was still in darkness. Once he had an overall view of what he wanted to create, he was able, by his exceptional spiritual force, to create, instantaneously, the four forces of the Universe.

'With these, he directed the first and the most gigantic atomic explosion of all time - what certain people on Earth call 'The Big Bang'. The Spirit was at its centre and induced it. Darkness was gone and the Universe was creating itself according to the will of the Spirit.

'The Spirit was thus, is still, and always will be, at the centre of the Universe for he is the Master and Creator of it...'

'Well then,' I interrupted, 'it's the story of God as the Christian religion teaches it - or just about - and I never believed in their nonsense...'

'Michel, I speak of no religion such as exists on Earth and especially not the Christian religion. Don't confuse religions with the Creation and the simplicity of all that ensued. Don't confuse logic with the illogical distortions of religions. We will have the opportunity to talk again later on this subject, and you are certainly in for some surprises.

'For the moment, I was trying to explain the Creation to you. During billions of years (for the Creator of course, it is eternally the 'present', but it is more at the level of our understanding to count by billions of years), all the worlds, suns and atoms were formed, as you are taught in schools, the planets revolving around their suns, and sometimes with their own satellites etc. At certain times in certain solar systems, some planets cool down - soil is formed, rocks solidify, oceans are formed and landmasses become continents.

'Finally, these planets become habitable for certain forms of life. All this was in the beginning, in the imagination of The Spirit. We can call his first force the 'Atomic force'.

'At this stage, by his second force, he conceived the primary living creatures and many of the primary plants, from which later derived the sub-species. This second force we will call the 'Ovocosmic Force', as these creatures and plants were created by simple cosmic rays, which ended up with cosmic eggs.

'At the very beginning, The Spirit imagined experiencing feelings through a special creature. He had imagined Man by means of the third force that we will call the 'Ovoastromic Force'. Thus Man was created. Have you ever considered Michel, what intelligence it took to create a human being or even an animal? Blood that circulates thanks to the heart that beats millions of times independently of the will...lungs that purify the blood by means of a complex system...the nervous system...the brain which gives the orders, aided by the five senses...the spinal cord which is ultra-sensitive and which will make you [instantly] withdraw your hand from a hot stove so you won't burn yourself – the one tenth of a second it would have taken the brain to issue the order to prevent your hand from being burnt.

'Have you ever wondered why, that of the billions of individuals on a planet like yours, there are no two fingerprints the same: and why, what we call the 'crystalline' of the blood, is just as unique among individuals as the fingerprint?

'Your experts and technicians on Earth, and on other planets, have tried and still try to create a human body. Have they succeeded? In regards to the robots they have made, not even the most highly perfected will ever be more than a vulgar machine in comparison with the human mechanism.

'To go back to the crystalline I mentioned just now, it is best described as a certain vibration particular to the blood of each individual. It has nothing to do with the blood group. Various religious sects on Earth believe absolutely in the 'rightness' of refusing blood transfusions. Their reasons relate to the teachings and books of their religious teachings and their own interpretations of these, whereas they should look to the real reason, which is the impact the different vibrations have on each other.

'If it is a large transfusion, it can have an influence on the recipient to a degree and, for a length of time, which varies according to the volume of the transfusion. This influence, of course, is never dangerous.

'After a time, which never exceeds one month, the vibrations of the recipient's blood takes over, leaving no trace of the vibrations of the donor's blood.

'It shouldn't be forgotten that these vibrations are much more than a feature of the physiological and fluidic body than that of the physical body.

'But I notice that I have deviated greatly from my subject, Michel. In any case, it is time now to rejoin the others. We are not far from arriving at Thiaoouba.'

I didn't dare ask Thao then, about the nature of the fourth force, for already she was heading for the exit. I left my seat and followed her back to the command post. There, on the panel and in close-up view, a person was talking slowly and almost continuously. Numbers and figures, with luminous dots of different bright colours were continually crossing the screen, interspersed with symbols.

Thao sat me down in the seat I had previously occupied and asked me not to interfere with my security system. She then moved away, to confer with Biastra who seemed to be supervising the astronauts, each of who was busy at her respective desk. Finally, she came back and sat down in the seat next to mine.

'What is happening?' I asked

'We are reducing speed progressively as we approach our planet. We are now 848 million kilometres away and will arrive in about twenty-five minutes.'

'Can we see it now?'

'Patience, Michel. Twenty-five minutes is not the end of the world!' She winked, evidently in good humour.

The close-up view on the panel was replaced by a wide-angle shot, allowing us a general view of the command room of the intergalactic base, as we had seen earlier. Now each operator was deep in concentration at her particular desk. Many of the 'desk-computers' were operated orally, rather than manually, responding to the operators' voices. Figures, accompanied by luminous dots of various colours, crossed the screen rapidly. No one in the spacecraft remained standing.

Suddenly, there it was, right in the middle of the panel. The intergalactic centre had been replaced by... Thiaoouba!

My guess *had* to be correct - I could *feel* it. Thao immediately telepathised an affirmative, leaving me in no doubt.

As we approached and Thiaoouba grew on the panel, I couldn't take my eyes off the sight, for what I saw before me was indescribably beautiful. Initially, the first word which sprang to mind was 'luminous' - this then was juxtaposed with 'golden' - but the effect produced by this colour was beyond any description. If I were to invent a word, perhaps one that might apply would be 'lumino-vapour- golden'. In fact, one had the impression of plunging into a luminous and golden bath - almost as if there were very fine gold dust in the atmosphere.

We were descending gently on to the planet and the panel no longer showed its contours, but rather, the contours of a continent could be distinguished, ending abruptly at an ocean, that was sprinkled with a multitude of islands of different colours.

The closer we came, the greater was the detail discernible - the zoom lenses were not used at the time of landing, for a reason which was explained to me later. What captivated me most, was the *colour* before me - I was *dazzled!*

All the colours were, in each tonal variation more vivid than ours. A bright green, for example, almost shone - it radiated colour. A dark green had the opposite effect - it 'kept' its colour. It is extremely difficult to describe, for the colours on this planet could not be compared with any that exist on Earth. A red could be recognised as red, but it wasn't the red we know. There is a word in Thao's language which defines the types of colours on Earth and on planets similar to ours. Our colours are *Kalbilaoka* which I translate as 'dull', theirs, on the other hand, are *Theosolakoviniki* which means they radiate their colours from within.

My attention was soon drawn to what looked, on the screen, like eggs - yes, eggs![2] could see the ground dotted with eggs, some half covered with vegetation, and others quite bare. Some seemed bigger than others and some lay down. Others were upright with what looked like the pointed end towards the sky.

I was so astonished by this sight that I turned again towards Thao to ask her about these 'eggs', when suddenly on the screen, there appeared a round form surrounded by several spheres of different sizes, and, slightly further away, yet more 'eggs'. These ones were enormous.

I recognised the spheres to be space vessels just like ours.

'Affirmative', said Thao from her seat, 'and the round form you see is the cell in which our spacecraft will be accommodated in a few moments, for we are in the process of docking.

'And the gigantic eggs, what are they?'

Thao smiled. 'Buildings, Michel, but just now, there is something more important that I must explain to you. Our planet contains many

---

[2] I should say *half an egg*, as we shall see later on, the description would be more appropriate.

surprises for you, but there are two, which could have harmful effects on you. I must therefore ensure that you take certain elementary precautions. Thiaoouba does not have the same gravitational force as your planet. Your weight would be 70 kilograms on Earth - here it will be 47 kg. When you leave the spacecraft, if you aren't careful, you risk losing your sense of equilibrium in your movements and your reflexes. You'll be inclined to take too great a stride, and perhaps fall and injure yourself...'

'But I don't understand. In your spacecraft, I feel fine.'

'We have related the internal gravitational pull to correspond with that of Earth - or almost.'

'Then you must be extremely uncomfortable, for you must weigh about 60 kilograms more than your normal weight, given your size.'

'It's true that under this force, our bodies are heavier, but we have counter-balanced this by a semi-levitation, thus we are not uncomfortable, and at the same time, we have the satisfaction of seeing you move among us at ease.'

A slight jolt indicated we had docked. This extraordinary trip was over - I was going to put my foot on *another planet.*

'The second point,' Thao resumed, 'is that you will be obliged to wear a mask, for a while at least, for the brightness and the colours will literally intoxicate you, just as if you had drunk alcohol. The colours are vibrations that act on certain points on your physiological body. On Earth, these points are so slightly stimulated, so little exercised, that here, consequences could be unfortunate.'

The security force field of my seat had just been 'turned off liberating me again, to move about as I pleased. The panel was blank but the astronauts were still busy. Thao led me towards the door and back into the room I'd first entered where I had lain for three hours. There, she took a helmet, very light, which covered my face from my forehead to just below my nose.

'Let's go, Michel, and welcome to Thiaoouba.'

Outside the spacecraft, we walked along a very short walkway. Immediately, I felt lighter. The sensation was very pleasant, although somewhat disconcerting, since several times I lost balance and Thao had to steady me.

We saw no one, a fact that surprised me. Earthly perspective had led me to expect to be welcomed by a crowd of reporters, cameras flashing...or something similar - perhaps a red carpet! Why not the head of state in person? For heaven's sake, these people wouldn't be visited by an extra-planetarian every day! But nothing...

After a short distance, we arrived at a round platform, to the side of the walkway. Thao sat down on one of the circular seat inside the platform and signalled that I should sit down opposite her.

She took out an object the size of a walkie-talkie and immediately I felt myself pinned to the seat, just as I had been in the spaceship, by an invisible force field. Then, quite gently and with a barely perceptible hum, the platform rose by several metres and moved off rapidly towards the 'eggs', about 800 metres away. The thin and slightly perfumed air was lashing the exposed area of my face below my nose, which was very nice, its temperature being around 26 degrees Celsius.

In just seconds, we arrived, and passed through the walls of one of the 'eggs', as if we'd passed through a cloud. The platform stopped and came to rest gently on the floor of the 'building'. I looked around me in all directions.

It seemed absurd, but the 'egg' had disappeared. We had indeed, entered the 'egg' and yet around us, as far as the eye could see, stretched the countryside. We could see the landing ground and the docked spaceships just as though we were outside...

'I understand your reaction, Michel,' said Thao who knew what I was thinking, 'I'll explain the mystery to you later.'

Not far from us, were gathered twenty or thirty people, all busy to some extent, in front of desks and screens which flashed with coloured lights - similar to inside the spacecraft. A type of music played very softly, elevating me to a state of euphoria.

Thao signalled me to follow her and we headed towards one of the smaller 'eggs' situated near the 'supposed inside walls' of this larger one. As we went, we were greeted with happiness by all we passed.

I must mention here, that Thao and I made an odd couple as we moved across the room. The great difference in our heights meant that, as we walked side by side, she was obliged to move slowly so that I didn't have to run to keep up - my movements were more like ungainly jumps, for each time I tried to hurry, I exacerbated the problem. I had the task of coordinating muscles that were accustomed to moving a weight of 70 kilograms and now had only to move 47 kilograms - you can imagine the effect we created.

We headed for a light that was shining on the wall of the small 'egg'. In spite of my mask, I was very conscious of its brilliance. We passed beneath the light and went through the wall into a room that I immediately recognised as the one featured on the screen in the spaceship. The faces too, were familiar to me. I realised I was in the intergalactic centre.

Thao took off my mask. 'It's all right for now, Michel, you won't need it here.'

She introduced me personally to each of the dozen people there. They all exclaimed something and put a hand on my shoulder as a gesture of welcome.

Their faces wore expressions of sincere joy and goodness and I was deeply touched by the warmth of their reception. It was as if they considered me one of them.

Thao explained that their principal question was: why is he so sad - is he ill?

'I am not sad!' I protested.

'I know, but they are not accustomed to the facial expressions of the people of Earth. Faces here, as you can see, reflect a perpetual happiness.'

It was true. They looked as though every second, they received excellent news.

I had been aware that something was strange about these people and suddenly it *hit me:* Everyone I had seen, seemed to be of the same age!

Learning to live
on another planet

It seemed that Thao was also very popular here and she found herself answering numerous questions - always with her natural, broad smile. Before long, however, several of our hosts were required to resume their duties and we took this as our cue to leave. My mask was put on again and we left these people, as well as those in the larger room, amidst many gestures of friendship and goodwill.

We rejoined our vehicle and immediately accelerated away in the direction of a forest, which could be seen in the distance. We flew at a height of approximately five or six metres and at a speed I would have estimated to be 70 or 80 kilometres per hour. The air was warm and fragrant and I again felt euphoric, in a way I had never experienced on Earth.

We arrived at the edge of the forest and I remember having been greatly impressed by the size of the largest trees. They looked to rise about 200 metres into the sky.

'The tallest is 240 of your metres, Michel.' Thao explained without me having to ask, 'and between 20 and 30 metres in diameter at the base.

'Some of these are 8000 of our years old. Our year consists of 333 days of 26 *karses.* A karse is a period of 55 *lorse,* a lorse comprising 70 *kasios,* and a kasio being almost equivalent to one of your seconds. (Now there's a sum for you...) Would you like to go to your 'apartment' or to have a look at the forest first?'

'Let's visit the forest first, Thao.'

The vehicle greatly reduced its speed and we were able to glide between, or indeed, stop and observe more closely, the trees at heights that ranged from almost ground level to 10 metres above the ground.

Thao was able to guide our 'flying platform' with amazing precision and expertise. Our vehicle, and Thao's manner of driving it, put me in mind of a flying carpet, which was taking me on a magical tour of this magnificent forest floor.

Thao leaned towards me and removed my mask. The undergrowth was luminous and softly golden but I found it quite tolerable.

'It is a good time to begin accustoming yourself to the light and colour, Michel. Look!'

Following her gaze, I spotted, very high among the branches, three butterflies, vividly coloured and of enormous size.

These lepidoptera, which must have had one metre wingspans, fluttered high in the foliage, but we were lucky to see them fly closer and closer to us, on wings of blue, green and orange. It is as clear to me as if it were yesterday. They brushed against us with their wings that were strangely fringed, to create the most beautiful and breathtaking effect. One of them came to rest on a leaf just a few metres from us and I was able to admire its body, ringed with silver and gold, and its jade-green antennae. Its proboscis was golden and the tops of its wings were green with streaks of bright blue alternated with dark orange diamond shapes. The under-sides were dark blue, but luminous, as though they had been illuminated from above by a projector.

For the duration of time this giant insect remained on the leaf, it seemed to emit a soft whistling sound and I was quite surprised by this. I had certainly not heard a lepidopteran on Earth make any sound at all. Of course, we were no longer on Earth but on Thiaoouba, and this was only the beginning of a long series of surprises for me.

On the forest floor, grew an incredible variety of plants, each one stranger than the next. They covered the ground completely, but I noticed very few bushes among them. I imagine the forest's giants prevented them from developing.

In size, these plants varied from a ground-covering moss-like plant, to one the size of a large rose bush. One kind, with leaves as thick as a hand in various shapes - sometimes heart-shaped or circular, sometimes very long and thin - was of a colour tending much more towards blue than to green.

Flowers of every shape and colour, even of the purest black, entwined each other. From our altitude of several metres, the effect was absolutely glorious.

We rose till we were up among the highest branches and I put my mask back on according to Thao's direction. We emerged from the canopy and moved slowly, just above the foliage of those enormous trees.

Above the forest the light was, once again, incredibly intense and I had the impression of travelling through a landscape of pure crystal.

Marvellous birds were perched on the tops of the taller trees, watching us pass, without fear. Their colours, varied and rich, were a veritable feast for my eyes in spite of the subduing effect of my mask. Here were varieties of macaw, with blue, yellow, pink and red plumage; and, among them a type of bird of paradise strutted amidst a cloud of what appeared to be hummingbirds.

These hummingbirds were of a brilliant red colour flecked with gold. The red, pink and orange tail feathers of the birds of paradise, would have measured 250 centimetres in length and their wingspans almost two metres.

When these 'jewels' took flight, the underside of their wings revealed a very soft, misty pink, with just a touch of bright blue on the tips - so unexpected, especially as the tops of their wings were of an orange-yellow colour. Their heads wore plumes of impressive size, each feather being a different colour: yellow, green, orange, black, blue, red, white, cream...

I feel frustrated that my attempts to describe the colours I saw on Thiaoouba are so inadequate - I feel I need a whole new lexicon, as my language fails me. I had the constant impression that the colours came from *within* the objects I looked at, and the colour was *more* than I had known it to be. On earth, we know perhaps 15 shades of red; here there must have been over a hundred...

It wasn't only the colours that claimed my attention. The sounds that I had heard since we began to fly over the forest inspired me to seek an explanation from Thao. It was almost a background music, very light and soft, similar to a flute which continually played the same air but at a distance.

As we moved on, the music seemed to change, only to return to the original tune.

'Is that music I hear?'

'It is vibrations emitted by the thousands of insects which, when combined with the vibrations of the colours reflected by solar rays on to certain plants, such as the *Xinoxi,* for example, produce the very musical results that you hear. We, ourselves, only hear it if we particularly attune to it, for it comprises an integral part of our life and our environment. It is restful, isn't it?'

'Absolutely.'

'According to the experts, if these vibrations were to cease, we would experience considerable eye trouble. This will perhaps seem odd at first, since these vibrations appear to be perceptible to the ear rather than the eye. However, experts are experts, Michel, and, in any case, it is of little concern to us, for they also say that the chance of their ceasing is as remote as the chance of our sun extinguishing itself tomorrow.'

Thao turned our vehicle and in a few moments, we had left the forest tops and were flying over a plain, across which flowed a jade-green river.

We descended to an altitude of about three metres and followed its course. Now we were able to follow the movements of strange fish - fish that resembled platypuses more than fish, as I knew them to be. The water was pure, like crystal, and at this altitude we could distinguish everything down to the smallest pebble.

Looking up, I saw we were approaching the ocean. Palm trees resembling coconut palms waved their majestic fronds at impressive heights, on the edge of a beach of golden sands. The blue of the ocean contrasted pleasantly with the bright red of rocks encrusted in small hills, which overlooked a section of its beach.

A hundred or so people basked on the sand or swam, entirely naked, in the transparent waters of the ocean.

I felt a little dazed, not only because of the new and wondrous things I was constantly discovering, but also because of the perpetual sensation of lightness, due to the change in gravity. This sensation was my reminder of *Earth* - what a strange word, and how difficult it was to visualise Earth now!

The auditory and visual vibrations were also affecting my nervous system enormously. Usually a highly-strung person, I was feeling completely relaxed - as if I had plunged into a warm bath, allowing myself to float in the bubbles while soft music played.

No, even more relaxed than that - so relaxed I felt like crying.

We proceeded, quite rapidly, across the waters of the immense bay, flying about 12 metres above the waves. On the horizon, I could distinguish several dots - some larger than others, and I realised these were islands; no doubt those I had seen prior to our landing on Thiaoouba.

As we headed for the smallest island, I looked below and saw that we were being followed by numerous fish, amusing themselves by criss-crossing the shadow our vehicle projected on the water.

'Are they sharks?' I asked.

'No, they're Dajiks - the brothers of your dolphin. You see? They are as fond of playing as your dolphins are.'

'Look!' I interrupted Thao. 'Look!'

Thao looked to where I was pointing and began laughing - I was astonished to see a group of people approaching us, seemingly without the aid of a vehicle.

They were about two metres above the water, in a vertical position, and not only floating in the air, but moving quite rapidly towards us.

Soon our paths crossed and grand gestures of friendship were exchanged. At the same instant, a wave of well-being flowed through me lasting several seconds. It was the same sensation Latoli had produced and I recognised it as a sign of greeting from these 'flying people'.

'How do they do that? Is it levitation?'

'No, they have a Tara[3] on their waists and a Litiolac[4] in their hands. These produce certain vibrations that neutralise the cold magnetic force of the planet, allowing neutralisation of the gravitational force. Even a weight of millions of tonnes compares with that of feathers. Then, by other vibrations resembling those of ultra-sound, they can steer themselves precisely to wherever they choose, as they are doing now. On this planet, everyone wanting to travel some distance uses this method.'

'Then why are we using this vehicle?' I asked, for I would have loved to experiment with such equipment, which, by the way, was absolutely noiseless.

'Michel, you are impatient. I have brought you by this means because you are not capable of flying with a Litiolac. Without practice, you could hurt yourself. Later, perhaps, if there is time, I will teach you how to use it. Look, we are nearly there.'

Indeed, we were fast approaching an island and could clearly see a

---

[3] The Tara is an apparatus worn like a belt when you wish to fly.
[4] The Litiolac works in concert with the Tara to fly, but is held in the hand.

golden beach where several people basked in the sun. Almost immediately, we were flying beneath palm fronds along a wide path, bordered with two rows of flowering and very fragrant bushes. The area was alive with the sound and colour of insects, butterflies and birds.

The vehicle proceeded slowly at ground level and, after a final bend in the path, we arrived before a 'little egg', nestled among small trees and flowering vines. It seemed that every building on this planet had the shape of an egg, most often lying on their 'sides' but occasionally upright, as I have said, with the pointed end upwards. The 'shells' were off-white in colour and had no windows or doors.

This particular egg lay on its side, apparently half buried in the ground. It was about 30 metres long and 20 metres in diameter - quite small in comparison with those I'd seen so far.

Thao stopped the vehicle in front of a bright light centred on the wall of the egg. Leaving the platform, we entered the habitation. As we did so, I felt a light pressure, with no more force than the weight of an eiderdown. I remembered experiencing the same sensation earlier, when we passed
through the wall of the space centre.

Having neither doors nor windows on these buildings is extraordinary in itself, but once inside, it was stranger still. As I have mentioned before, the overall impression was of still being outside.

The startling beauty of colour was everywhere; the greenery; the branches of the trees dissecting the blue-mauve sky above; the butterflies; the flowers...I recall a bird that came to rest right in the middle of the 'roof, so that we could see the bottom of its feet. It was as though it had miraculously stopped in mid-air - the effect was quite extraordinary.

The only contrast with the outside was provided by the floor that was covered in a type of carpet on which were arranged comfortable looking seats and large pedestal tables. All of these furnishings were, of course, on a large scale - appropriate to these 'large-scale' people.

'Thao,' I asked, 'how are your walls transparent and yet we can't see in from the outside? And how can we pass through your walls as we did?'

'First of all, Michel, let's take off this mask of yours. I will regulate the internal light so that it will be bearable for you.'

Thao approached an object on the floor and touched it. When I removed my mask, I found the light to be no less tolerable than with it on, although the shiny quality was restored.

'You see, Michel, this habitation exists because of a magnetic field that is quite special. We have copied the forces of nature and the creations of nature to our own ends. Let me explain. Every body - human, animal or mineral - possesses a field around itself. The human body, for example, is surrounded both by an Aura and by an etheric force of oval shape. You know that, don't you?'

I nodded.

'The latter comprises, in part, electricity and, to a greater extent, vibrations that we call *Ariacostinaki*.

'These vibrations occur continuously for your protection while you are alive, and they are not to be confused with the vibrations of the Aura. With our habitations, we have copied nature in creating a field of mineral electro-etheric vibrations around a nucleus.' Thao indicated an 'egg', the size of an ostrich egg, located in the middle of the room between two seats. 'Will you push this seat please, Michel?'

I looked at Thao, surprised by her request, considering the size of the seat and the fact that she had never before asked anything of me. I tried to oblige, but with some difficulty for the seat was indeed heavy; however I succeeded in moving it about 50 centimetres.

'Very good,' she said. 'Now you will pass me the egg.'

I smiled. In comparison, this would be a simple task. I could lift it with one hand and without any effort; but in order not to drop it, I took it in two hands and...fell to my knees! I had not expected it to be so heavy and had overbalanced. I stood up and tried again, this time with all my strength...nothing happened.

Thao touched my shoulder. 'Watch,' she said. Turning towards the seat I had found so difficult to move, she placed one hand under it and raised it above her head. Still with one hand, she set it down again, apparently with no effort. Next, she took the egg in both hands and pushed and pulled with all her might till the veins swelled in her neck. Still the egg didn't move a tenth of a millimetre.

'It is welded to the floor,' I suggested.

'No, Michel, it is *the* Centre and *cannot* move. It is the nucleus I spoke of earlier. We have created a field around it, so strong that the wind and the rain can't penetrate this field. As for the sun's rays, we can regulate the extent to which they penetrate. The birds too, which come to rest above, are not heavy enough to pass through the field and, if by chance a heavier bird does land, he will start to sink. This produces such a frightening sensation for the bird that he will fly away immediately without having come to any harm.'

'It's so ingenious,' I said, 'but what is the significance of the light at the entrance? Couldn't we pass through the walls anywhere we chose?'

'Indeed, we could. It's just that from the outside, it's not possible to see the interior and so you can't know that you won't hit a piece of furniture on the other side. The best place to enter is always indicated by an external light. Come, let me show you around.'

I followed her and discovered, behind a richly decorated partition, a truly magnificent setting. There was a miniature swimming pool that seemed to be of green porphyry and, nearby, a matching basin over which a porphyry swan was bending, its beak open...the effect was beautiful.

Thao held her hand under the swan's beak and immediately the water began to flow over her hand and into the basin. She withdrew it and the flow ceased. She indicated that I should try. The basin was about 150 centimetres above the floor so that I had to lift my arm quite high but I managed and the water spurted out again.

'How clever!' I explained. 'Do you have water which is drinkable on this island, or have you had to sink bores?'

Again Thao's face lit with her smile of amusement. It was quite familiar to me, appearing each time I said something that, to her, seemed 'quaint'.

'No, Michel, we don't procure our water as you do on Earth. Under this magnificent stone bird, is an apparatus which draws air from outside and transforms it into drinking water as required.'

'That's wonderful!'

'We are merely exploiting a natural law.'

'And what if you want hot water?'

'Electro-vibratory force. For warm water, you put your foot here, and for boiling water, you put it there.

'Cells positioned on the side, control the functioning of the apparatus...but these are only material details and of no great significance. 'This here,' said Thao, following the direction of my gaze, 'is the relaxation area. You can stretch out there.' She pointed to a thick mat that was on the floor, a little further down towards the base of the egg.

I lay down and immediately felt as though I were floating at ground level. Although she continued to speak, I could no longer hear Thao's voice. She had disappeared behind a misty curtain, so that I had the impression of being enveloped in a thick fog of cotton wool. At the same time, musical vibrations could be heard, and the total effect was marvellously relaxing.

I stood up again and after several seconds, Thao's voice was audible again, growing louder as the 'fog' lifted and disappeared completely.

'What do you think of that, Michel?'

'It really is the height of comfort!' I replied enthusiastically. 'But there is one thing I haven't yet seen and that is the kitchen - and you know how important the kitchen is to the French!'

'This way,' she said, smiling again and taking several steps in another direction. 'Do you see this transparent drawer? Inside you have various compartments. From left to right: fish, shellfish, eggs, cheese, dairy products, vegetables and fruits, and here in the last, we have what you call 'manna', which is our bread.'

'Either you are teasing me or you are making fun of me. All I see in your drawer is red, green, blue, brown and blends of these colours...'

'What you see are concentrates of the various foods - fish, vegetables etc, of the best quality prepared by excellent cooks using various special methods. When you taste it, you will find all this food excellent and very nourishing.'

Thao then uttered several words in her own language and, in a few moments, I had before me on a tray, selected items of food arranged in a manner pleasing to the eye. When I tasted it, my palate was agreeably surprised. It was indeed, excellent, although very different from anything I had ever eaten before in my life. The manna I had already tasted in the spaceship. I ate some of it again and found it a good accompaniment to the dishes presented.

'You tell me that, on Earth, this bread is known as 'manna'. How is it that it exists on Earth at all?'

'It is a product we always carry on our intergalactic spacecraft. It is very practical, being easily compressed and highly nourishing. In fact, it's a complete food. It comes from wheat and oats and you could live on it alone for months.'

Just then, our attention was drawn by the approach of some people, flying at ground level beneath the branches of the trees. They set down at the entrance to the 'egg', unfastened their Taras and placed them on a block of marble, no doubt there for the purpose. One after the other, they entered and I recognised with pleasure, Biastra and Latoli and the rest of the crew from the spacecraft.

They had changed from their space uniforms into long Arabian-style robes of shimmering colours. (Later, I was to understand why the colour of each robe was so flattering to the individual who wore it.) For the moment, it was difficult to believe these were the same people I had known and spoken with on the spacecraft, they were so completely transformed.

Latoli approached me, a radiant smile lighting up her face. Placing her hand on my shoulder she said, telepathically, 'You seem somewhat stunned, my dear. Are our habitations not to your liking?'

She 'read' my affirmative and admiring response and was delighted by it. Turning back to the others, she relayed my response, and comments flew thick and fast, everyone talking at once. They had all sat down, looking much more at home in their seats than I felt in mine. I felt as odd as a duckling among chickens in that my size corresponded with nothing that had been built on their scale.

Thao went to the 'kitchen' and filled a tray with things to eat. Then, at a word from her, all hands were held out in the direction of the tray, which rose slowly in the air.

It moved around the room, stopping before each guest, without her having to touch it. Finally, it stopped in front of me and, with great caution, lest it fall (which vastly amused everyone) I took a glass of hydromel. The tray departed of its own accord, returning to its place of origin, and all hands were lowered.

'How is that done?' I asked Thao. My question was understood telepathically by everyone and there was a general burst of laughter.

'By what you would call 'levitation', Michel. We can, as readily, lift ourselves in the air, but that serves no great purpose other than our own amusement.' Having said that, Thao, who was sitting cross-legged, began to rise above her seat and floated about the room, finally coming to rest in mid-air. I stared at her, but soon realised I was the only one fascinated by her accomplishment. Indeed, I must have looked idiotic, for all eyes were fixed on me. Evidently, Thao's behaviour was perfectly normal to my friends but they were more interested in the astonished expression on my face.

Thao descended slowly on to her seat.

'That demonstrates one of the many sciences you have lost on Earth, Michel - apart from a few individuals who are still capable of doing it.

'There was a time when it was practised by many, along with many other skills.'

We passed the time pleasantly that afternoon, my new friends and I, communicating telepathically in a light-hearted way, until the sun was low in the sky.

Then Thao explained, 'Michel, this 'doko', as we call our habitations on this planet, will be your home during your brief stay on Thiaoouba. We'll be leaving you now for the night, to let you sleep. If you wish to bathe, you know how to arrange it and you can sleep on the relaxation bed. But try to be organised within the next half-hour, as there is no lighting in this habitation. We are able to see as well by night, as by day, and have no need of it.'

'Is this building secure? Am I safe here?' I asked worriedly.

Again Thao smiled. 'On this planet, you could sleep on the ground in the middle of town and you would be safer than in a building with armed guards, dogs and alarms on Earth.

'Here, we have only very evolved beings and certainly, none resembling the criminals you have on Earth. In our eyes, they must be likened to the worst of savage beasts. On that note, good night.'

Thao about-turned and passed through the 'wall' of the doko to rejoin her friends. They must have brought a 'Litiolac' for her because she flew off with the group.

I prepared then, to spend my first night on Thiaoouba.

The Seven Masters and
the Aura

A huge flame burned blue; orange yellow and red flames burned around it. An enormous black snake slid straight through the flames, heading for me. Giants appeared from nowhere, running, and trying to catch the snake. It took seven of them together, to stop it before it reached me. But it turned and swallowed the flames, only to spit them back out, like a dragon, at the giants. They were transformed into immense statues just as they were - mounted on the tail of the snake.

The reptile became a comet and carried the statues off - to Easter Island. Next, they were greeting me, wearing strange hats. One of the statues, resembling Thao, caught me by the shoulder and said, 'Michel, Michel...wake up.' Thao was shaking me and gently smiling.

'My goodness!' I said, opening my eyes, 'I was dreaming you were an Easter Island statue and that you caught hold of me by the shoulder...'

'I *am* an Easter Island statue, and I *did* take you by the shoulder.'

'Anyway, I'm not dreaming now, am I?'

'No, but your dream was really quite strange, for on Easter Island, there is a statue which was sculptured a very long time ago to immortalise me and which was given my name.'

'What are you telling me now?'

'The simple truth, Michel, but we will explain all that to you in good time. For now, we will try on these clothes I've brought for you.'

Thao handed me a richly-coloured robe which quite delighted me and, after a warm and perfumed bath, I dressed in the garment. A feeling of euphoria, which was totally unexpected, overwhelmed me. I mentioned it to Thao, who was waiting with a glass of milk and a little manna for me.

'The colours of your robe were chosen according to those of your Aura; that's why you feel so good. If people on Earth were able to see Auras, they too could choose colours, which suit them and thereby enhance their feeling of well-being. They'd make use of colour rather than aspirin.'

'What do you mean, exactly?'

'I'll give you an example. Do you ever remember saying of someone: 'oh, those clothes don't suit you at all. He, or she, has no taste'?'

'Yes, quite often, in fact.'

'Well, in such cases, those people have simply chosen their clothes less skilfully than others, or mixed them less successfully. As you say in French, they *jurent* or 'clash', but more in the eyes of others than in their own. However, such people will not feel good in themselves, without

realising why. If you were to suggest it be because of the colours they were wearing, they would think you odd. You could explain that the vibrations of the colours were in discord with those of their Auras, but they would be no more inclined to believe you. On your planet, people only believe in what they see or touch...and yet the Aura can be seen...'
'The Aura is actually coloured?'
'Of course. The Aura vibrates constantly with colours that vary. At the top of your head is a veritable bouquet of colours, where almost all the colours you know are represented.

'Around the head too, is a golden halo, but it is only really obvious in the most highly spiritual people and in those who have sacrificed themselves in order to help someone else. The halo resembles a golden mist, much like painters on Earth depict the haloes of 'saints' and of Christ. The haloes were included in their paintings because, in those times, some of the artists actually saw them.'
'Yes, I have heard mention of that, but I love to hear it from you.'
'The colours are all there in the Aura: some shine more strongly, others are dull. People in poor health, for example, or people with bad intentions...'
'I would like so much to see the Aura. I know there are people who can see it.' 'Many people on Earth could see it and read it a very long time ago, but there are few now. Calm yourself, Michel. You will see it, and not only one but several. Including your own. Now, though, I'll ask you to follow me, because we have so much to show you and little time available.'

I followed Thao, who placed my mask on my face and led the way to the flying platform we had used the day before.

We took our places and immediately Thao began manoeuvring the machine so that it dodged below the branches of trees.

In a matter of moments, we had emerged on the beach.

The sun had just risen behind the island and lit up the ocean and surrounding islands. From water level - the effect was magical. As we proceeded along the beach, I could see other dokos through the foliage, nestled among flowering bushes. On the beach, the inhabitants of these dwellings bathed in transparent waters or strolled together on the sand. Apparently surprised to see our flying platform, they followed our progress as we passed. It occurred to me that this was not the usual means of transport on the island.

I should mention too, although swimmers and sunbathers are always completely naked on Thiaoouba, those who stroll or move any significant distance, always dress to do so. On this planet, there is neither hypocrisy, exhibitionism nor false modesty (this will be explained later).

It was not long before we reached the end of the island and, accelerating, Thao guided the vehicle at water level.

We headed in the direction of a large island, which could be seen on the horizon. I could not help but admire the dexterity with which Thao piloted the flying machine, especially when we arrived at the shore of the island.

Approaching the coast, I could recognise enormous dokos, their points as usual towards the sky, I counted a group of nine, but the island was sprinkled with others, smaller and less visible amongst the vegetation. Thao took us higher and we were soon flying over what Thao called *Kotra quo doj Doko* - 'The City of the nine Dokos'.

Skilfully, Thao brought us down between the dokos, to a beautiful park located in their midst. In spite of my mask, I was aware that the golden mist that enveloped Thiaoouba was much denser around these dokos than elsewhere.

Thao confirmed I was not mistaken in my perception, but she was not then able to explain the phenomenon, as they were waiting for us.

She led me beneath an archway of greenery and along a path, which ran beside small ponds. Here wonderful water birds frolicked and little waterfalls murmured.

I found myself almost running to keep up with Thao, but didn't like to ask her to slow down. She appeared preoccupied in a way that was not typical of her. At one point, there was almost a catastrophe when I tried to jump, as much to amuse myself as to catch up with Thao. Due to the difference in gravity, I misjudged my leap and had to catch hold of a tree, which grew right on the water's edge, to prevent myself from falling in.

Eventually, we reached the Central Doko and stopped below the entrance light. Thao seemed to concentrate for several seconds, then she took me by the shoulder and we passed through the wall.

She immediately removed my mask, advising at the same time, that I half-closed my eyes, which I did. Light filtered through my lower lids and after a time, I was able to open my eyes normally.

I must say, that this brightness, more golden that in my own doko, was considerably uncomfortable at first. I was most curious now, especially since Thao, who was usually very free and without protocol in her relations with everyone, seemed to have abruptly changed in her manner. Why?

This doko must have been 100 metres in diameter. We headed directly, although more slowly, for the centre, where seven seats, each occupied, were arranged in a semi-circle. The occupants sat as though petrified and, at first, I thought them to be statues.

In looks they resembled Thao, although their hair was longer and their facial expressions more serious, giving them the air of being older. Their eyes seemed to be illuminated from within, which was somewhat disturbing. What struck me most of all, was the golden haze, even stronger here than outside, which seemed to concentrate in haloes around their heads.

Since the age of fifteen, I don't recall ever having been in awe of another person. No matter how grand a personage: no matter how important he or she was, (or thought they were) I have not felt intimidated by position: neither have I had qualms about expressing my opinion to anyone. To me, the president of a nation is still just a person and it amuses me that people regard themselves as VIPs. I mention this to make it clear I am not impressed by mere status.

In the doko, all that changed.

When one of them raised a hand to indicate Thao and I should each take a seat facing them, I was indeed *awestruck,* and the word is feeble. I could not have imagined it possible that such radiant beings could exist: it was as though they were on fire inside and emitting rays from within.

They sat on block-like seats, fabric-covered, with straight backs. Each seat was of a different colour - some only slightly different and others vastly different from their neighbours. Their clothes too, differed in colour, suiting each wearer perfectly. All of them sat in what we call on Earth, the 'lotus position' that is, the sitting position of Buddha, with hands resting on knees.

As previously mentioned, they formed a semi-circle and, since there were seven of them, I reasoned that the central figure had to be the principal one, with three acolytes on either side. Of course, at the time, I was too overcome to note such details. It only occurred to me later.

It was the central figure who addressed me, in a voice so melodious and, at the same time, so authoritarian. I was stunned by it, particularly since he spoke in *perfect French.*

'You are welcome among us, Michel. May The Spirit assist and enlighten you.' The others echoed: 'May The Spirit enlighten you.'

He began to rise gently above his seat still in the lotus position, and floated towards me. This did not entirely surprise me since Thao had previously demonstrated this technique of levitation. I wanted to rise before this undoubtedly great and highly spiritual personage, as a measure of the infinite respect inspired in me. In trying to move, I found I couldn't - as though paralysed in my seat.

He stopped just above and in front of me, placing both his hands on my head; the thumbs joined on my forehead above my nose, opposite the pineal gland, and the fingers joined at the top of my head. It was Thao who described these details to me later, for at the time, I was overwhelmed by such a sensation, that the details didn't register.

During the time his hands were on my head, it seemed that my body no longer existed. A gentle warmth and delicate perfume originated within me, emanating in waves and blending with soft music that was barely audible.

Suddenly, I could see amazing colours surrounding the figures opposite me and, as the 'leader' returned slowly towards his seat, I could see a multitude of radiant colours around him; ones I had been unable to perceive before. The principal colour was a mass of pale pink which enveloped the seven figures, as though in a cloud, and their movements caused that wonderful, glowing pink to encircle us also!

When I had sufficiently recovered my senses to turn towards Thao, she too, was surrounded with wonderful colours, although less brilliant than those around the seven figures.

You will notice that, in speaking of these great personages, I instinctively use 'he' rather than 'she'. In explaining this, I can only suggest that the personalities of these special beings were so strong and their bearings so imposing, that I recognised more of the masculine in them than the feminine - I *mean no offence to women* - my reaction was instinctive. It's a bit like imagining Methuselah as a woman... However, women or men, they had transformed me. I knew that the colours surrounding them were their *Auras*. I was capable of *seeing* Auras - who knew for how long - and I wondered at what I saw.

The 'leader' had resumed his seat and all eyes were fixed on me, as if they wanted to see inside me, which indeed, is what they were doing. Silence reigned for a time, which seemed interminable. I watched the varied colours of their Auras vibrate and dance around them, sometimes far in the distance and recognised the 'bouquet of colour' Thao had spoken of earlier.

The golden haloes, clearly defined, were almost saffron coloured. It occurred to me, they could not only see my Aura, but possibly *read* it as well. I suddenly felt quite naked before this learned assembly. The question that haunted me was: why have they brought me here?

Abruptly, the 'leader' broke the silence. 'As Thao has already explained to you, Michel, you have been chosen by us, to visit our planet, in order to report certain messages and to offer enlightenment on several important issues when you return to Earth. The time has come when certain events *must* occur. After several thousand years of darkness and savagery on the planet Earth, a so-called 'civilisation' appeared and, inevitably, technology was developed - a development, which was accelerated during the last 150 years.

'It has been 14 500 years since a comparable level of technological advance existed on Earth. This technology, which is nothing compared with true *knowledge,* is nevertheless, sufficiently advanced to become harmful to the human race on Earth in the very near future.

'Harmful, because it is only material knowledge and not spiritual knowledge. Technology should *assist* spiritual development, not confine people, more and more, within a materialistic world, as is happening now on your planet.

'To an even greater extent, your people are obsessed with a single goal - affluence. Their lives are concerned with all that the pursuit of wealth entails; envy, jealousy, hatred of those richer and contempt for those poorer. In other words your technology, which is nothing compared with what existed on Earth more than 14 500 years ago, is dragging your civilisation down, and pushing it closer and closer to moral and spiritual catastrophe'.

I noticed that each time this great personage spoke of materialism, his Aura and those of his acolytes, flashed with a dull and 'dirty' red, as though momentarily, they were in the middle of burning bushes.

'We, the people of Thiaoouba, are assigned to assist, guide and sometimes punish the inhabitants of planets under our guardianship.'

Fortunately, Thao had briefed me on Earth's history during our journey to Thiaoouba. Otherwise, I'd have surely fallen off my seat on hearing such a speech.

'I think,' he resumed, 'that you already know what we mean by 'harmful to the human race'. Many people on Earth believe atomic arms to be the major danger, but it is not so. The greatest danger concerns 'materialism'. The people of your planet seek *money* - to some it's a means of attaining power; to others it's a means to acquire drugs, (another curse) yet to others, it's a way of possessing more than their neighbours possess.

'If a businessman owns a large store he then wants a second, then a third. If he commands a small empire, he wants to increase it. If an ordinary man owns a house in which he could live happily with his family, he wants a larger one or to own a second one, then a third...

Why this folly? Besides, a man will die and have to abandon all he has amassed. Perhaps his children will squander his legacy and his grandchildren will live in poverty? His whole life will have been preoccupied with purely material concerns, with insufficient time allowed for matters of the spirit. Others with money turn to drugs in their endeavour to procure an artificial paradise and these people pay more dearly than do the others.

'I see,' he continued. 'I am going much too fast and you are not following me, Michel. You should be able to follow, however, since Thao has already initiated your education in these matters during your voyage.'

I felt ashamed, almost like when reprimanded by a teacher at school; the only difference being, here I was not able to cheat by saying I had understood when it wasn't true. He could read me like an open book.

He deigned to smile at me and his Aura, which had been flaming like a fire, returned to its original hue.

'Now, once and for always, we will teach you and provide you with what you French call 'the key to the mystery'.

'As you have heard, in the beginning there was the Spirit alone and he created, by his immense force, all that exists materially. He created the planets, the suns, plants, animals, with one goal in mind: *to satisfy his spiritual need.* This is quite logical since he is purely spirit. Already I see you are wondering why the need to create material things in order to attain spiritual fulfilment. I offer this, by way of explanation: the creator sought spiritual experiences through a material world. I see you still have difficulty following - but you are making progress.

'In order to have these experiences, he wanted to embody a tiny part of his Spirit in a physical entity. To do this, he called on the Fourth force - the force which Thao has not yet spoken of and which concerns only spirituality. In this domain, Universal Law also applies.

'You most certainly know that the pattern of the Universe dictates that nine planets revolve around their sun. It is also the case that these suns revolve around a bigger sun, which is the nucleus for nine such suns, and their nine planets. So it continues, right to the centre of the Universe from where the explosion referred to by the English as the 'Big Bang' originated.

'Needless to say, certain accidents occur and sometimes a planet will disappear in a solar system, or perhaps enter it, but later in time, the solar system will revert and base its structure again on the number nine.

'The Fourth force had a very important role to play: it had to bring to fruition all that the Spirit had imagined. It 'inserted' thus, an infinitesimal part of the Spirit in the human body. This comprises what you could call the Astral body, which forms one ninth of the essential human being and consists of one ninth of a 'Higher-self, which is sometimes called 'overself. The Higher-self of man is, in other words, an entity which sends one ninth of itself into a human body, becoming the person's Astral being. Other physical bodies are inhabited, similarly, by other ninths of the same Higher-self and yet each part remains integral to the central entity.

'Further, the Higher-self is a ninth part of a superior Higher-self which, in turn, is a ninth part of a more superior Higher-self. The process continues as far back as the *source,* and allows the enormous filtration of spiritual experience required by the Spirit.

'You must not think that the Higher-self of the first category is insignificant in comparison with the others. It functions at a lower level, but is nevertheless extremely powerful and important. It is capable of curing illness[5] and even resuscitating the dead. There are many instances of people, declared clinically dead, who are brought back to life in the hands of doctors who had abandoned all hope for them. What generally happens in these cases, is that the person's Astral body meets with the Higher-self. This portion of the Higher-self has left the physical body during the period of 'death'. It perceives its physical body below, and the doctors trying to resuscitate it; it can also perceive loved ones who mourn for it. In his present state, the Astral body, the person will feel perfectly well - even blissful. Usually he abandons his physical body, frequently the source of much suffering, to find himself catapulted down a 'psychic canal', at the end of which is a wondrous light and beyond, a state of bliss.

'If before passing through this canal into the blissful light which is his Higher- self he has the *least* will not to die - not on his own account but

---

5 What is known on Earth as Spiritual Healing, can be achieved with the help of the Higher-self of the healer, without the patient being present. Providing the patient gives permission, the competent healer can assist the patient from anywhere in the world.

for the sake of those who need him, young children for example, he will ask to return. In certain cases it *will* be permitted.

'You are in constant communication with your Higher-self by means of your cerebral canal. Acting as a transmitting and receiving post, it conducts special vibrations directly between your Astral body and your Higher-self. Your Higher- self monitors you continually, by day and by night and can intervene to save you from an accident.

'Someone, for example, who is to catch a plane, finds that the taxi breaks down on the way to the airport; a second taxi called also breaks down - just like *that...just like that*? Could you really believe in such a coincidence? The plane in question crashes thirty minutes later, leaving no survivors. Another person, an old and rheumatic woman and barely able to walk, starts to cross a street. There is a loud horn blast and a screeching of tyres, but this person is miraculously able to leap to safety.

'How is this explained? It was not yet her time to die and so her Higher-self intervened. In one hundredth of a second the Higher-self triggered a reaction in her adrenaline glands which, for a few seconds, provided enough strength to her muscles to enable her to execute the leap which saved her life. Adrenaline released into the blood can make it possible to flee from imminent danger, or to defeat the 'unbeatable' through anger or fear. In too strong a dose, however, adrenaline becomes a lethal poison.

'It isn't only the cerebral canal which is able to conduct messages between the Higher-self and the Astral body. Another channel exists sometimes in dreams - or, I should even say, in sleep. At certain times during sleep, your Higher-self is able to call your Astral body to itself and, either communicate instructions or ideas, or to regenerate it in some way, replenishing its spiritual strength or enlightening it in regard to solutions to important problems. For this reason, it is essential your sleep is undisturbed by intrusive noise or by nightmares resulting from harmful impressions received during the day. Perhaps you will better understand the importance of your old French saying: 'Night brings counsel'.

'The physical body in which you exist at the moment is already very complex, but still, it is nothing compared with the complexity of the process of evolvement which occurs with Astral bodies and Higher-selves. In order to allow ordinary people on your planet to understand as easily as possible, I will make my explanation in the most simple terms.

'Your Astral body, which inhabits every normal human being, transfers to its Higher-self all the sensations that are experienced during a lifetime in a physical body. These sensations pass through the immense 'filter' of nine Higher-selves before arriving in the etheric 'ocean' that surrounds the Spirit. If these sensations are based essentially on materialism, the Higher-selves have enormous trouble filtering them, just as a water filter clogs quicker if it filters dirty water than if the water was already clear.

'If, through the numerous experiences you have in your life, you ensure your Astral body benefits in a spiritual sense, it will acquire more and more spiritual understanding. In time, which can vary from 500 to even 15 000 of your Earth years, your Higher-self will have nothing more to filter.

'This part of itself, embodied in the Astral being of Michel Desmarquet, will be so spiritually advanced, it will have arrived at the next stage where it will have to contend directly with the more superior Higher-self.

'We can compare this process with a nine-stage filter, intended to rid the water passing through, of nine elements. At the end of stage one in the process, one will have been completely eliminated, with eight remaining. Of course, to make this information easier to digest, I am making enormous use of imagery...

'This Astral body then, will have completed its cycle with the Higher-self of the first category and will then detach itself from Higher-self number one to rejoin the Higher-self of the second category; the entire process will be repeated. By the same token, the Astral body will be sufficiently spiritually advanced to pass to a planet of the next category, as well.

'I see you are not following me very well and I am anxious that you will understand absolutely, all that I explain to you.

'In his wisdom, The Spirit, by means of the Fourth force, provided for nine categories of planets. At present, you are on the planet Thiaoouba which is in the ninth category; that is, at the top of the scale.

'Earth is a planet of the first category and therefore at the bottom of the scale. What does this mean? The planet Earth could be likened to a kindergarten with the emphasis on teaching basic social values. A planet of the second category would then correspond with a primary school where further values are taught - in both schools, adult guidance is imperative. The third category would comprise secondary schools where a foundation of values allows exploration beyond. Next, you would go to university, where you are treated as an adult, for you would not only have attained a certain amount of knowledge, but you would also start to accept civic responsibility.

'This is the type of progress occurring with the nine categories of planets. The more spiritually advanced you are, the more you will benefit, on a superior planet, by an environment and general way of life which is superior. The very way in which you procure food is much easier, which in turn, simplifies the process of organising your way of life; the consequence is more effective spiritual development.

'On the higher planets, Nature itself, enters the stage to assist 'the pupil' and, by the time you reach planets of the sixth, seventh, eighth and ninth category, not only is your Astral body highly evolved, your physical body has also benefited from your development.

'We know you have already been favourably impressed by what you have seen on our planet. As you see more, you will appreciate that it is what you would call on Earth, 'a paradise'; and yet, compared with true happiness, when you become a pure spirit, it is still nothing.

'I must be careful not to make this explanation too long, for you must report it word for word, changing nothing in the book that you will write. It is absolutely essential you allow no personal opinion to intrude.

'No, don't get anxious - Thao will help you with the details when the time comes to start writing...

'From this planet, it is possible either to remain in a physical body or be reunited with the Great Spirit in the ether.'

As these words were uttered, the Aura surrounding the leader shone more brightly than ever and I was surprised to see him almost disappear in a golden mist, only to reappear a second later.

'You have understood that the Astral body is a body which inhabits your physical body recalling and noting all the understanding acquired during the course of its various lives.

'It can only be enriched spiritually - not materially. The physical body is merely a vehicle which, in most cases we abandon when we die.

'I will elaborate, for I see that 'in most cases' has confused you. By this, I mean that some of us, including all on our planet, are able to regenerate the cells of our bodies at will. Yes, you have already noticed that most of us seem to be of the same age. We are one of three planets that are the most highly evolved in this galaxy. Some of us can, and do, directly join what we call the *great ether.*

'So, on this particular planet, we have arrived at a stage near perfection, both materially and spiritually. But we have our roles to perform, as does every creature existing in the universe; in fact, everything, including a single pebble, has its role.

'Our role, as beings of a superior planet, is to guide - to help with spiritual development and even, sometimes, materially. We are in a position to give material assistance because we are technologically the most advanced people. Indeed, how could a father give spiritual guidance to his child if he were not older, more educated and more skilled in diplomacy than the child?

'If the child should require physical punishment, as unfortunately, is sometimes the case, isn't it important that the parent be physically stronger than the child? Certain adults, who refuse to listen and who are absolutely stubborn, also need to be corrected by physical means.

'You, Michel, come from the planet Earth, which is sometimes called 'The Planet of Sorrows'. Indeed, the name is appropriate, but it is this way for a precise reason - it is intended to provide a learning environment of a quite specific kind. It is not because life there is so difficult that you have to intervene - you cannot lightly go against Nature, destroying rather than conserving what the Creator has put at your disposal; that is, interfering with ecological systems, which have been intricately designed. Certain countries, like Australia, where you are from, are beginning to show great respect for ecology and it is a step in the right direction; but even in that country, what case is made of pollution - both water and air pollution? What is ever done about one of the worst forms of pollution? *Noise.*

'I say 'worst' because people such as Australians pay virtually no attention to it at all.

'Ask someone if traffic noise bothers him and the response will surprise you - eighty five per cent of the time it will be; 'What noise? What are you talking about? Oh that noise - we get used to it.' And it is precisely because they 'get used to it' that the danger exists.'

Just then, Thaora, as this high figure was called, made a gesture and I turned around. He was replying to a question I had mentally posed; 'How can he speak of percentages and know so much about our planet with so much precision?'

Turning around, I almost uttered a cry of surprise for, behind me, stood Biastra and Latoli. In itself, this was nothing surprising, but the friends I knew who measured 310 and 280 centimetres in height respectively, were now reduced in size to correspond with my height. My mouth must have continued to gape, for Thaora smiled.

'Can you understand, that sometimes, and very often in these days, some of us live among *your* people on Earth? - and there is my answer to your question.

'To continue on the very important subject of noise, it is such a danger that, if nothing is done, catastrophe is certain.

'Let us take the example of a discotheque. The people who expose themselves to music that is typically played three times too loudly, are subjecting their brains and their physiological and astral bodies to vibrations which are so harmful. If they could see the damage that is caused, they would vacate the discotheque quicker than if there was a fire.

'But vibrations don't only come from noise; they also come from colours and it is astonishing that, on your planet, experiments conducted in this field have not been followed up. Our 'agents' reported a particular experiment involving a man who was capable of lifting a certain weight. It was found, after staring for a moment at a pink-coloured screen, he consistently lost thirty per cent of his strength.

'Your civilisation pays no attention to such experimentation. In fact, colours can enormously influence the behaviour of human beings and yet, control of this influence requires that an individual's Aura be taken into account. If for example, you want to paint or wallpaper your bedroom with the colours that are truly appropriate for you, you must be aware of the colours of certain principal points of your Aura.

'By matching the colours of your walls with those of your Aura, you can improve your health or maintain good health. Further, the vibrations emanating from these colours are essential for good mental balance, exerting their influence even while you sleep.'

I was wondering how we could be expected to know these significant colours in our Auras when, on Earth, we were not capable of perceiving Auras.

Of course, Thaora replied immediately, without me having to say a word aloud.

'Michel, it is now very important that your experts invent the special equipment necessary, to enable perception of the Aura, as this, in turn, will ensure that correct choices are made at the critical cross-roads ahead.

'The Russians have already photographed the Aura. This is the beginning, but the results obtained allow them only to read the first two letters of the alphabet, as it were, in comparison with what we are able to decipher. The reading of the Aura in order to heal the physical body is nothing compared with what such a reading can achieve for the psychic body, or the physiological body. It is in the area of the psyche that, on Earth, your greatest problems exist.

'At the moment, most responsibility is taken for the physical body, but this is a serious mistake. If your psyche is poor, it will influence your physical appearance accordingly, but, regardless, your physical body will wear out and die one day, whereas your psyche, being part of your Astral body, never dies. On the contrary, the more you cultivate your mind, the less you will be burdened by your physical body and the quicker you will proceed through your cycle of lives.

'We could have brought you to our planet in Astral body, but instead, we have brought you here in physical body - and for an important reason. I see you already understand our reason. This pleases us and we thank you for your willingness to assist us in our task.'

The Thaora stopped talking and seemed to lapse into thought, at the same time, fixing me with his luminous eyes. I cannot say how much time elapsed. I know my state became more and more euphoric and I was aware that the Auras of the seven personages were gradually changing. The colours became more vivid in places, softer in others, while the outer edges became misty.

This mist became more golden and pink as it spread, gradually blurring the seven figures. I felt Thao's hand on my shoulder.

'No, you are not dreaming, Michel. It's all quite real.' She spoke very loudly and, as if to prove her point, she pinched my shoulder so hard, she left a bruise that could be seen for several weeks.

'Why did you do that? I would not have thought you capable of such violence, Thao.'

'I'm sorry, Michel, but sometimes strange means are employed. The Thaori always disappear - and sometimes appear in this manner - and you might have thought it part of a dream. I am entrusted with the task of ensuring that you recognise what is real.'

With these words, Thao pivoted me around and I followed her, as we departed by the same route we had come.

The Continent of Mu
and Easter Island

Before leaving the doko, Thao fitted a mask on my head - a mask that was different from the one I'd worn previously. I was able to see colours that were much more vivid and much more luminous.

'How do you feel in your new *voki* Michel? Do you find the light tolerable?'

'Yes...it's...fine, it's so beautiful and I feel so...' With that, I collapsed at Thao's feet. She took me in her arms and carried me to the flying platform.

I awoke in my doko, quite astonished. My shoulder was hurting; quite instinctively I put my hand to the pain, and grimaced.

'I am really sorry, Michel, but it was necessary.' There was just a hint of remorse in Thao's expression.

'What happened to me?'

'Let's say that you fainted, although the word is not quite appropriate; rather, you were overwhelmed with beauty. Your new voki allows fifty per cent of the vibrations of colour on our planet to pass, whereas your former voki subdued all but twenty per cent.'

'Only twenty per cent? - that's incredible! All those marvellous colours I could see - the butterflies, the flowers, the trees, the ocean... No wonder I was overcome. I remember, during a journey I made from France to New Caledonia, we called in at the island of Tahiti. While there, I toured the island with family and friends, in a hired car. The islanders were delightful and made such a charming picture, with their straw hats constructed on the banks of lagoons amidst bougainvillea, hibiscus and exoras - red, yellow, orange and purple, surrounded by well-kept lawns and shaded by coconut trees.

'The backdrop to these scenes was provided by the blue of the ocean. We spent all day touring the island and I described it in my journal as having been an entire day of inebriation for my eyes. I was, indeed, intoxicated by the beauty around me; and yet, now, I admit all that was nothing compared with the beauty here on your planet.'

Thao had listened to my description with marked interest, smiling all the while. She placed her hand on my forehead and said, 'Rest now, Michel. Later you will feel better and will be able to come with me.'

I fell asleep immediately and slept peacefully, without dreaming, I think for about 24 hours. When I awoke, I felt rested and refreshed.

Thao was there, and Latoli and Biastra had joined her. They had regained their normal size and I commented on the fact straight away.

'Little time is required for such a metamorphose, Michel,' explained Biastra, 'but that is not important. Today we are going to show you something of our country and introduce you to some very interesting people.' Latoli approached me and touched my shoulder with her fingertips, just where Thao had bruised me. Instantly, the pain vanished and I felt quivers of well-being run through my whole body. She returned my smile and handed me my new mask.

I still found that, outside, I had to squint against the light. Thao gestured to me indicating that I should climb on to the *Lativok* as our flying platform was called. The others chose to fly independently, fluttering about our vehicle, as though playing a game - and no doubt they were. On this planet, the inhabitants seemed perpetually happy; the only ones I had found to be serious - in fact, even a little severe, despite their air of benevolence - were the seven Thaori.[6]

We flew at high speed, several metres above the water and, although my curiosity was constantly aroused, I often had to close my eyes to allow them to 'recover' from the brightness.

Still, it appeared I was going to become accustomed to it...I wondered how I would cope though, if it occurred to Thao to give me a mask which permitted seventy per cent of the light to penetrate - or even more?

We rapidly approached the coast of the mainland, where waves were breaking over rocks of green, black, orange and gold. The iridescence of the water, crashing against the rocks, under the perpendicular rays of a midday sun, created a memorably lovely effect. A band of light and colour was formed, one hundred times more crystalline than a rainbow on Earth. We rose to an altitude of about 200 metres and proceeded to travel over the continent.

Thao flew us over a plain on which I could see animals of all sorts - some were two-legged and resembled little ostriches; others were four-legged creatures, similar to mammoths, but twice as big. I also watched cows graze side by side with hippopotamuses. The cows were so similar to those we have on Earth, I couldn't help but remark on it to Thao, pointing as I did so, at a particular herd, just like an excited child at the zoo. She laughed heartily.

'Why shouldn't we have cows here, Michel? Look over there and you'll see donkeys and there, giraffes - although they are somewhat taller than on Earth. See how lovely those horses are as they run together.'

I was thrilled, but wasn't I constantly thrilled by this experience -sometimes a little more, sometimes a little less? What really rendered me speechless, to the amusement of my friends, was the sight of horses bearing the heads of very pretty women - some blonde, others auburn or brown and even some with blue hair. As they galloped, they would often soar for tens of metres. Ah yes! In fact, they had wings, folded back

---

[6] Thaori is the plural of Thaora

against their bodies, which they made use of from time to time - something like the flying fish which follow or precede ships. They lifted their heads to see us and tried to rival the speed of the Lativok.

Thao reduced speed and altitude, enabling us to approach within several metres of them. There were more surprises ahead of me, as some of these horse-women cried out to us in a language that was recognisably human. My three companions answered in the same language, and the exchange was obviously a pleasant one. We didn't linger long at that low altitude, however, as some of the horse-women soared to such heights, they almost touched our vehicle, thereby risking injury to themselves.

The plain we flew over was, in places, embossed with small knolls, all of about the same size. I remarked on them and Biastra explained that, millions of years ago, these knolls had been volcanoes. The vegetation below us had none of the exuberance of the forest I had 'experienced' on my arrival. On the contrary, here the trees were grouped in small stands, reaching no more than 25 metres in height. As we passed, large white birds took flight by the hundreds, only to land again, a 'safe' distance away. A wide water-course flowed to the horizon, dissecting the plain with its lazy wanderings.

I could make out some small dokos grouped together on a bend of the river. Thao guided the Lativok above the river, reducing altitude to water level as we approached the settlement. We landed in a small square between two dokos and were immediately surrounded by the inhabitants. They didn't scramble or push to get near us; rather, they stopped what they were doing and calmly approached us. They formed a circle large enough to be comfortable and for all to have equal opportunity to see an alien face to face.

Again, it struck me that these people all seemed to be of the same age, apart from about half a dozen that could have been older. Age, here, did not detract but added a quality of surprising nobility.

I had also been struck by the absence of children on the planet; and yet, in this settlement and among the crowd that approached, I saw six or seven of them. They were charming and appeared to be quite level headed for children. According to Thao, they would have been eight or nine years old.

Since my arrival on Thiaoouba, I had not yet had occasion to meet so great a number of these people. Glancing around the circle, I could appreciate a calmness and reserve about them, as well as the great beauty in their faces that I'd grown to expect. There was a strong resemblance between them, as if they were all brothers and sisters; and yet, isn't that our first impression when we encounter a group of blacks or Asians together? In fact, the same physical variety in facial features existed among these people, as exists within races on Earth.

In height, they varied from 280 to 300 centimetres, their bodies being so well- proportioned, they were a pleasure to behold - neither too muscly nor too puny, and without deformity of any kind. Their hips were somewhat larger than you would expect in a man, but then I'd been told that some of them gave birth to children.

All possessed magnificent heads of hair - most of a golden-blond colour, others platinum-blond or coppery-blond and occasionally, a bright chestnut colour. There were also some, like Thao and Biastra, with a fine down of hair on the upper lip, but, apart from this, these people had absolutely no other body hair. (This is not, of course, an observation that I made at the time but one which I made later, when I had occasion to see from quite near, a group of naked sunbathers.) Their skin-type reminded me of Arab women who protect themselves from the sun - it was certainly not the pale skin typical of blondes with such light eyes. So light, indeed, were the mauve and blue eyes around me, that I might have wondered if they were blind, had I been on Earth.

When I speak now, of their long legs and rounded thighs - they reminded me of our female long-distance runners, as well as their beautifully proportioned breasts, firm and shapely in every case, the reader will understand my error in believing Thao to be a female giant when first we met. It occurred to me that women on Earth would be most envious of the breasts of these people - and men would be most delighted by them...

I have already commented on the beauty of Thao's face, and others in this crowd had similar 'classic' features; still others I would describe as 'charming' or 'alluring'. Each face, though slightly different in shape and features, seemed to have been designed by an artist.

Each had been given its own unique charm; but, above all, the quality most evident in their faces and in their manner and deportment, was the quality of intelligence.

In all, I could find no fault with these people who grouped around us, beaming smiles of welcome which revealed rows of perfect white teeth. This physical perfection did not surprise me, since Thao had explained their ability to regenerate their body cells at will. There was no reason, therefore, that these magnificent bodies should age.

'Are we interrupting them in their work?' I asked Biastra, who happened to be by my side.

'No, not really,' she replied. 'Most of the people in this town are on vacation - it is also a place where people come to meditate.'

Three of the 'elders' approached and Thao asked that I address them in French, and loudly enough for everyone to hear. I believe I said; 'I am very happy to be among you and to be able to admire your wonderful planet. You are fortunate people and I, myself, would like to live among you.'

This speech released a concert of exclamation, not only on account of the language, which most of them had never before heard spoken, but also for the sense of what I had said, which had been telepathically communicated.

Biastra signalled we should follow the three 'elders', who led us into one of the dokos. When the seven of us were comfortably installed, Thao began; 'Michel, I would like to introduce you to Lationusi.' She held her hand towards one of the three and I bowed. 'Lationusi was, about 14 000 of your years ago, the last King of the continent Mu on Earth.'

'I don't understand.'

'You don't want to understand, Michel, and, at this particular moment, you resemble many of your peers on Earth.'

I must have looked troubled, for Thao, Biastra and Latoli laughed loudly.

'Don't look like that, Michel. I just meant to jostle you a little. Now, in the presence of Lationusi, I am going to explain one of the mysteries that elude many experts on your planet - who, I might add, would do better to devote their precious time discovering more useful things. I am going to unveil not one, but several of the mysteries which obsess them.'

Our seats were arranged in a circle, Thao sat next to Lationusi and I sat facing them.

'As I already explained during our journey to Thiaoouba, the Bakaratinians arrived on Earth 1 350 000 years ago. Thirty thousand years later came the terrible cataclysm that gouged out seas and caused the emergence of islands and even continents. I made mention also, of an enormous continent which arose in the middle of the Pacific Ocean.

'This continent was called 'Lamar' but is better known to you as the continent of Mu. It emerged virtually in one piece, to be shattered 2000 years later, by seismic shock, into three principal continents.

'With the passing of years, vegetation established on these continents, large areas of which were located in equatorial regions. Grass grew, forests established and, gradually, animals migrated across the very narrow isthmus that bound Mu to North America.

'The yellow race that had better managed to come to terms with the disastrous consequences of the cataclysm, were first to construct ships and explore the seas. About 300 000 Earth years ago, they landed on the northwest coast of Mu, where they eventually founded a small colony.

'This colony barely grew over the course of centuries as there were difficulties in expatriating, which would take too long to explain and which does not concern us now.

'About 250 000 Earth years ago, the inhabitants of planet Aremo X3, on which we stopped to take samples during our journey here, embarked on an interplanetary voyage of exploration penetrating your solar system. After having skirted Saturn, Jupiter, Mars and Mercury, they landed on the planet Earth in China, where their spacecraft caused considerable panic among the populace. Their legends refer to 'fire dragons' descending from the sky. The fear and mistrust of the Chinese, led them eventually, to attack the aliens, who were forced to use violence in order to defend themselves. This they hated, for they were not only technologically advanced but also highly spiritual people who abhorred killing.

'They moved on, continuing their exploration of the planet. It turned out, that the continent of Mu had most appeal for them for two main reasons. First, the continent appeared to be virtually uninhabited and second, by virtue of its latitude, it was a veritable paradise.

'They had become particularly cautious since their confrontation with the Chinese and felt it would be wise to establish a base to which they could retreat, should they encounter further hostilities of a serious nature from Earth people. I have not yet explained that their reason for exploring Earth was their intention of resettling several million people from Aremo X3 - a planet that was becoming uncomfortably over-populated. This operation was much too serious to take risks of any kind. Thus, it was decided that their base of retreat would be set up, not on Earth, but on the moon, which was quite close and considered very safe.

'Fifty years were spent establishing the lunar bases and it wasn't until they were ready that emigration to Mu began. All went well. The small Chinese colony that had existed in the north-west of Mu had been totally destroyed some decades after their first visit, so in effect, they had the entire continent to themselves.

'Work began immediately on the construction of towns, canals and roads, which they paved with immense flagstones. Their usual means of transport was a flying chariot, not unlike our Lativoks.

'From their planet, they imported animals such as the dog and the armadillo - which they were very partial to on Aremo X3, and also the pig.'

When she told me about all those imported animals, I remembered how astonished I'd been to see pigs and dogs on that famous planet during our earlier visit. Suddenly, everything was very clear to me.

'In height, these people averaged 180 centimetres for the males, and 160 centimetres for the females. Their hair was dark, their eyes of a beautiful black and their skin lightly bronzed. You saw some of their kind when we stopped at Aremo X3 and I believe you have already guessed them to be the ancestors of the Polynesians.

'So they established settlements throughout the length and breadth of the continent, including 19 large cities, seven of which were sacred. Small villages were also numerous, for these people were highly skilled farmers and graziers.

'Their political system was modelled on that of Aremo X3. They had long ago discovered that the only way to govern a country properly was to place at the head of government, seven men of integrity, representing no political party, but sincerely committed to doing what they could for their nation.

'The seventh among them was the Supreme Judge whose vote on council was worth two. If four were against him and two with him on a particular issue, they were at deadlock, and hours or days of debate would ensue, until at least one of the seven was persuaded to change his vote. This debate was conducted within a context of intelligence, love and concern for the people.

'These high figures received no great material benefits for leading the nation. It was their vocation to lead and they did it for the love of serving their country - this avoided the problem of hiding opportunists among the leaders.'

'The same can't be said of our national leaders now,' I remarked with a hint of bitterness. 'Where were such men found?'

'The procedure was as follows: In a village or district, a man of integrity was elected by referendum. No one with a record of bad conduct or a tendency towards fanaticism could be chosen - the chosen one would have demonstrated integrity in all spheres. He would then be sent to the nearest town, along with other representatives from neighbouring villages, and there, further elections would be held.

'For example, if there were 60 villages, there would be 60 men elected by the people for their *integrity* and *not* for promises which they made, but *couldn't keep.*

'Representatives from all over the nation would meet together in the capital city. They would be divided into groups of six and each group assigned a particular conference room. For the next ten days the group would be together - holding discussions, sharing meals, enjoying shows and, eventually, they would elect a group leader. So, if there had been 60 representatives, divided into ten groups, there would be ten group leaders. Of these ten, seven would be elected by the same process, and from the seven, an eventual Supreme Leader would emerge. He was given the title of King.'

'So, he was a republican King,' I said.

Thao smiled at my remark and Lationusi gave a slight frown.

'The King was elected in this way only if his predecessor died without having nominated a successor, or if the successor was not unanimously accepted by the council of seven. He was given the title of King, first because he was the representative on Earth of the Great Spirit, and second because nine times out of ten, he would be the son or near relative of the preceding King.'

'Something like the Roman method, then.'

'Yes indeed. However, if this King manifested the slightest tendency towards dictatorship, he was overthrown by his council of peers. But let's go back now to our emigrants from Aremo X3...

'Their capital city, given the name Savanasa, was situated on a plateau overlooking the Gulf of Suvatu. The plateau was 300 metres high and, except for two hills - one in the south-west and one in the south-east, this was the highest point on the continent of Mu.'

'I'm sorry, Thao - may I interrupt? When you explained the cataclysm which knocked the Earth off its axis, you said that refuge on the moon was not possible because it didn't exist - and yet now, you say that safety bases were established on the moon for these emigrants...'

'There *was* no moon at the time when the blacks populated Australia, or for a very long time afterwards. There had been two very small moons much earlier - about six million years ago, which revolved around Earth, eventually colliding with it. Earth was not inhabited at the time so, although terrible cataclysms followed, it didn't really matter.

'About 500 000 years ago, Earth 'captured' a much larger moon - the one which exists now. It was passing too close to your planet and was attracted into an orbit. This often happens with moons. Further catastrophes were provoked by this event...'

'What do you mean when you say 'passing too close' to Earth? Why didn't it crash? And anyway, what *is* a moon?'

'It could have crashed indeed, but that doesn't often happen. A moon is originally a small planet revolving around its sun in a spiral that becomes increasingly tight. The smaller planets spiral more rapidly than the larger ones, whose inertial force is less.

'Their spiral being faster, the smaller planets often catch up to the larger planets and, if they pass too closely, the gravitational attraction of the planet will be stronger than that of the sun. The smaller planet begins to orbit the larger one, still in a spiral, which will sooner or later result in a collision.'

'Are you saying that our beautiful moon celebrated in poem and song, will one day fall on our heads?'

'One day, yes...but not for about 195 000 years.'

I must have seemed relieved and my fright somewhat comical, for my hosts all laughed.

Thao continued. 'When that happens - when the moon collides with the Earth - that will be the end of your planet. If the people of Earth are not sufficiently spiritually and technologically advanced at the time, it will mean a holocaust; but, if they are, they will have evacuated to another planet. Everything in its time though, Michel - for now, I must finish off my story concerning the continent of Mu.

'Savanasa then, was situated on a vast plateau overlooking plains which rose, on average, no more than 30 metres above sea level. On this plateau and in the centre, an enormous pyramid was constructed. Each stone used in its construction, some weighing more than 50 tonnes, was cut precisely to within one fifth of a millimetre, using what we can call 'ultrasonic vibratory systems'. This was done in the quarries of Holaton, now found on Easter Island, which was the one place on the entire continent where this special rock could be found. There was, however, another quarry at Notora, south-west of the continent.

'The enormous stones were transported using anti-gravitational techniques well known to these people. (They were carried on platforms, 20 centimetres above the paved roads, and were constructed using the same principals as those of the pyramids.) Roads such as these were built all over the country, converging, like a massive spider's web, on the capital, Savanasa.

'The huge stones were taken to Savanasa and put into position according to directions from the 'master' or chief architect on the project. When finished, the pyramid measured exactly 440.01 metres in height and its four faces were oriented *precisely* towards the four points of the compass.

'Was this intended to be the King's palace, or his tomb?' Everyone wore the same indulgent smile that often appeared when I asked a question.

'Nothing of the sort, Michel. This pyramid was much more important - it was a tool. An enormous tool, I admit, but a tool just the same. So, too, was the Pyramid of Cheops, in Egypt, though it was much smaller in size.'

'A tool? Please explain - I'm no longer with you.' It was true I was having trouble following Thao, but I could sense one of the great mysteries was about to be revealed to me - one which had provoked so much inquiry and had been the subject of so much writing on Earth.

'You will have realised,' Thao resumed, 'that these were highly advanced people. They possessed a profound understanding of Universal Law and used their pyramid as a 'captor' of cosmic rays, forces and energies, as well as terrestrial energies.

'Inside, rooms positioned according to a precise plan, served the King and certain other great initiates, as powerful communications centres, enabling (telepathic) communication with other planets and other worlds in the universe. Such communication with extra-terrestrials is no longer possible for people on Earth; but the people of Mu in those days, by natural means and by exploiting cosmic forces, were in constant communication with other beings and were even able to explore parallel universes.'

'Was this the sole purpose of the pyramid?'

'Not quite. Its second use was to make rain. By a system of plates, made of a special alloy incorporating silver as its major component, these people were able, in a few days, to cause the accumulation of clouds above the country, and so, to have rain as they needed it.

'Thus, they were able to create, virtually, a paradise over the whole continent. Rivers and springs never dried up, but flowed lazily across the numerous plains of a land that was essentially flat.

'Fruit trees were laden with fruit, bowing under the weight of oranges, mandarins or apples, according to latitude. Exotic fruits, of kinds that actually no longer exist on Earth, were harvested in abundance. One such fruit, called the *Laikoti*, possessed a property that caused an excitation of brain activity, allowing whoever ate it to solve problems which would normally be beyond them. This property was not actually a drug but the fruit was, nevertheless, condemned by the sages. The Laikoti was only authorised to be planted in the gardens of the King. [7]

'Man being what he is, however, the fruit was secretly planted in various places throughout the continent. Those caught with the fruit were harshly punished for they had directly disobeyed the King of Mu. In matters of religion and government, he was to be obeyed absolutely, as he was the representative of the Great Spirit.

'As such, the King was not one to be worshiped - he simply represented another.

'Those people believed in Tharoa - the God, The Spirit, the One and Only, the Creator of all things and, of course, they believed in reincarnation.

'What concerns us here, Michel, are the great events which occurred on your planet, in times long gone, so that you will be able to enlighten your people. I won't, therefore, elaborate on my description of the continent that was home to one of the best-organised civilisations to have existed on Earth. However, you should know that, after a period of 50 000 years, the population of Mu was eighty million.

'Expeditions were undertaken regularly, to explore and research aspects of the planet. For these expeditions, they used flying ships, similar to what you call 'flying saucers'. It was known that most of the planet was populated by black, yellow and also white races, although the latter had regressed into a primitive state due to their loss of technical understanding right at the beginning. These white people had actually arrived on Earth in very small numbers at a time in between the arrival of the Bakaratinians and the colonising of Mu. They had settled on a continent known to you as Atlantis, but, as much for material as spiritual reasons, their civilisation failed completely.'

'What do you mean by 'material reasons'?'

'Natural disasters, which effectively destroyed their towns and almost all that might have allowed them to advance technologically.

'I must emphasise the following point: prior to embarking on their exploratory expeditions of the planet, the inhabitants of Mu had conducted research by means of the Pyramid of Savanasa. As a result of this research, it was decided to send forth the flying ships and to colonise New Guinea and the southern Asiatic region - that is, all to the west of Mu. Simultaneously, they set up colonies in South America and Central America.

'Most importantly, they established a colonial base, which grew into a huge town, in the area known to your archaeologists as Thiacuano, located not far from Lake Titicaca. The Andes did not exist at the time, the mountains formed some time later, as you will soon see.

---

7 In writing this book, I feel it is interesting to emphasise the striking similarity between this prohibition from eating the Laikoti - for reasons relating to knowledge - and, in the Bible, Adam being forbidden to eat the apple on similar grounds.

'At Thiacuano, an enormous seaport was built. In those days, North and South America were flat and eventually, a canal was constructed to link an inland sea, existing where Brazil is now, with the Pacific Ocean. This sea also had an outlet into the Atlantic Ocean, so that it was possible to pass from one ocean to the other and so, to colonise the continent of Atlantis...'

'But you say they had flying ships - why wouldn't they use them? If they pierced a canal, they must have intended to use boats.'

'They used their flying machines just as you now use aeroplanes Michel, but for very heavy loads, they used machines of anti-gravitation, exactly like the heavy vehicles are now used on Earth.

'So, as I said, they colonised the continent of Atlantis. Many white people from Atlantis preferred, at the time, to emigrate to the region of Northern Europe, as they didn't accept the new government and the new religion coming from Mu. These white people set off in their sea vessels propelled by steam and wind. Indeed, the white race had discovered steam power, having passed through a period you would call 'prehistoric'. I must also explain that Britain was not an island, at this time as it was joined to northern Europe, and the Straits of Gibraltar didn't exist either, as Africa reached to the south of Europe. Many white people from Atlantis emigrated to North Africa, mixing with the cross-bred black-yellow race of the area. Interbreeding created new races in North Africa, which have perpetuated themselves over thousands of years and which you know as Berbers, Tuaregs and others.

'We often visited Earth during those times. When we judged the time opportune, we went overtly, to visit the King of Mu and, according to his request or the information he gave us, we would visit the new colonies. In India, for example, or in New Guinea, the people of Mu sometimes experienced great difficulties assimilating their civilisation with that already in existence. We would arrive, openly and publicly, in vessels quite like the one that brought you to Thiaoouba, although different in shape.

'Our size, which has always been large and our radiant beauty, meant that we passed as gods in the eyes of people who were not greatly advanced and, in some cases, were even cannibals.

'According to our mission, it was important that we impress as *friendly* gods in the eyes of the colonisers so that war could be avoided, something which they abhorred on account of their advancement, their beliefs and their religion.

'It is because of our frequent visits, during this period, that there are so many legends on Earth, describing 'giants' and 'chariots of fire' from the heavens.

'We were great friends with the inhabitants of Mu and my astral entity at the time, existed in a body quite similar to the one I'm 'wearing' now.

'Artists and sculptors gave us much consideration. They consulted the King of Mu and, with his consent, worked to immortalise us. The immense statues at Holaton[8] (Easter Island) are examples of such work. They were, for the civilisation of the time, the ultimate of great art - being in size and shape, what you would describe as 'stylised'.

'This is how a statue of me came to be sculpted. It was finished and ready to be transported on one of the enormous platforms that serviced the length and breadth of the country, terminating always in Savanasa. The Master of the time erected these statues either in the King's gardens or along the path that led to the pyramid. Unfortunately, when the statue representing me, along with several others, was about to be transported, a cataclysm occurred which destroyed the continent of Mu.

'However, Holaton was partially spared. When I say 'partially', you must realise that the quarries had been ten times as extensive as the vestiges that remain today. The part that wasn't swallowed up in the cataclysm was the area where my statue stood.

'My stylised image is thus preserved on Easter Island. When you told me you had dreamed of me in the form of a statue on Easter Island and I confirmed that I was, you thought I was being metaphorical, but that was only half right. You see, Michel, certain dreams, and yours most definitely, are influenced by *lacotina*. This is something for which there is no corresponding word in any Earth language. It is not necessary for you to understand the phenomenon, but, under its influence, it is a *true* dream.'

Thao ended her account at that point, flashing her familiar smile and adding: 'If you have difficulty remembering all that, I will help you in good time.'

With that, she rose, and we all did likewise.

---

8 Holaton (Easter Island) was situated at the south-east of the Continent of Mu.

Delving into the psychosphere

We followed Lationusi who led us into another part of the doko - the relaxation area where one can relax completely and no external sound can penetrate. Here, Latoli and two of the 'elders' left us. Lationusi, Thao, Biastra and I remained.

Thao explained that, because my psychic powers were not sufficiently developed and refined, and, in order to participate in an important and very special experience, I would be obliged to take a special elixir. It was a matter of 'delving' into the psychosphere, of the planet Earth at the time of the disappearance of Mu, that is, 14 500 years ago, she explained.

My understanding of the term 'psychosphere' is as follows:

Around each planet, since its creation, is a kind of psychosphere or vibratory cocoon, which turns at a speed seven times that of light. This cocoon acts as a blotter, as it were, absorbing (and remembering)[1] absolutely every event occurring on the planet. The contents of this cocoon are inaccessible to us on Earth - we have no way of 'reading the story'.

It is well known that, in the USA, researchers and technicians are employed to develop a 'time machine' but, up to the present time, their efforts have been without success. The difficulty exists, according to Thao, in adapting to the vibrations of the cocoon, rather than to wavelengths. The human being, comprising an integral part of the universe can, because of his Astral body and if he is correctly trained, draw what knowledge he seeks from within the psychosphere. Of course, great skill is required for this. 'This elixir will allow you access to the psychosphere, Michel'.

All four of us made ourselves comfortable in a special bed. I was placed in the centre of a triangle formed by Thao, Biastra and Lationusi. I was handed a goblet containing a liquid, which I drank.

Biastra and Thao then placed their fingers lightly on my hand and my solar plexus, while Lationusi put his index finger above my pineal gland. They told me to relax completely and not be afraid, regardless of what happened. We would be travelling in Astral body and I would be under their guidance and so, quite safe.

That time is engraved on my memory forever. The longer Thao spoke to me softly and slowly, the less afraid I was.

I must confess however, that initially, I was very frightened. Suddenly, in spite of my closed eyes, I was dazzled by the colours of the whole spectrum, which danced and shone. I could see my three companions around me, radiant with colour, but at the same time, translucent.

The village slowly blurred below us.

I had the bizarre impression that four silver cords attached us to our physical bodies, which were assuming the proportions of mountains.

Suddenly, a flash of blinding white gold crossed my 'vision' and for some time afterwards, I neither saw nor felt anything.

A ball, brilliant like the sun but silver in colour, appeared in space and approached at an incredible speed. We hurried through, I should say, *I* hurried through for, at that moment, I was no longer aware of the presence of my companions. When I had penetrated this silvery atmosphere, I could make out no more than the 'fog' that surrounded me. It's impossible to say what time period was involved but, quite suddenly, the fog dissipated, revealing a rectangular room, with a low ceiling, in which two men sat cross-legged on marvellously coloured cushions.

The walls of the room were of finely sculptured stone blocks, scenes of contemporary civilisation, with clusters of grapes which seemed transparent, fruits which I couldn't recognise and animals too - some of which had human heads. There were also human figures with the heads of animals.

I noticed, then, that my three companions and I formed a 'unit' that was a gaseous mass, and yet we were able to distinguish each other.

'We are in the main chamber of the Pyramid of Savanasa,' said Lationusi. It was incredible - Lationusi had not opened his mouth and yet he spoke to me in French! The explanation came in a flash: 'it's true telepathy, Michel. Ask no questions, all will unfold naturally and you will learn what you must know.'

(Since my duty, in writing this book, is to report on my experiences, I must try to explain as clearly as possible that, in the state I was in at the time - my Astral body had passed into the psychosphere - the words *saw, heard* and *felt,* were not appropriate, merely useful, as sensations occur 'spontaneously' in a very different way from that which we normally experience - and even from that which we experience when we travel in Astral body.

Events occur rather as they do in a dream, and sometimes very slowly, other times with a disconcerting speed. Afterwards, each thing seemed self-evident and I learned later, this was because of the state I was in and because of the close supervision that my mentors exercised over me.)

Very rapidly, I saw an opening in the ceiling of the room and, right at the end, a star. I was aware that the two figures were exchanging 'visible' thoughts with the star. From their pineal glands, streamed threads of what looked like silvery cigarette smoke that passed through the opening in the ceiling and went to join the star in distant space.

The two figures were perfectly immobile and, around them, floated a soft golden light. I know, thanks to the constant tutelage of my companions, that these figures not only couldn't see us, but neither could they be disturbed by us, since we were spectators in another dimension. I examined them more attentively.

One of them was an old man with long white hair falling past his shoulders. On the back of his head, he wore a skullcap of saffron-coloured fabric similar to that worn by rabbis.

He was dressed in a loose-fitting, yellow-gold tunic, with long sleeves, which enveloped him totally. In the position he sat, his feet were not visible but I 'knew' they were bare. His hands met, touching only at the fingertips and I could clearly see little bluish flashes around his fingers, bearing testimony to the immeasurable force of his concentration.

The second figure seemed to be about the same age, in spite of his shiny black hair. Apart from the colour of his tunic, which was bright orange, he was dressed in the same manner as his companion. So completely motionless were they that they didn't appear to be breathing.

'They are in communication with other worlds, Michel,' it was explained to me.

Suddenly, the 'scene' vanished, to be immediately replaced by another. A palace, in the shape of a pagoda, with roofs covered in gold, stood before us with its towers, its portals, its immense picture windows opening on to splendid gardens and its enamelled pools in which the water of fountains gushed and fell, forming rainbows under the rays of a sun at its zenith. Hundreds of birds flitted in the branches of trees scattered throughout immense parks, adding splashes of colour to an already magical setting.

People dressed in tunics of various styles and colours strolled in groups, beneath the trees or near the pools. Some sat in meditation beneath floral bowers specially provided for their comfort and shelter. The whole scene was dominated by a structure that loomed in the distance beyond the palace - a gigantic pyramid.

I 'knew' that we had just left this pyramid and that I was now admiring the marvellous palace of Savanasa, the capital of Mu.

Beyond the palace, in all directions, stretched the plateau Thao had spoken of. A pathway, at least 40 metres wide, seemed to be made of a single stone block, led out on to the plateau from the centre of the gardens. It was bordered by two rows of massive shade trees interspersed with huge, stylised statues. On some of these statues were hats, red or green, with wide rims.

We glided along this pathway amidst people on horseback and others riding strange four-legged animals with heads resembling dolphins - animals to which I had never heard any reference made: animals whose existence took me by surprise.

'These are *Akitepayos*, Michel, which have long been extinct,' it was explained to me.

This animal was the size of a very large horse, with a multi-coloured tail, which he sometimes spread like a fan, similar to the tail of a peacock. Its hindquarters were much broader than those of a horse; its body was of a comparable length; its shoulders emerging from the body like the carapace of a rhinoceros; and its forelegs were longer than its hindlegs.

All of its body, except for the tail, was covered in long grey hair. When it galloped, I was reminded of the way our camels run.

I sensed quite strongly that I was being led elsewhere by my companions. We quickly passed the people on their walks - *very* quickly, and yet I was able to 'take in' and note a feature of their language. It was very pleasant to the ear and seemed to comprise more vowels than consonants.

Immediately, we were presented with another scene, similar to a film, when one scene is cut and another shown. Machines, exactly like the 'flying saucers' dear to the writers of science fiction, were lined up in an immense field on the edge of the plateau. People were disembarking and boarding the 'flying machines' that took them to an enormous building, which no doubt served as an air terminal.

On the landing field, the flying machines emitted a whistling sound that was quite tolerable to the 'ear'. I was told that our perception of the sound and its intensity was comparable with that of the people who were part of the scene before us.

It struck me that I was witnessing the daily life of people who were remarkably advanced, and who had been *dead* for thousands of years! I recall taking note also, of the pathway beneath our 'feet' and realising that it was not one huge stone block, as it appeared to be, but, in fact, a series of large flagstones, so precisely cut and positioned that the joins were barely visible.

From the edge of the plateau, we had a panoramic view over an immense city and seaport, and beyond, the ocean. Then, instantaneously, we were in a wide street of the city, bordered by houses of varying sizes and architectural designs. Most of the houses had terraces surrounded by flowers, where at times, we glimpsed a very pretty species of bird. The more modest houses without terraces had, instead, beautifully made balconies - also flower-filled. The effect was quite delightful - like walking in a garden.

In the street, the people either walked or flew, about 20 centimetres above the road, on small flying platforms that made no sound at all. This seemed a very pleasant way to travel. Yet others rode on horseback.

When, at the end of the street, we found ourselves in a large town square, I was surprised to see no boutiques or the like. Instead, there was a covered market where 'stalls' displayed all manner of goods that the heart, or palate, might desire. There were fish, among which I recognised tuna, mackerel, bonitoes and rays; there was meat of many varieties as well as an incredible assortment of vegetables. Most predominant however, were the flowers that seemed to fill the area. It was clear these people delighted in flowers, which were either worn in the hair or carried in the hands of everyone. The 'shoppers' helped themselves to what they wanted, giving nothing in exchange - neither money nor anything which might substitute. My curiosity drew our group into the heart of the marketplace, right through the bodies of the people - an experience that I found most interesting.

All my questions were answered as they occurred to me: 'they use no money as everything belongs to the community. No one cheats - communal life is perfectly harmonious. With the passing of time, they have been taught to obey well- established and well-studied laws that suit them very well'.

Most of these people were between 160 and 170 centimetres in height, with light brown skin and black hair and eyes - very similar to our present day Polynesian race. There were also some white people among them, larger in size, about two metres tall, with blond hair and blue eyes and, in greater numbers, some blacks. The latter were tall, like the whites, and appeared to be of several 'kinds', including one like the Tamils and another, strikingly like our Aborigines in Australia.

We went down towards the port where vessels of all shapes and sizes were moored. The quays were constructed from gigantic stones which I was 'told', came from the Notora quarry in the south-west of the continent.

The entire port had been artificially made. We were able to see some very sophisticated pieces of equipment in operation - ship-building equipment, loading equipment machines carrying out repairs...

The vessels in port represented, as I have said, a huge range - from eighteenth and nineteenth-century-style sailing ships to modern style yachts; from steam boats to ultra modern hydrogen powered cargo vessels. The enormous ships at anchor in the bay were the anti-magnetic, anti-gravitational vessels I'd been told about.

Out of action, they floated on the water: however, when carrying their several thousand tonne loads, they travelled, at speeds of 70 to 90 knots, just above the water - and that, without making any noise.

It was explained to me that the 'classic' vessels represented in the port, belonged to people of distant lands - India, Japan, China - which had been colonised by Mu, but which did not yet have the capacity to take advantage of technological advance. In this regard, I also learned from Lationusi, that the leaders of Mu kept secret much of their scientific knowledge, for example, nuclear energy, antigravitation and ultra-sounds. This policy ensured that they maintained their supremacy on Earth and guaranteed their security.

The scene was 'cut' and we found ourselves back on the landing field, looking at a night view of the city. It was lit up, quite uniformly, by large globes, as was The Path of Ra, the road which led to the palace of Savanasa. Globes positioned in the sculptured colonnades along the avenue illuminated it, as though it were day.

It was explained to me that these globes, which were spherical in shape, converted nuclear energy into light and had the capacity to be working thousands of years into the future without extinguishing. I confess I didn't understand, but I believed it must be so.

Another scene change - and it was daylight. The grand avenue and the palace gardens had been invaded by crowds of people brightly dressed and there was an enormous white ball attached to the top of the pyramid.

Apparently, the King, whom I had seen meditating in the pyramid, had died just prior to the gathering of the crowd.

With much noise, the ball exploded and a unanimous cry of joy rose from the people. This astonished me, as death usually inspires tears, but my companions explained it as follows:

'Michel! You don't remember the lessons we taught you. When the physical body dies, the Astral being is liberated. These people also know it and celebrate the event. In three days time, the Astral body of the King will leave Earth to rejoin the Great Spirit, for this King has conducted himself in an exemplary manner during this final life on Earth, despite very difficult responsibilities and tasks required of him.'

I had no answer and I felt ashamed of being caught out by Thao for my forgetfulness.

Suddenly the decor changed again. We found ourselves on the front steps of the palace. A huge crowd stretched before us for as far as the 'eye' could see, and, beside us, was an assembly of dignitaries, including a figure dressed in the finest attire imaginable. This was to be the new King of Mu.

Something about him drew my attention. He was familiar - it was as though I knew him but didn't quite recognise him, made up as he was. In a flash I had the answer from Lationusi: 'it's *me*, Michel, during another life. You don't recognise me but you are aware of my astral vibrations in that body.'

In effect, Lationusi was experiencing the extraordinary *within* the extraordinary! Lationusi was seeing himself living a previous life while he was still existing in his present life!

From the hands of one of the dignitaries, the new King received a magnificent head-piece which he put on himself.

A shout of joy rose from the crowd. The continent of Mu - the most highly developed nation on the planet and ruler over more than half of it, had a new King.

The crowd seemed delirious with joy. Thousands of small balloons, garnet- coloured and bright orange, soared into the sky, and an orchestra began to play. The musicians of the 'orchestra', who numbered two hundred at least, played from stationary flying platforms located all around the gardens, the palace and the pyramid. On each platform, a group of musicians played together on indescribably strange instruments and in such a way that the sound was distributed as though through gigantic stereophonic speakers.

The 'music' was not at all the music we are familiar with. Apart from a type of flute that produced notes of a very special frequency, the instruments all modulated the sounds of nature; for example, the howling wind, the hum of bees in the flowers, the songs of the birds, the sound of rain falling on to a lake or of the waves crashing on a beach. It was all so skilfully arranged - the sound of a wave might originate in the gardens, roll towards you, pass over your head and finish by crashing on the steps of the Great Pyramid.

I never would have imagined that human beings, no matter how advanced, could accomplish such a feat as that orchestral arrangement.

The crowd, the nobles and the King seemed to 'experience' the music from within their souls, so entranced were they. I would have liked to stay too, to listen and listen more, to allow myself to be impregnated by this song of nature. Even in my astral-psychospheric situation, the music 'penetrated' and the effect was spell binding. I was 'reminded' that we were not there for the pleasure...The scene vanished.

Immediately, I was witnessing an extraordinary meeting, presided over by the King and restricted to his six advisers. I was told the matter was serious when the King met only with these six.

The King had aged significantly, for we had leapt forward in time by twenty years. Everyone present looked grave, as they discussed the technical worth of their seismographs and I was able to understand it all within one-hundredth of a second: I could follow the course of their discussions as if I was one of them!

One of the advisers was claiming that the equipment had, on occasions, proved unreliable but there was no great cause for concern. Another stated that the seismograph was perfectly accurate since that very model had proven itself at the time of the first catastrophe, occurring in the west of the continent...

As they spoke, the palace began to tremble, like leaves on a tree in the wind. The King rose, his eyes wide with surprise and fear: two of his advisers fell from their seats. Outside, a great din seemed to come from the town.

The scene changed and suddenly, we were outside. The moon was full and illuminated the gardens of the palace. All had become calm again - too calm. The only sound heard was a dull rumbling, coming from the edge of town...

Suddenly, the servants ran from the palace and scurried in all directions. Several of the columns supporting the globes that lit up the avenue lay on the ground - smashed. Emerging quickly from the palace, the king and his 'entourage' climbed on to a flying platform and headed immediately for the airport. We followed them. Around the flying vessels on the field, and in the terminal, confusion reigned. Some people were making a dash for the vessels, screaming and shoving. The King's flying platform moved quickly towards one of the vehicles that stood apart from the others: he and his followers boarded it. Other craft were already taking off, when a deafening sound rose from the depths of the Earth - a strange, continuous sound like thunder.

The airfield suddenly ripped apart like a sheet of paper, and an enormous column of fire enveloped us. The vessels that had just taken off were trapped in the middle of the flames and exploded. The people who had been running on the airfield were lost in the crevasse. The king's vessel, still on the ground, caught fire and exploded.

At this moment, as if the King's death had been a signal, we saw the great pyramid topple in a single block into the crevasse, which was extending along the plateau, widening by the second. The pyramid had balanced for a moment on the edge of the crevasse, then, with a violent shudder, it was swallowed into the flames.

Again the scene changed. We had a view of the seaport and the town, which seemed to undulate like waves on the ocean. Buildings began to collapse accompanied by screams of terror in the scenes of horror that appeared and disappeared among the flames.

Deafening explosions occurred, originating I learned, from deep below the surface of the Earth. Entire 'suburbs' plunged into the earth; then huge pieces of the continent followed suit. The ocean rushed in to fill the immense chasms being created and suddenly, the entire plateau of Savanasa sunk into the waters, like an enormous foundering liner, but much quicker. Powerful whirlpools were formed and, within them, I could see people desperately clinging to wreckage, trying in vain, to survive.

It was horrifying for me to witness such a cataclysm, even knowing that it had occurred 14 500 years ago.

We began a very rapid 'tour' of the continent, finding everywhere, the same disasters. Water rushed in gigantic waves over the remaining plains, submerging them. We approached a volcano that had just erupted, and nearby, we saw rocks begin to move with a regular motion, as though a gigantic hand was lifting them above the lava flow and creating a mountain before our very eyes. This seemed to take as little time in happening, as the plateau of Savanasa had taken to disappear.

The scene vanished again, to be repeated by another.

'We are arriving in South America, Michel, where the cataclysm has not yet had effect. We'll have a look at the coast here and the port of Thiacuano. In time, we've gone back to just prior to the first tremor, when the King of Mu was meeting with his advisers.'

We were on the quays of the large seaport of Thiacuano. It was night and a full moon lit up the land, although quite soon it would set. In the east, a faint lightening of the sky heralded the approach of dawn. All was quiet. Watchmen patrolled the quays where numerous boats were moored.

A few rowdy revellers were entering a building on which a small night light shone. Here, we could see some of the spherical globes of Mu - but just a few.

We flew over the canal, where several ships could be seen heading in the direction of the inland sea (now Brazil).

Our group 'came to rest' on the bridge of a pretty sailing ship. A gentle breeze coming from the west pushed the vessel from behind. It carried little sail, as it negotiated a zone congested with numerous boats. There were three masts on deck, quite modern in style, and of about 70 metres in length. Judging by the shape of its hull, it would be capable of significant speed in open waters.

A moment later, we found ourselves in a large seaman's cabin, furnished with a good dozen bunks, all occupied.

Everyone was asleep, apart from two men of about thirty years of age, who, by their physical appearance, probably came from Mu. They sat at a table, engrossed in a game, which might well have been mahjong. My attention was drawn to one of the pair - perhaps older than his companion - whose long dark hair was tied back in a red scarf. I was attracted to him as a piece of iron is to a magnet and, in an instant I was upon him, taking my companions with me.

As I passed through him, I felt an almost electric stimulation - and a sensation of love, such as I had never felt before, invaded my being. I felt an indefinable oneness with him and I passed through him again and again.

'This is easily explained, Michel. In this man, you are reunited with your Astral body. This is *you,* in one of your previous lives. However, you are here as an observer and no purpose is served by trying to re-live this time. Do *not* get involved.'

With regret, I 'followed' my companions back to the bridge.

Suddenly, in the distance to the west, a loud explosion was heard, then another nearer. Still in the west, the sky began to glow. Closer still, amid much sharper explosions, we watched the eruption of a volcano that lit up the western sky for about a 30 kilometre radius.

On the canal and in the port, we were aware of a feverish agitation as cries rang out and sirens sounded.

We heard running footsteps and the sailors from below spilled on to the bridge. Among them, I could see the sailor who 'wore' my Astral body, just as frightened as his companions and I felt an enormous wave of sympathy for the panic- stricken 'self.

On the outskirts of the town, in the glow of the volcano, I saw a shining sphere fly very rapidly up into the sky, and eventually, disappear from sight.

'Yes, that was one of our spacecraft,' explained Thao. 'It will observe the cataclysm from very high. There are seventeen people on board, who will do what they can to help survivors, but this will be very little. Watch.'

The ground began to shake and rumble. Three more volcanoes surged from beneath the surface of the ocean near the coast, only to be engulfed by the waters as quickly as they had appeared. At the same time, it caused a tidal wave of about 40 metres in amplitude to surge towards the coast with an infernal noise. Before it reached the town however, the land beneath us began to rise. The port, the town and the countryside beyond - a whole section of the continent - rose rapidly, blocking the assault of the waves. In order to see better, we rose higher. I was reminded of a gigantic animal arching its back as it stretched, after extricating itself from a burrow.

The cries of the people reached us as a Dantean screech. They were mad with panic, for they were rising with the town, as though in a lift, and it seemed their ascent would never stop.

The boats had been smashed to pieces on rocks hurled from the ocean, and I watched as the sailor we had left behind was literally pulverised. One of my 'selves' had just returned to its source.

It seemed the Earth was completely remodelling its shape. The town disappeared as thick black clouds rolled in rapidly from the west, showering the land with lava and ash, spewed from the volcanoes. Two words of description came to mind at that moment: 'grandiose' and 'apocalyptic'.

Everything blurred and I felt my companions close around me. I was aware of a silvery-grey cloud moving away from us at a dizzying speed and then Thiaoouba appeared. I had the impression that we were pulling on the silvery threads, in order to return quickly to our physical bodies that seemed to be waiting for us - huge like mountains and shrinking as we approached.

My astral eyes appreciated the beauty of the colours here on this 'golden' planet, after enduring the nightmares we had just left behind.

I felt the hands which were touching my physical body let go. Opening my eyes, I looked around me. My companion stood up, smiling, and Thao asked me if I was all right.

'Very well, thank you. I am very surprised it is still light outside.'

'Of course it is still light, Michel. How long do you think we were away?'

'I really don't know. Five or six hours?'

'No,' said Thao, amused. 'No more than fifteen lorses - about fifteen minutes.'

Then each taking me by a shoulder, Thao and Biastra guided me out of the 'relaxation chamber', bursting with laughter at my dumbfounded air. Lationusi followed, less exuberant in his amusement.

Our 'so-called' civilisation

When I had paid my respects and said my goodbyes to Lationusi and his companions, we left the village and boarded the flying platform once again, to retire to my doko. We took a different route this time, flying over large cultivated fields, and pausing long enough for me to admire the crops of wheat which grew there with very large ears. Our route also took us over an interesting looking city - not only were all the buildings 'dokos', from the largest to the smallest, but there were also no actual streets linking them. I understood the reason for this: the people here were able to move from place to place by 'flying' - with or without a Lativok so that proper streets were unnecessary. We passed close by people entering and leaving huge dokos, similar in size to those at the spaceport.

'These are the 'factories' where our food is prepared,' explained Thao. 'The manna and the vegetables you were eating yesterday in your doko, would have been prepared here.'

We didn't stop but flew on, over the city and then over the ocean. Before long, we had reached the island where my doko was situated. Leaving our vehicle in the usual place, we went inside.

'Do you realise,' said Thao, 'that you have eaten nothing since yesterday morning? You are going to lose weight at this rate. Aren't you hungry?'

'Surprisingly, I'm not particularly hungry, and yet, on Earth, I have four meals per day!'

'It's not really so surprising, my friend. Our food here is prepared in such a way that the calories contained in the food are released at regular intervals over a two- day period. We continue to be nourished without overloading our stomachs. This also allows our minds to remain clear and alert and, after all, our minds must be a priority - isn't that so?' I nodded my agreement.

We helped ourselves to various coloured dishes and a little manna, then, as we enjoyed a glass of hydromel, Thao asked, 'What do you think of your stay on Thiaoouba, Michel?'

'What do I think of it? Perhaps after my experience of this morning, you should rather be asking what I think of the planet Earth! It seemed to me during those... fifteen minutes - that years had passed by. Some moments were, obviously, dreadful, but others were enthralling. May I ask you, why did you take me for that journey in time?'

'A very good question, Michel. I am glad you have asked. We wanted to *show* you that, prior to your present so-called civilisation, there had been, on Earth, 'true' civilisations. We didn't 'kidnap' you, as you might say, and bring you several billion kilometres just to show you the beauty of our planet.

'You are here because you belong to a civilisation that has taken a wrong turn. Most of the nations on Earth believe themselves to be highly advanced, which is not so. Rather, their cultures are decadent, from the leaders and so-called elite classes. The whole system is distorted.

'We know this because we have kept a very close watch over the planet Earth, particularly during recent years, as the great Thaora explained to you. We are able to study what is happening in a whole range of ways. We can live among you in physical bodies or in astral presence. We are not just present on your planet - we are able to influence the behaviour of certain of your leaders, fortunately for you. For example, our intervention prevented Germany from being the first nation to have the use of the atomic bomb, for it would have been disastrous for the rest of the people on Earth if Nazism had triumphed at the end of the Second World War. As you will appreciate, any totalitarian regime signifies a great backward step for civilisation.

'When millions of people are sent to the gas chambers simply because they are Jews, their murderers cannot pride themselves on being a civilised people.

'Still less, could the Germans believe themselves to be the chosen people. To act as they did, they had to have fallen lower than any tribe of cannibals.

'The Russians who send thousands to work in concentration camps and who eliminate thousands more, on the grounds they represent a danger to 'the regime' are no better.

'On Earth, there is a great need for discipline, but 'discipline' does not mean dictatorship. The Great Spirit, the Creator himself obliges no creature, human or otherwise, to do anything against its will. We all have free will and it is up to us to discipline ourselves in order to improve spiritually.

To impose one's will on another, in a way which deprives the individual of the privilege of exercising his own free will, is one of the greatest crimes that man can commit.

'What is happening now in South Africa is a crime against all humanity. Racism itself is a crime...'

'Thao,' I interrupted, 'there is something I don't understand. You say that you prevented the Germans from being the first to have the atomic bomb, but why did you not prevent all countries from having it? You must admit that, at the point we have arrived at with atomic arms, we are sitting on a volcano. What do you say of Hiroshima and Nagasaki - don't you feel in some way responsible?'

'Michel, of course you look at such things in a very simplified way. Everything for you is black or white, but there are also many shades of grey. If the Second World War had not been stopped, as it was by the bombing and destruction of those two cities, there would have been many more deaths - three times as many as there were victims of the atomic bombs. As you say in your language, we chose the lesser of the two evils.

'As I have told you before, we can 'lend a hand' but we don't concern ourselves with the fine details of a situation. There are very strict rules to be followed. The bomb had to exist - just as on all planets it is eventually discovered. Once in existence we can either watch what ensues, as spectators, or we can intervene. If we intervene, it is to give an advantage to the 'side' which is most sincere and most respectful of individual liberty.

'If certain of the leaders who read your book *don 't believe you,* or *doubt what is written,* challenge them to explain the disappearance of billions of 'needles' put into orbit around Earth several years ago. Ask them also to explain the second disappearance of billions more 'needles' again put into orbit. They will know what you are referring to, never fear. We are responsible for the disappearance of these 'needles', judging them to be potentially disastrous for your planet.

'We do, at times, prevent your experts from 'playing with matches' but it is important that our assistance not be relied upon when mistakes are made. If we judge it appropriate to 'lend a hand', we do so, but we can't, and we don't wish to save you from disaster automatically - that would be to contravene Universal Law.

'You see, Michel, atomic weaponry seems to cast fear into the hearts of people of Earth, and I admit that it is a sword of Damocles suspended over your heads, but it is not the real danger.

'The real dangers on Earth, in order of 'importance' are: first *money* then *politicians;* third *journalists and drugs* and fourth *religions.* These dangers in no way relate to nuclear arms.

''If the people on Earth are wiped out by a nuclear cataclysm, their Astral beings will go where they must after death and the natural order of death and rebirth will be maintained. The danger does not lie in the death of the physical body, as millions believe: the danger exists in the way in which one lives.

'On your planet, money is the worst of all evils. Try now, to imagine life without money...

'You see,' said Thao who had 'read' my efforts, 'you can't even imagine such a life, for you are caught up in the system.

'However, just two hours ago, you saw that the people of Mu were able to meet their needs without spending any money. You noticed, I know, that the people were very happy and highly advanced.

'The civilisation of Mu revolved around the community - both spiritually and materially, and it thrived. Of course, you must not confuse 'community' with 'communism', as exists in certain countries on Earth. Communism, as practised on Earth, is the essential part of totalitarian regimes rather than democratic, and, as such, is degrading for Man.

'Unfortunately, as regards money, it is difficult to help constructively on Earth for your whole system is based on it. If Germany needs 5000 tonnes of Australian wool, it can't send, in exchange, 300 Mercedes and 50 tractors. Your economic system doesn't work this way; it is, therefore, difficult to improve the system.

'On the other hand, much could be achieved in regard to politicians and political parties. You are all in the same boat...and there is a useful comparison to be made between a country or planet and a boat. Every boat must have its captain, but to run well it requires skill and a spirit of cooperation among the sailors, as well as their respect for their captain.

'If, as well as being knowledgeable, experienced and quick thinking, the captain is also fair and honest, the chances are great that his *crew* will do its best by him. It is, ultimately, the *intrinsic worth* of the captain - regardless of his political or religious leanings - that will determine the effectiveness of his operation.

'Imagine, for example, that a captain had to be elected by his crew, more for reasons of politics than for his skill in navigation and his cool-handedness in times of danger. To imagine the situation better, let's suppose we are watching an actual election. We are standing on a leading dock where 150 crew members are assembled with three candidates for command of a ship. The first is a democrat, the second, a communist, and the third a conservative. Among the crew members, there are 60 with communist leanings, 50 democrats and 40 conservatives. Now, I am going to show you that this affair cannot be conducted appropriately.

'The communist candidate is obliged to make certain promises to the democrats and conservatives if he wants to win; because he is only 'guaranteed' 60 of the votes. He must convince at least 16 men from the other parties that it is in their interests to elect him. But will he be able to keep the promises he makes? And, of course, the same applies to the other two candidates.

'When one or the other of these captains is at sea, he will always find that a significant number of his crew are fundamentally opposed to his having command, so there is always a significant risk of mutiny.

'Of course, this is *not* the method by which a captain achieves his command - fortunately. I merely wished to illustrate the dangers that are inherent in electing leaders on the basis of political bias rather than for their ability to lead people, honestly, in appropriate directions.

'While on the subject, I must emphasise another point. When our 'captain-elect' is at sea, he is the one and only leader of the vessel, whereas, when a party leader is elected as head of state, he is immediately confronted with a 'Leader of the Opposition'. From the very beginning of his leadership, whether his decisions are good or bad, he will be systematically criticised by an opposing party bent on his demise. How can a country be properly governed under such a system, Michel?'

'Do you have a solution?'

'Of course, and it has already been described to you. The only solution is to follow the example of the government of Mu.

'This is to place as head of state a leader whose unique goal is the wellbeing *of the people* - a leader not motivated by false pride or party and personal pecuniary ambition; to do away with political parties - and the resentment, the grudges, the hatred that go with them; and to hold out your hand to your neighbour - to accept him and work with him, regardless of differences you may have. He is after all, in the same boat with you, Michel. He is part of the same village, the same town, the same nation, the same planet.

'What is the house which shelters you made of, Michel?'

'Of bricks...of wood, tiles, plaster, nails...'

'Indeed, and what are all these materials made of?'

'Atoms, of course.'

'Perfect. Now these atoms, as you know, have to connect very closely in order to form a brick or any other building material. What would happen if these atoms repelled each other instead of combining as they do?'

'Disintegration.'

'And there we are. When you push away your neighbours, your son or your daughter - if you aren't always ready to help even those whom you don't like, you contribute to the disintegration of your civilisation. And this is what is happening on Earth more and more, through hate and *violence*.

'Consider two examples well known to all on your planet, which prove that violence is not a solution.

The first is Napoleon Bonaparte: by the use of arms he was able to conquer all of Europe, and he established, as national leaders, his own brothers to diminish the risk of treason. It is widely accepted that Napoleon was a genius and, indeed, a competent organiser and legislator since, 200 years later, many of his laws still exist in France. But what has become of his empire, Michel? It quickly disintegrated because it had been established through the use of arms.

'Hitler, similarly, sought to conquer Europe by force and you know what happened there.

'Violence does not pay, and never will. The solution lies, rather, in *love* and the cultivation of minds. Have you ever noticed that, all round the world, and particularly in Europe, you had many more great writers, musicians and philosophers emerging in the nineteenth and early twentieth centuries?'

'Yes, I believe it is so.'

'Do you know why?'

'No.'

'Because, along with the advent of electricity, the internal combustion engine, the automobile, the aeroplane and such like, the people of Earth neglected the cultivation of their spirituality and focused on the material world.

'Now, as the great Thaora explained, materialism poses one of the greatest threats to your present life and your future lives.

'After politicians, you have the problem of journalists and reporters. There are some among them, although unfortunately rare, who try to do their job of disseminating information honestly and sincerely, attending carefully to their sources; but we are greatly alarmed that most of them seek only sensationalism.

'Your television stations too, screen more and more scenes of *violence*. If those responsible were obliged to study psychology before being able to undertake such grave responsibilities, a step in the right direction would have been taken. Your reporters seem to seek and even prey on scenes of violence, murder, tragedy and disaster; we are sickened by their behaviour.

'The leaders of a country, the journalists, in fact anyone who, by their position, is able to exert influence on the people, has an enormous responsibility towards millions of people who are no more nor less than his fellow creatures. Too often, even those who have been elected to their positions by the people, forget the obligations they have in this regard - until, that is, a few months prior to a new election, when it occurs to them that the people are dissatisfied and might vote them out.

'This is not the case with journalists though, as they have not needed to inspire confidence in the people in order to attain their positions; and yet they have a similar power to influence in ways which are good or bad.

'Indeed, they are capable of doing much good when they alert public attention to danger and injustice - and this should be their *main* function.

'To return to the need for such high profile people to understand and apply psychology, I will give you a good example to illustrate what I mean. On TV we see the following report: A young man has just taken a rifle and killed seven people including two women and two young children. The reporter shows the bloodstains and the bodies, adding that the killer had imitated the style of an actor, well known for his violent roles in films. And the result? The murderer is going to be proud of himself - not only has he achieved 'national notoriety', he has also been compared with one of the most popular heroes of violent modern films. But, beyond that, another such madman who sees the reports and hears the commentaries of reporters who pay unwarranted attention to this odious crime, will be inspired to seek his own moment of national 'glory'.

'Such a person is usually a failure - someone repressed, frustrated, inhibited; someone ignored, who yearns for recognition. He has just seen the report and he knows that all violence is reported, and sometimes exaggerated, by TV reporters and journalists. Perhaps his picture will appear on the front page of all the newspapers - and why not? Then he will go before the courts and perhaps be referred to by a name like 'Jack the Ripper' or 'The Strangler with the Velvet Glove'. No longer will he rank among ordinary mortals. The harm that such irresponsible reporting can do is unimaginable. Thoughtlessness and irresponsibility are not qualities apparent in civilised nations. That's why I say, on Earth, you have not even achieved the first letter of the word *civilisation.*'

'So, what is the solution?'

'Why do you ask such a question, Michel? You have been chosen because we know how you think, and I know that you know the answer to your question. Still, if you insist, you will hear it from my mouth. Journalists, reporters and anyone else whose function it is to disseminate information should devote no more than two to three lines to such cases of murder. They could simply say: 'we have just learned of the murder of seven people by an irresponsible lunatic. This murder occurred at whatever location and is a sorry event in a country that considers itself to be civilised.' Full stop'.

'Those who seek their day or weeks of glory would surely side step murder as a means of attaining it, if their efforts received so little publication in return. Don't you agree?'

'What, then, should their reports comprise?'

'There are so many worthwhile things to show - reports of worthwhile events which improve the psyche of Earth people rather than brainwashing them in a negative way. Reports such as the risking of life to rescue a child who was drowning, for example, or of assistance given to the poor to improve their lot.'

'Of course, I agree with you entirely, but I'm sure the circulation of newspapers depends on the sensational news they contain.'

'And there we are, back at the *root of all evil* that I mentioned earlier - *money*. This is the curse that undermines your entire civilisation; and yet, in this particular case, the situation could be reversed if those responsible were motivated to change. On no matter which planet, the greatest dangers to humankind are, ultimately, of a psychological, rather than material nature.

'Drugs, similarly, affect the psyche of the individual - not only do they ruin physical health, they also reverse the individual's process of universal evolution. At the same time as they induce states of euphoria or artificial paradise, they are also directly attacking the Astral body. I will elaborate on this, for it is of great importance.

'The Astral body can only be harmed by two things: drugs and the vibrations occasioned by certain kinds of noise. Considering only drugs, it must be understood that they have an influence that is totally against Nature. They 'remove' the Astral body to another sphere where it should not be. The Astral body should be either in a physical body or with its Higher-self, of which it is a part. When drugged, an individual's Astral body is as though 'asleep' experiencing artificial sensations that completely distort his or her judgement. It is in the same situation as a physical body is during an important surgical operation. If you like, it's like a tool that we bend or break by using it incorrectly or for a task for which it was not intended.

'According to the length of time that a person is under the influence of drugs, his or her Astral body is going to decline or, more exactly, it is going to become saturated with false data. 'Recovery' for the Astral body can take several lifetimes: for this reason, Michel, drugs should be avoided at all costs.'

'There is something I don't understand then,' I interrupted. 'Twice, now, you have given me drugs to take in order to release my Astral body from my physical body. Haven't you, thereby, done me a disservice?'

'No, not at all. We used a drug that is not an hallucinogen, in order to assist a process which could occur quite naturally with adequate training. It is not a drug that 'blinds' and therefore presents no danger to your Astral body and its effects are very short-term.

'Returning to the problems of your planet, Michel, the solution depends on love - not money. It requires that people rise above hate, resentment, jealousy and envy, and that each person, whether he be street sweeper or community leader, put his neighbour before himself, offering his hand to whoever needs it.

'Everyone has need, both physically and mentally, of his neighbour's friendship - not only on your planet, but on all planets. As Jesus said, when we sent him to you almost 2000 years ago: 'Love each other' - but of course...'

'Thao!' I interrupted again, almost rudely this time. 'What did you just *say* in regard to *Jesus?*

'Jesus, Michel was sent to Earth from Thiaoouba almost 2000 years ago - just as Lationusi also went to Earth and has returned.'

Of all that had been explained to me, it was this unexpected revelation which shocked me most. At the same time, Thao's Aura rapidly changed colour. The soft gold 'mist' around her head become almost yellow, and the gentle shower of colours from the top of her head, blazed forth with new energy.

'A great Thaora is calling us, Michel. We must go immediately.' Thao stood up.

I adjusted my mask and followed her outside, most intrigued by this sudden interruption and uncustomary haste. We boarded the flying platform and rose, vertically, above the branches of the trees. Soon we were flying over the beach, and then the ocean, travelling at a speed much greater than ever before. The sun was quite low in the sky and we skimmed over waters that were emerald green or a perfect azure blue - if I can describe colours in Earthly terms.

Huge birds, with a wingspan of about four metres, crossed our path just in front of us and the sun's rays lit up the bright pink feathers of their wings and the bright green feathers of their tails.

Before long we had reached the island and Thao brought the platform down again in the park, in which seemed to be precisely the same spot as before. She signalled that I should follow her and we set off - she walking and I running behind her.

This time we did not head for the central doko, but took a different path, which led us eventually to another doko, of the same huge size as the central doko.

Two people, both taller than Thao, were waiting for us under the entrance light. Thao spoke to them in a low voice; then moved nearer to them and engaged in a brief consultation, from which I was excluded. They stood still, casting curious glances my way, but not smiling at all. I could see their Auras, which were less brilliant than Thao's - a sure indication that they were not as highly evolved in spirit.

For a considerable time, we waited without moving. The birds from the park approached, watching us. No one, apart from me, paid them any attention; my companions were apparently deep in thought. I remember clearly, a bird, resembling a bird of paradise, came and stationed itself between Thao and me, for all the world as though it wanted to be admired.

The sun would soon set and I remember watching its last rays high up in the trees, igniting sparks of purple and gold among the branches. A flock of birds fluttered noisily in the canopy, breaking the silence that had been established. As if this had been a signal, Thao asked me to take off my mask, close my eyes and to take her hand that she might guide my steps. Much intrigued, I did as she asked.

Moving forward, I felt the light resistance, now familiar to me, as we entered the doko. I was told telepathically to keep my eyes half-closed and lowered, and to follow in Thao's wake. We advanced about 30 paces before Thao stopped and placed me at her side. Still by telepathy, she indicated that I could now open my eyes and look around; this I did quite slowly. Before me were three figures remarkably like those I had met previously. Like the others, they sat cross-legged, straight backed, on fabric-covered blocks, each seat being of a colour that complemented the occupant.

Thao and I were standing beside two similar seats until, telepathically, and without a gesture, we were invited to sit down. I looked around discretely, but saw no trace of the two characters who had met us at the entrance: perhaps they were behind me..?

Like before, the eyes of the Thaori gave the impression of being illuminated from within but, by contrast, this time I was immediately able to see their Auras, resplendent with bright colours all so pleasing to the eye.

The central figure rose by levitation, without altering his position, and slowly floated towards me. He stopped before and slightly above me, placing one of his hands at the base of my cerebellum and the other on the left side of my skull. Again, I felt my body invaded by the fluid-like feeling of well-being, but this time I almost fainted.

Removing his hands, he returned to his seat. Perhaps I should explain that the details concerning the position of his hands on my head were provided later, by Thao, as, once again, it was beyond me at the time to register such details. And yet I remember a thought that occurred to me - a thought rather out of place at such a time - when he resumed his seat: 'I'll probably never get to see one of these figures use his two legs as everyone else does.'

A different alien
and my former lives

A period of time had elapsed, I've no idea how long, when, instinctively, I turned my head towards the left. I'm sure my mouth fell open and remained that way. One of the two people I had met earlier was coming towards us from the left, leading a person, very odd in appearance, by the shoulder. For a moment I thought this person to be a Red Indian chief such as we see in films. I will try to describe him as best I can.

He was very small in stature, perhaps 150 centimetres but what was most striking about him was that he was as wide as he was tall - just like a square. His head was completely round and sat directly on his shoulders. What had at first sight brought to mind an Indian chief, was his hair, which was more like feathers, coloured yellow, red and blue, rather than hair. His eyes were quite red and his face was 'flattened' almost like a Mongoloid face. He had no eyebrows but lashes that were four times as long as mine. He had been given a robe like mine, although quite different in colour. The limbs that extended beyond the robe were of the same light blue colour as his face. His Aura, silvery in places, shone brightly and around his head was a strong halo of gold.

The shower of colour from the top of his head was much smaller than Thao's, rising only a few centimetres into the air. He was, telepathically, invited to take a seat, about ten paces to our left.

Again, the central figure levitated towards the new arrival and placed his hands on his head, repeating the procedure I had experienced.

When we were all seated, the great figure began to address us. He spoke in the language of Thiaoouba and I was completely stunned at finding I understood everything he said, just as if he had spoken in my mother tongue!

Seeing my agitation, Thao telepathised, 'Yes Michel, you have a new gift. It will be explained later.'

'Arki,' the Thaora was saying, 'this is Michel, from the planet Earth. I welcome you to Thiaoouba, Arki. May The Spirit enlighten you.'

Addressing me, he continued. 'Arki has come to visit us from the planet X'. (I am not allowed to reveal the name of this planet, nor the reason I have been forbidden to do so.) 'And we thank him in the name of The Spirit and all the Universe, just as we thank you, Michel, for your willingness to collaborate with us in our mission.

'Arki has come in his Agoura[9] at our request, especially to meet you,

---

9 Spacecraft of the planet X which travels at a speed slightly below the speed of light.

Michel.

'We wanted you to see with your own eyes and touch with your own hands, an extra-planetarian quite different from our own race. Arki inhabits a planet of the same category as Earth, although it is very different in certain respects. These 'differences' are essentially physical and have contributed, over the course of time, to the physical appearance of the people.

'We also wanted to show you several things, Michel. Arki and his fellow beings are highly evolved both technologically and spiritually which might surprise you considering you will find his appearance 'abnormal', even monstrous. However, you can see by his Aura that he is highly spiritual and good. We also wanted to show you, by this experience, that we can give you for a time, the gift not only of seeing Auras, but of understanding all languages - and that, without recourse to telepathy.'

So that was it, I thought to myself.

'Yes, that was it,' Thaora replied. 'Now, move closer, the two of you. Talk together, touch each other if you want to - in a word, make each other's acquaintance.

I stood up and Arki did likewise. When he was upright, his hands almost touch the floor. Each had five fingers, like ours, but the fifth included two thumbs - one in the same position as ours and the other where our little fingers are.

We approached each other and he held his arm out to me, the wrist forward and fist closed. He was smiling at me, revealing a set of straight, even teeth, just like ours, but green. I held my hand out in return, not knowing what else to do, and he addressed me in his own language - now perfectly comprehensible to me.

'Michel, I am very pleased to meet you and would have liked to be welcoming you as a guest on my own planet.' I thanked him warmly, and filled with such emotion, began the sentence in French and finished it in English, which he, likewise, had no difficulty understanding!

He continued. 'At the request of the great Thaora, I have come to Thiaoouba from planet X, a planet that resembles yours in many ways. It is twice larger than Earth, with 15 billion inhabitants but, like Earth and other planets of the first category, it's a 'Planet of Sorrows'. Our problems are much the same as yours: we have had two nuclear holocausts during our existence on our planet and we have experienced dictatorships, crime, epidemics, cataclysms, a monetary system and all that is associated with it, religions, cults and other things.

'However, eighty of our years ago (our year lasts four hundred and two 21- hour-days) we initiated a reform. In fact, the reform was set in motion by a group of four people from a small village on the shores of one of our largest oceans. This group, comprising three men and one woman, preached peace, love and freedom of expression. They travelled to the capital city of their country and requested an audience with the leaders. Their request was denied for the regime was dictatorial and military. For six days and five nights, the four slept in front of the palace gates, eating nothing and drinking little water.

'Their perseverance attracted public attention and by the sixth day, a crowd of 2000 had gathered in front of the palace. With feeble voices, the four preached to the crowd of uniting in love to change the regime - until guards put an end to their 'sermon' by shooting the four and threatening to shoot members of the crowd if they did not disperse. This they quickly did, in genuine fear of the guards. Nevertheless, a seed had been sown in the minds of the people. On reflection, thousands of them came to realise that, without a peaceful understanding, they were powerless, absolutely powerless.

'Word was passed around among the people - rich and poor, employer and employee, worker and foreman, and one day, six months later, the entire nation came to a standstill.'

'What do you mean by 'came to a standstill'?' I asked.

'The nuclear power stations shut down, transport systems halted, freeways were blocked. Everything stopped. The farmers didn't deliver their produce; radio and television networks ceased transmitting; communication systems shut down. The police were helpless in the face of such unity, for, in a matter of hours, millions of people had joined the 'cease work'. It seemed, for that time, the people had forgotten their hates, jealousies, differences of opinion as they united against injustice and tyranny. A police force and an army comprise human beings and these human beings had relatives and friends among the crowd.

'It was no longer a question of killing four subversive individuals. Hundreds of thousands would have had to be killed just to 'liberate' one power station.

'In the face of the people's determination, the police, the army and the Dictator were forced to capitulate. The only deaths to occur during this incident were the 23 fanatics who comprised the Tyrant's personal guard - the soldiers were obliged to shoot them in order to reach him.'

'Was he hanged?' I asked.

Arki smiled. 'Why, no, Michel. The people were through with violence. He was deported instead, to a place where he could do no further harm, and, in fact their example inspired his reform. He found, again, the path of love and respect for individual liberty. He died, eventually, repentant for all that he had done. Now, that nation is the most successful on our planet, but, as on yours, there are other nations under the domination of violent totalitarian regimes and we are doing all in our power to help them.

'We know that all we do in this life is an apprenticeship, offering us the possibility of graduating to a superior existence and even freeing us forever of our physical bodies. You must know, too, that the planets are categorised and that it is possible for entire populations to emigrate to another, when their planet is in danger, but no-one can do so if the new planet is not of the same category.

'Being, overpopulated ourselves and, having highly advanced technology, we have visited your planet with a view to establish a settlement there - an idea we decided against since your degree of evolution would bring us more harm than good.'

I was not very flattered by this reflection and my Aura must have indicated as much to Arki. He smiled and continued. 'I'm sorry, Michel, but I am saying my piece without hypocrisy. We still visit Earth but only as observers, interested in studying, and learning from you, your errors. We never intervene because that is not our role, and we would never invade your planet, as this would be a backward step for us. You are not to be envied - materially, technologically or spiritually.

'Going back to our Astral bodies, an Astral body absolutely cannot change to a superior planet until sufficiently evolved. We are speaking, of course, of spiritual evolution and not technological. This evolution occurs thanks to the physical body. You have already learned of the nine categories of planets — ours are at the bottom of the scale that improves as it progresses right up as far as this planet. We, in our present physical bodies, can be permitted only nine days' stay here. According to Universal Law, on the tenth day, our physical bodies would die and neither Thao nor the great Thaora, within whose power it is to revive the dead, would be able to prevent or reverse the process. Nature has very inflexible rules with well-established safeguards.'

'But if I were to die here, perhaps my Astral body could stay here and I could be reincarnated as a baby on Thiaoouba...?' I was full of hope, forgetting, for the moment, the family I loved back on Earth.

'You don't understand, Michel. Universal Law would require that you be reincarnated on Earth, if you had not yet finished your time there. But it *is* possible that when you do die on Earth - when your moment has come - your Astral body will reincarnate in a body on another, more advanced planet...a second or perhaps third category planet, or even this one, depending on your present degree of development.'

'It's possible then, to skip all categories and find ourselves reincarnated on a ninth category planet?' I asked, still full of hope, for, most decidedly, I regarded Thiaoouba as a veritable paradise.

'Michel, can you take some iron ore and some carbon, heat them to the right temperature, and produce pure steel? No. First you must skim the rubbish from the iron; then it goes back to the pot to be processed again and again and again... for as long as it takes to produce first-class steel. The same applies to us; we must be 'reprocessed' over and over until we emerge perfect, for eventually we will rejoin The Spirit who, being perfect himself, cannot accept the slightest imperfection.'

'That seems so complicated!'

'The Spirit, who has created everything, wanted it this way and I'm sure that, for him, it's very simple; but for a poor human brain, I admit, it is at times difficult to comprehend. And it gets more difficult, the closer we try to get to the Source. For this reason, we have tried, and in several places with success, to abolish religions and sects. They apparently want to group people together and help them to worship God or gods and to understand better; and yet they make it all much more complicated and quite incomprehensible by introducing rituals and laws invented by priests who look to their own personal interests rather than following nature and Universal Law. I see by your Aura that you already realise certain of these things.'

I smiled, for it was true, and asked, 'On your planet, can you see Auras, and read them?'

'A few of us have learned to, myself included, but in this domain we are little more advanced than you. However, we study the subject enormously because we know this is what's necessary for our evolution.'

He stopped there, quite suddenly, and I realised it was a telepathic order coming from the great personage that made him do so.

'I must go now, Michel and I will be completely happy to do so if in having spoken to you, I have been able to assist you and your fellow creatures - on Earth and across the Universe.'

He held his hand out to me and I did likewise. In spite of his ugliness, I would have liked to kiss him and hold him in my arms. I wish I had...

I later learned that he had been killed, along with five others, when his spacecraft exploded just an hour after leaving Thiaoouba. I hoped that life would continue for him on a more hospitable planet...but perhaps he would return to his own in order to help his people - who knows? I had met, across the Universe, a brother who, like me, existed on a Planet of Sorrows - studying, at the same school, how one day, to gain eternal happiness.

When Arki had left the room with his mentor, I sat down again near Thao. The Thaora who had given me the gift of understanding all languages, addressed me again.

'Michel, as Thao has already told you, you were chosen by us to visit Thiaoouba, but the essential motive for our choice has not been revealed. It is not only because you have a mind already awakend and open, but also - and *principally* - because you are one of the rare *soukous* inhabiting Earth at the present time. A 'soukou' is an Astral body that has lived eighty-one lives in human physical bodies, and that on different planets or different categories. For various reasons, the 'soukous' return to live on inferior planets, like Earth, when they could just as well continue to 'climb the ladder' without ever going backwards. You know that the number nine is the number of the Universe. You are here in the City of Nine Dokos, founded on Universal Law. Your Astral body has nine times nine lives, which brings you to the end of one of the great cycles.'

Once again, I was completely flabbergasted. I suspected I wasn't living my first life, especially after my journey to Mu - but eighty-one lives! I didn't know one lived so many...

'It's possible to live many more, Michel,' said the Thaora,

interrupting my thoughts. 'Thao is up to her 216th, but other entities live far fewer. As I said, you have been chosen from among very few 'soukous' living on Earth, but, in order that you acquire a thorough understanding during the trip to our planet, we have planned another journey in time for you. So that you will better understand what reincarnation is, and what its purpose is, we will permit you to revisit your previous existences. This journey in time will be useful to you when writing your book as you will fully comprehend its purpose.'

He had barely finished speaking, when Thao took me by the shoulder and spun me around. She led me towards the relaxation chamber - a feature, it seemed, of each and every doko. The three Thaori followed us, still by levitation.

Thao indicated that I should lie down on a large piece of fabric that was just like an air cushion. The 'chief Thaora positioned himself behind my head, the other two each holding one of my hands. Thao cupped her hands above my solar plexus.

The leader then placed the index fingers of both hands over my pineal gland, telepathically ordering me to stare at his fingers.

Seconds later, I had the impression of sliding backwards at incredible speed, through a dark, endless tunnel. Then, abruptly, I emerged from the tunnel into what seemed to be a gallery of a coal mine. Several men, wearing small lamps on their foreheads were pushing carts; others, a little further away, were attacking the coals with picks or shovelling it into carts. I moved towards the end of the gallery where I was able to examine one of the miners closely. I seemed to know him. A voice that came from within me said, 'It's one of *your* physical bodies, Michel.' The man was quite tall and well built. He was covered in sweat and coal dust and laboured as he shovelled coal into a cart.

The scene changed abruptly, just as it had when I was in the psychosphere on Mu. I learned that he was called Siegfried, when one of the other miners at the entrance to the mine shaft called his name in German, which I understood perfectly - and I do not speak or understand that language. The other miner asked Siegfried to follow him. He headed towards an old shed, somewhat larger than all the others in this apparent main street of the village. I followed them both inside, where oil lamps were burning and men sat at tables.

Siegfried joined a group of them. They shouted something at a brute wearing a dirty apron and, shortly afterwards, he brought them a bottle and some pewter goblets.

Another scene was superimposed on this one. It seemed that it was several hours later. The shed was the same, but now, Siegfried was staggering out, visibly drunk. He headed towards a row of smaller sheds, all of which had chimneys from which blackish smoke curled. Brusquely, he opened the door of one of them and entered, with me hot on his heels.

Eight children, progressing in ages from one year upwards, each twelve months apart, sat at a table plunging their spoons into bowls full of unappetising looking gruel. They all lifted their heads at the sudden appearance of their father, watching him with fearful eyes. A woman, medium in size but strong looking, with hair of a dirty blonde colour, addressed him aggressively: 'Where have you been and where is the money? You know very well that the children haven't had beans in a fortnight, and, yet again, you're drunk!'

She rose and approached Siegfried. As she raised her hand to slap his face, he grabbed her arm and, with his left fist, punched her so hard that she was sent flying backwards.

She fell to the floor, hitting the back of her neck on the chimney hearth as she did so, and was killed instantly.

The children were crying and screaming. Siegfried leaned over his wife whose wide-open eyes stared lifelessly into his.

'Freda, Freda, come on, get up,' he cried, his voice filled with anguish. He took her in his arms to help her, but she couldn't stand. Suddenly, as she continued to stare fixedly, he realised she was dead. Sobered now, he rushed towards the door and fled into the night, running on and on, as if he had lost his mind.

Again the scene changed and Siegfried appeared, firmly bound between two guards, one of whom was putting a hood over Siegfried's head. The executioner also wore one with holes cut in it for his eyes. He was a huge man and held within his enormous hand the handle of a wide blade axe. The guard made Siegfried kneel, bending forward so that his head rested on the execution block. Now the executioner came forward and assumed his position. A priest hastily recited prayers as the executioner slowly raised his axe over his head. Quite suddenly, he let it fall on the neck of Siegfried. The victim's head rolled across the ground, causing the crowd to recoil several steps.

I had just witnessed the violent death of one of *my* many physical bodies...

The sensation was *so* strange. Until the moment of his death, I had been filled with a great fondness for this man, and although he had done wrong, I felt great pity for him. At the moment of his death, however, as his head rolled across the ground amid the murmurs of the crowd, I felt an overwhelming sense of relief - on his account as well as my own.

Immediately, I was presented with another scene. Before me was a lake, its shining blue waters reflecting the rays of two suns which hung quite low on the horizon.

A small boat, richly yet delicately decorated with sculptures and paintings, proceeded across the lake. It was guided by men, of medium size and reddish complexion, using long poles which they plunged into the water. Beneath a type of canopy and seated on an ornately decorated throne, was a lovely young woman with golden skin. Her oval shaped face was lit up by pretty almond eyes and long blonde hair that fell to her waist.

She was relaxed and smiling as the young company, which hovered around her, entertained her light-heartedly. I *knew* instantly that this pretty creature was myself in another life.

The boat proceeded steadily towards a landing pier, from which led a wide pathway bordered by tiny flowering shrubs. This path disappeared among trees that surrounded what appeared to be a palace, with roofs at various levels and of various colours.

With a change of scene, I was transported inside the palace to find myself in a lavishly decorated room.

One wall opened up on to a garden - a very orderly miniature garden of astonishing variety and colour.

Servants with reddish skin, dressed in bright green loincloths, busied themselves with serving one hundred or so guests. These 'guests' were of both sexes and all richly dressed. They had the same type of light golden skin colour as the woman on the boat. In contrast to the complexions of the servants, these people had skins of the colour that blonde women on Earth can attain after numerous suntanning sessions.

The pretty young woman from the boat, sat, in what appeared to be the place of honour, in a high-backed seat. Music, soft and enchanting, could be heard and seemed to emanate from the far end of the room as well as from the garden.

One of the servants opened a large door to admit a tall young man - perhaps 190 centimetres in height and of similar golden complexion. His bearing was proud and his build athletic.

Copper blond hair framed a face of regular features. He advanced with a purposeful stride towards the young woman and bowed before her. Whispering something to him, she gestured to the servants who brought forward an armchair similar to her own and placed it beside hers. The young man sat down and the woman gave him her hand, which he held in his.

Suddenly, on a signal from her, a gong sounded several times, and silence fell. The guests turned towards the couple. In a voice loud and clear, directed towards the servants as well as the guests, the young woman spoke: 'to all of you gathered here, I want you to know that I have chosen a companion. This is he, Xinolini, and he will have, from this moment and according to my agreement, all of the royal rights and privileges, after me. Indeed, he will be the second power in the kingdom, after myself, the Queen and the head. Any subject disobeying him or doing wrong by him in any way will answer to me. The first child that I bear Xinolini, whether male or female, will be my successor. I, Labinola, Queen of the land, have decided this.'

She signalled again, and the sound of the gong indicated the end of her speech. One by one, the guests bowed low before Labinola, kissing first her feet and then Xinolini's in gestures of subservience.

This scene disappeared in a blur to be replaced by another, in the same palace but another room, where the royal family sat in thrones. Here, Labinola was administering justice. All sorts of people paraded before the Queen and she listened attentively to them all.

An extraordinary thing happened. I found I was able to enter into her body. It's quite difficult to explain, but for a considerable time, while I listened and watched, I *was* Labinola.

I could understand absolutely all that was said, and when Labinola pronounced her judgement, I was in total agreement with her decisions.

I could hear in the murmuring of the crowd, reflections of admiration for her wisdom, never once did she turn towards Xinolini and never did she ask his advice. I felt a great pride invade me, knowing that I had been this woman in another life and I felt, during this time, the light tingling sensation that I was starting to recognise.

Everything disappeared again and then I was in the most luxurious of bedrooms. It proved to be that of Labinola, who lay, completely naked, on the bed. Three women and two men hovered nearby. As I approached, I could see her face, streaming with perspiration and disfigured with the pain of labour.

The women, midwives, and the men, the most eminent doctors in the kingdom, seemed worried. The child was arriving in a breech position and Labinola had lost a lot of blood. This was her first child and she was exhausted. Fear was evident in the eyes of the midwives and doctors and I *knew* that Labinola already realised she was going to die.

The scene moved forwards two hours in time and Labinola had just breathed her last breath. She had lost too much blood. The child, too, had died, suffocating before it could emerge into the world. Labinola, this pretty creature of twenty- eight years, so beautiful and good had just released her Astral body - my Astral body, to live another life.

Further scenes were already appearing, revealing other lives on other planets - as men, women and children. Twice I was a beggar, and three times a sailor. I was a water carrier in India, a goldsmith in Japan where I lived till ninety-five years of age; a Roman soldier; a black child at Chad devoured by a lion at the age of eight years; an Indian fisherman on the Amazon, dead at forty-two years leaving twelve children; an Apache chief dead at eighty-six years; several times a peasant farmer, on Earth as well as on other planets; and twice an ascetic in the mountains of Tibet and on another planet.

Apart from when I was Labinola, ruling Queen of one-third of a planet, most of my lives were very modest. I saw scenes from all eighty of my previous lives - some of which impressed me a lot. I do not have time to detail them all in this book, as they would fill a volume on their own. Maybe one day I will write it.

At the end of the 'show', I had the impression of moving backwards in the 'tunnel' and, when I opened my eyes, Thao and the three Thaori were smiling kindly. When it was established that I was indeed back in my present skin, the leader addressed me in the following words:

'We wanted to show you your past lives, that you might notice they vary, as though they were attached to a wheel. Because a wheel is made

115

to turn, any point on it that is on top will soon be at the bottom - it is inevitable, do you see?

'One day you are a beggar and then you can be a Queen, such as Labinola who, of course, was not only at the top of the wheel but also learned a lot and greatly helped others. And yet, in many cases, a beggar will learn as much as a king and in some instances he will learn much more.

'When you were an ascetic in the mountains, you assisted many more individuals than in most of your other lives. What counts most is *not* appearances, but what is *behind* them.

'When your Astral body takes on another physical body it is, quite simply, in order to learn more, and even more...

'As we have explained to you, it is for the sake of your Higher-self. It is a process of continual refinement, which can occur just as effectively in the body of a beggar as in that of a king or a miner. The physical body is but a tool. A sculptor's chisel and hammer are tools; they will never reach beauty on their own, but they contribute to it in the hands of an artist. A wonderful statue could not have been created with the artist's bare hands.

'You should always bear in mind this main point: An Astral body, in all cases, must conform to Universal Law, and, by following nature as closely as possible, it can achieve the ultimate goal by the fastest path.'

With that, the Thaori resumed their places and we resumed ours.

During my stay in the doko, the sun had set; however, they didn't deem it necessary to explain the luminous ambience that allowed us to see at least fifteen metres in distance inside the doko.

My attention was still focused on the Thaori. They were looking at me with kindness, surrounded by a golden mist that became more and more dense, into which they disappeared - just as they had on my first visit.

This time, Thao gently placed her hand on my shoulder and asked me to follow her. She led me towards the entrance of the doko, and in an instant we were outside. It was completely dark and no light shone anywhere apart from over the entrance. I could see no more than three metres in front of me and wondered how we were going to find the flying platform. I then remembered that Thao could see as well by night as by day. I was curious to see evidence of this - like a typical Earthling, I sought proof! It was provided immediately. Thao lifted me up effortlessly and sat me on her shoulders, just as we on Earth carry our little ones.

'You could stumble,' she explained, as we proceeded along the path - and indeed, she seemed to know exactly where she was going, just as though it were daylight.

Before long, she put me down on the seat of the Lativok and sat herself next to me. I placed my mask, which I had been holding in my hand, on my knees, and almost immediately we took off.

I must say that, in spite of my confidence in Thao, I felt uneasy at flying 'blind'. We flew between the immense trees of the park and I couldn't even see the stars that usually shone so brightly. Great clouds had formed after sundown and our surroundings were completely obscured in darkness. Next to me, however, I could see Thao's Aura and the 'bouquet' at the top of her head, which was particularly bright.

We picked up speed and I'm sure we travelled as fast in the darkness as we did by day. I felt some drops of rain sting my face. Thao moved her hand towards a point on the machine and I felt the rain no more. At the same instant, I had the impression that we were stopping and I wondered what was happening, for I knew we were over the ocean. Occasionally, in the distance on our left, I could make out coloured lights that moved.

'What is it?' I asked Thao.

'The lights at the entrances to the dokos on the coast.'

I was trying to understand why the dokos were moving, when suddenly, through the darkness which seemed even thicker, a light came directly towards us and stopped beside us.

'We are at your place,' said Thao. 'Come on.'

She lifted me again. I felt a slight pressure as when one enters a doko and then felt the rain full on my face. The downpour was very strong but, in a few strides, Thao was under the light and we entered the doko.

'We got here just in time,' I remarked.

'Why? For the rain? No, it's actually been pouring for a short while now. I activated the force field - didn't you notice? You stopped feeling the wind, didn't you?'

'Yes, but I thought we had stopped. I don't understand at all.'

Thao burst into laughter, which put me at ease again and suggested that the explanation to the mystery was about to unfold.

'The force field not only keeps the rain out but also the wind, so you had no reference point by which to judge whether we moved or not. You see, one must not rely on perception.'

'But how could you find this place in such darkness?'

'As I told you, we can see as well by night as by day. That's why we don't use lighting - I realise that is not convenient for you, you can't see me now, but, in any case, we have had a very full day and I think it would be best for you to rest now. Let me help you.'

She led me to the relaxation area, wishing me a good night. I asked her if she was going to stay with me, but she explained that she lived quite nearby, not even requiring the vehicle to transport her there. With that, she left and I stretched out and soon fell asleep.

The next morning, I awoke to the sound of Thao's voice as she leaned over me, whispering in my ear.

I observed as I had the first time, that this relaxation area was well deserving of its name, for I would not have heard Thao, had she not leaned over me to speak, sound being extremely muffled here. Further, I had slept soundly, without waking once. I was perfectly rested.

I got up and followed Thao towards the pool. It was at this time that she told me of the accident that had befallen Arki. I was greatly saddened by the news and tears sprang to my eyes. Thao reminded me that Arki was proceeding to another existence and should be remembered as a friend who has left us to go elsewhere.

'Indeed it is sad, but we must not be selfish, Michel. Other adventures and other joys are probably in store for Arki.'

I washed and when I rejoined Thao, we enjoyed a very light meal and drank some hydromel. I didn't feel hungry. Looking up, I could see the grey sky and the rain falling on the doko. It was interesting to watch, as the raindrops didn't stream down the doko as they would have done over a glass dome. Instead, they simply disappeared when they reached the doko's force field. I looked at Thao and she smiled at me, having seen my surprise.

'The drops are dislocated by the force field, Michel. It is elementary physics - at least for us. But there are more interesting things to study and, unfortunately, you have so little time. There are still more things that I must teach you, so your fellow men might be enlightened when you write your book - such as the mystery of Christ which I mentioned yesterday when we were interrupted by Arki's arrival.

'First, I must speak to you of Egypt and Israel, as well as of Atlantis, the famous continent so often talked of on Earth and the subject of so much controversy.

'Atlantis, like the continent of Mu, did exist and was situated in the northern hemisphere, in the middle of the Atlantic Ocean. It was attached to Europe, and linked to America by an isthmus and to Africa by another isthmus at about the latitude of the Canary Islands. Its area was slightly greater than that of Australia.

'It was inhabited by the people of Mu, approximately 30 000 years ago - in fact, it was a colony of Mu. There was also a white race there - tall blond people with blue eyes. It was the Mayas, very learned colonisers from Mu, who governed the country, and they constructed there, a replica of the Pyramid of Savanasa.

'Seventeen thousand years ago, they explored the Mediterranean thoroughly, going via the north of Africa where they acquainted the Arabs, (descendants of the cross-breeding between yellow and black Bakaratinians) with much new knowledge - material as well as spiritual. The numerical script, for example, still used by the Arabs, came from Atlantis, and from Mu, of course.

'They went to Greece where they founded a small colony and the Greek alphabet corresponds almost exactly to that of Mu.

'Finally they arrived in a land that the natives called Aranka and which you know as Egypt. There, they established a strong colony with a great man, by the name of Toth, at its head. Laws were established which embodied the beliefs of Mu and the organisational principles of Atlantis. Improved plants, new techniques for raising cattle, new methods of cultivation, pottery and weaving were all introduced.

'Toth was a great man of Atlantis, extremely knowledgeable materially as well as spiritually. He founded villages, built temples and, just before his death, he had constructed what you now call the Great Pyramid. Each time these great colonisers judged that the new colony had the potential to become great, materially and spiritually, they would construct a special pyramid - a tool - as you were able to see for yourself on Mu. In Egypt, they constructed the Great Pyramid on the same model as the Pyramid of Savanasa, but on a scale three times reduced. These pyramids are unique and, in order to fulfil their role as a 'tool', their dimensions and specifications must be precisely adhered to, as well as their orientation.'

'Do you know how much time it took?'

'It was quite fast - just nine years, for Toth and his master architects knew the secrets of anti-gravitation from Mu, and the secrets for cutting the rock and using - let's call them 'electro-ultra-sounds'.'

'But on Earth, the experts believe it to have been constructed by the Pharaoh Cheops.'

'It's not so, Michel. Of course, this is not the only mistake that the experts on Earth have made. On the other hand, I can confirm that the Pharaoh Cheops used this pyramid as it was meant to be used.

'The Maya-Atlanteans were not the only ones to explore and colonise. Gone for thousands of years, the Nagas had colonised Burma, India and finally they reached the shores of Egypt, at about the latitude of the Tropic of Cancer. They too, founded a successful colony and occupied upper Egypt. Both groups of colonisers introduced similar sorts of improvements. The Nagas established a large town called Mayou, on the banks of the Red Sea. The natives of the region went to their schools, gradually becoming assimilated with the colonists and producing the Egyptian race.

'However, about 5000 years ago, the Nagas in the north of Egypt and the Maya- Atlanteans began fighting for a reason that is quite ludicrous. The Atlanteans, whose religion differed significantly from the religion of Mu, believed in the reincarnation of the soul (Astral body) in the country of its ancestors. Thus, they claimed that the soul travelled westward to where they had come from. The Nagas held a similar belief except that they claimed the soul went back to the east, since they had come from the east.

'For two years they were actually at war over this difference but it was not a terribly cruel war, as both groups comprised of fundamentally peace loving people, and eventually they became allied and formed a unified Egypt.

'The first King of United Egypt, both upper and lower, was called Mena. It was he who established the town of Memphis. He was elected by the same method used in Mu - a method that did not long survive in Egypt, due to the rise of a powerful clergy which little by little put the Pharaohs under its thumb. This situation continued over the years with notable exceptions among the Pharaohs who yielded to the clergy. One such exception was the Pharaoh Athnaton who was poisoned by the priests. Before dying, he made the following statement: 'The time that I have spent on this Earth was an era in which the *simplicity* of Truth was not understood and was rejected by many.' As often happens in religious sects, the Egyptian priests distorted the Truth, simple though it was, in order to have a better hold over the people. They had them believing in the devil and in various divine beings as well as other such nonsense.

'It must also be said that prior to the war and the subsequent peace-pact which saw Mena installed as King of Egypt, the population, made up of Maya- Atlanteans and Nagas in equal proportions, had established a sophisticated civilisation in both upper and lower Egypt.

'The country was prosperous. Farming and grazing flourished and the (time of the) first King of Egypt, Mena, was, almost the consecration of this rising civilisation.

'Now, at this point, we must go back in time. Arki said that Earth is still being visited by extra-terrestrials and, as you know, it has been regularly visited in the past. But, I should elaborate on this.

'Earth is visited, as are many other inhabitable planets scattered throughout the Universe. Sometimes the inhabitants of certain planets are obliged to evacuate as their planet is dying. Now, as Arki also explained, you can't change planets as you might change houses. You must conform to a cycle that is well-established; otherwise, catastrophes can be the consequence. This is what happened 12 000 years ago. Human beings left the planet Hebra in order to visit the galaxy in search of a new planet of the same category as their own, for they knew that, in the millennium to come, their planet would become totally uninhabitable.

'A spacecraft, capable of extremely high speeds, experienced serious problems during its reconnaissance flight and was obliged to land on your planet. It landed in the region of Krasnodar, a town in Western Russia. Needless to say, at the time there was no town, no people, no Russia.

'On board the spacecraft were eight astronauts: three women and five men. These people were approximately 170 centimetres in height, with black eyes, fair skin and long brown hair. They made a successful landing and began repairs to their vessel.

'They found the gravitational force stronger than on their own planet and, initially, had some difficulty moving about. They established a camp near their spacecraft, expecting repairs to take some time. One day, during work, an accident occurred causing a terrific explosion that destroyed half of the vessel and killed five of the cosmonauts. The other three, being some distance away, were unharmed. They were Robanan, a man, and Levia and Dina, two women.

'They knew well what was in store for them. Coming from a planet of a superior category, they did not belong on Earth, where they were in fact prisoners, and thus they anticipated the misadventures that befell them.

The accident came as no great surprise.

'For several months, the three remained at the spot for the season was warm. They had some weapons and they were able to procure game - their provisions of manna and roustian having been lost in the explosion. Eventually the cold arrived and they decided to move further south.

'The gravitational force made walking long distances extremely difficult for them, so that their trek south to warmer climates became a veritable 'Road to Calvary'. They passed by the Black Sea heading in the direction of today's Israel. The journey took months but they were young people and, astonishingly, they made it. The weather became more clement, and even hot, as they reached lower latitudes. They stopped by a river, establishing there a permanent camp - all the more permanent since Dina was several months pregnant. At full term, she gave birth to a son whom they named Ranan. By then, Levia too, was pregnant and some time later, she also bore a son, Rabion.

'These people from Hebra acclimatised in this spot which was rich in game, honey and edible plants - and there they founded their line. It was quite some time later that they made the acquaintance of some nomads passing by. This was their first contact with Earthlings. The nomads numbered ten and, having found Robanan's women to their liking, they wanted to kill him and take all that he had, including the women.

'Robanan still had his weapon and, although a pacifist, he was obliged to use it and killed four of his attackers who fled in the face of such power.

'These people were greatly saddened that they had to resort to such a measure, and saw in it yet another sign that they were on a planet that was forbidden to them by Universal Law.

'I don't understand,' I interrupted. 'I thought that it wasn't possible to jump categories in a forward direction, but that it would be possible to go to inferior planets.'

'No, Michel, neither forwards nor backwards. If you go forward, disregarding Universal Law, you will die; if you go backwards, you expose yourself to worse conditions because your advanced spirituality can't exist in a materialistic environment.

'If you like, I can give you an analogy in the form of a childish comparison. Imagine a man immaculately dressed in polished shoes, white socks and pressed suit. You oblige this man to walk through a farmyard, 30 centimetres deep in mud. Further, you insist that he put this mud into a wheelbarrow with his hands. No need to ask what state he will be in when he has finished.

'Nonetheless, our group of extra-terrestrials founded their line that became the ancestors of present-day Jews.

'The Bible was written later by scribes who retraced the history of these people, distorting it, as legend became mixed with reality.

'I can affirm for you that the Adam of the Bible was, not only, *not* the first man on Earth, far from it, but he was called Robanan and he didn't have a wife called Eve but two wives named Levia and Dina. The race of

Jews developed from these three, without mixing with other races because, by atavism[1], they felt themselves superior - and indeed they were.

'However, I must assure you that the Bible is not the product of the scribes' imagination - nor is it embellished. There *was* much truth in it. I say 'was' because in the various councils of the Roman Catholic Church, the Bible has been greatly revised, for reasons which are clear: to serve the needs of Christianity. This is why I said yesterday, that religions are one of the curses of Earth. I must also enlighten you in regard to several other biblical points.

'Shortly after the arrival of the Hebrews on Earth, we helped them on several occasions. We also punished them. For example, the destruction of Sodom and Gomorrah was caused by one of our space vehicles. The people of those two towns were presenting a bad example and acting dangerously for the people in contact with them. We tried various means in an endeavour to put them back on the right track, but in vain. We had to be ruthless.

'Each time that you read in the Bible: 'And the Lord God said this or that' - you should read 'and the inhabitants of Thiaoouba said...'.'

'Why not save them in the beginning and take them back to their planet or to another of the same category?'

'That is, of course, a reasonable question, Michel, but there is a snag. We can't predict the future more than 100 years in advance. We thought, at the time, that, being such a small group, they might not survive and, if they did, they would mix with other races and thus be absorbed by other peoples and rendered 'impure'. We guessed that this would occur within a century - but such was not the case. Even now, as you know, the race is still almost as pure as it was 12 000 years ago.

'As I told you, by means of religious councils, priests erased or changed many things in the Bible, but others survived and can easily be explained.

'In Chapter 18, verse (1) the scribe refers to our appearance at that time, saying: 'The Lord God appeared unto him among the oaks of Mamre as he sat at the entrance to his tent in the heat of day.' The scribe is speaking of Abraham in this chapter.

'(2) He, Abraham, looked up and saw three men standing nearby. When he saw them he ran to them and fell to the ground before them.

(3) And he said, 'Lord and master, if I have found grace in your eyes, I beg you not to go far from your servant.' Abraham invites the three men to stay. The scribe refers to them as men one minute and yet one of them is also called 'the Lord God'. He speaks to them and each time, it is the one referred to as 'the Lord God' who replies. Now, the priests of the Roman Catholic Church find this in formal contradiction with their views, as do many other religions, for they will tell you that no one can imagine the face of God - that one would be blinded by it. In a sense they are right, since the Creator, being a pure spirit, has no face!

'According to the scribe, Abraham converses with the Lord God as he would with a high ranking lord on Earth. And the Lord God answers him and is accompanied by two other 'men' - the scribe does not speak of 'angels'. Isn't it odd that God comes down to Earth in the form of a man, accompanied, not by angels, but by men? Actually, there, and in many other places in the Bible, it is easy for someone of good faith to see that God has never spoken to any human being.

'He *could* not have done so, since it is astral bodies which aspire towards Him and not God who leans towards them. That would be like a river flowing backwards - you have never seen a river flowing from the sea to the mountaintop, have you? A passage from the Bible, two pages further on from the one just mentioned, is also quite amusing: Chapter 19, verse (1): 'The two angels arrived in Sodom, and Lot was seated at the gates to Sodom. When Lot saw them, he rose to go and kiss the ground in front of them' - then he manages to get them to go to his house, and suddenly, in verse five, 'They called Lot and said to him: 'Where are the *men* who entered your house?'. Now the scribe is referring to them as 'men'. Next, in verse (10), 'The men reached out, made Lot come inside and closed the door.' (11) 'And they struck blind everyone at the entrance to the house, from the smallest to the largest person, so that it was useless for them to try to find the door.'

'It is easy to see the lack of precision in this passage, where the scribe begins by speaking of two angels, then speaks of two men, and then describes two men striking people blind. According to the Bible, such a 'miracle' requires at least an angel! There my dear, is another good example of confusion in Earthly scripts. The 'men' were quite simply our men from Thiaoouba.

'Thus we guided and helped the Jews, for it would have been a shame to let a race so spiritually evolved sink back into ignorance and savagery only because it had accidentally committed the error of coming to a planet which was not appropriate for it. We helped them in the centuries that followed and it is this that certain scribes have tried to explain by writing the accounts that have formed the Bible. Often they were in good faith; at times, they have distorted the facts, although not purposely.

'The only times this distortion was purposely done, and for very specific reasons, as I have said, was by the Roman Church during the councils of Nicein AD 325, Constantinople in AD 381, Ephese in AD 431 and Chalcedoine in AD 451. There were others too, but of lesser significance. The Bible is not the *Book of God,* as many people on Earth believe it to be; it is simply a document of ancient history much modified and full of embellishments, added by writers different from the original scribes. For example, let's go back to Egypt and the time of the Exodus, which interests people on Earth. I'm going to restore the truth concerning this, for you and for others, before going further.

'Let's go back, then, to Egypt, where we find that the descendants of the cosmonauts have become the Hebrew people (the name deriving from that of their planet, Hebra). Since arriving accidentally on your planet, this race has experienced great difficulties - it experienced them then and it experiences them still.

'As you know, the Jews are very intelligent by comparison with other races; they have a religion which is quite different; and they don't mix with other races. Marriages are almost always among their own kind. Because of inexorable Universal Law, they have always suffered persecution, much of which has occurred in recent times. As a result, their astral bodies were liberated and therefore able to proceed directly to more highly evolved planets where they belong.

'As you also know, a group of Hebrews travelled with Joseph, son of Jacob, into Egypt, where they established a line, only to end up being hated by the Egyptians and always for the same unstated reasons - their intelligence and, particularly, their solidarity in the face of adversity. Action was needed.'

Who was Christ?

'This occurred during the time of the Pharaoh Seti I. It was a time when the people of Earth had all become materialistic. In Egypt, it was common in high society to take drugs; likewise, in Greece. Fornication with animals was by no means rare - something which is absolutely contrary to Nature and Universal Law.

'Our mission being to help when it was deemed necessary, we decided to change the course that history was taking, by intervening at this point. We had to get the Hebrews out of Egypt, for they could no longer evolve as a free people while under the evil domination of the Egyptians. It was decided to send a man, capable and just, to lead the Hebrews from Egypt and back to the land they had occupied previously, that is, soon after their arrival on Earth.

'On the planet Naxiti, a planet of the eighth category, a man by the name of Xioxtin had just died. His Astral body was waiting to be reincarnated on Thiaoouba, when it was put to him, that instead, he might be the liberator of the Hebrews. He agreed to this and went to Earth as Moses.

'Moses, then, was born in Egypt of Egyptian parents. His father was the equivalent of a sub-lieutenant in the army.

'Moses was not born a Hebrew - that is yet another error in the Bible. The story of the little Hebrew baby set adrift in the water and rescued by a princess is very romantic, but incorrect.'

'What a shame! I always loved that story. It's quite wonderful - like a fairy story!'

'Fairy tales are indeed very pretty, Michel, but you must concern yourself with the Truth - not fantasy. Promise me that you will only report what is the Truth?'

'Of course, have no fear, Thao - your instructions will be followed to the letter, so to speak.'

'I was explaining then, that Moses was born in an Egyptian, military family. His father's name was Lathotes. Until the age of ten, Moses played often with the Hebrew children. A pretty and amiable child, he was popular with the Hebrew mothers who indulged him with offerings of sweets. In turn, they won his heart and he came to love his Hebrew friends like brothers. This is why he was incarnated of course, but you must realise that, after having seen his life as Moses flash before him, and, after accepting to live that life, all details of it were erased from his memory. He passed through what certain Nagas have called 'The River of Oblivion' - this happens whether one accepts or rejects a possible reincarnation. Of course, there is a reason for it.

'If, for example, you *remembered* that, around forty years of age, you would lose your wife and two cherished children in a car accident and that you, yourself, would be confined to a wheelchair, the knowledge could tempt you to take your life rather than face up to your troubles, or it might lead you to behave badly in other spheres. So, the 'film' is erased, in something like the way you 'wipe out' a tape recording.

'Occasionally, by accident, the machine does not erase everything and you can hear brief portions of what should have been erased. Of course, my analogies are fanciful when I speak of 'films' and 'tape recordings' but I hope they give you an idea of what I am trying to explain. In reality, the process involves electrophotonics, which mean nothing, yet, to people on Earth. This, in fact, occurs often in the 'films' that the Higher-self shows to an Astral body, which is why most people say, on several occasions in the course of their lives 'I have seen that before' or 'I have heard that before' and they *know* what the very next action or word will be. In English, people call this feeling 'deja vu'.'

'Yes, I understand well what you are saying. The strangest such experience that I have had was when I was in French Equatorial Africa. I was in the army and we were on manoeuvres about 600 kilometres from base. We were approaching the Tchad border and I was standing with other soldiers in the back of a troop carrier facing the road.

'Suddenly, I 'recognised' the road as if I'd been there just a fortnight before. I was as though hypnotised by this stretch of road that ended with a right-angled bend. I 'recognised' the road, however, I was also sure that, around the bend, I was going to see a little straw hut, all by itself, sheltered by a mango tree. I was increasingly convinced that such would be the case and, when the truck took the bend, there it was - a lone straw hut beneath a mango tree. And then it was over - I 'recognised' nothing more. My face turned white.

'My nearest companion asked me if I was feeling all right, and I explained what had happened. His response was: 'You must have come here as a kid.' I knew that my parents had never set foot in Africa but I still wrote to them, so strongly had the experience affected me. Their reply was: 'No, and you never left us to make any such accompanied journeys when you were little.'

'So, my friend suggested that I might have gone there during a previous existence, for he was a believer in reincarnation. What do you think of that?'

'It's what I've just explained to you, Michel. Quite a long segment of your 'film' was not erased for you and I'm glad, for it illustrates very well what I was explaining to you in regard to Moses.

'He wanted to help the Hebrews but, as he chose to enter that world by the usual means - as a new born baby, he was obliged to 'forget' what the course of his life would be.

'However, in rare cases such as this one, the Astral body is so 'charged' with knowledge and experience from previous lives, that it has no trouble adapting to what it must learn in its new physical body. Moses was also advantaged in that he was sent to a good school with numerous facilities. He was enormously successful in his studies and gained entry into a much higher school of science, headed by priests and Egyptian experts. At this time, the Egyptians still had high schools which catered for a very limited elite, teaching some of the learnings Toth brought from Atlantis a long time previously. He was near finishing his studies, when he was witness to an incident that had great significance in his life.

'Still feeling great friendship towards the Hebrews, he often walked with them, despite the urgent recommendations of his father not to do so. The Hebrews were becoming increasingly despised by the Egyptians, and his father advised Moses not to mix with this race.

'Nevertheless, on this day he was walking in the vicinity of a building site where Hebrews were working under the directions of Egyptian soldiers. From afar he saw a soldier hit a Hebrew, who fell to the ground. Before he could intervene, a group of Hebrews threw themselves on the soldier and killed him; then they buried him quickly in foundations being made to hold an enormous column.

'Moses didn't know what to do, but he was seen by a couple of the Hebrews as he moved away. Believing he would denounce them, the Hebrews panicked and hastened to spread the word that it was Moses who had killed the soldier. When he arrived home, his father was waiting for him and advised him to go, immediately, into the desert. The Bible story that he went to the country of Madian is true, as is the report of his marriage to the daughter of the priest of Madian. I am not going to elaborate further on the details. We wanted to save these people from the slavery into which they'd fallen and, worse, from the clutches of evil priests who were a danger to their psyche.

'More than a million years earlier, we had saved another group of people from the hands of other dangerous priests, if you recall, and, interestingly, it was in practically the same location. Do you see how history is just a perpetual recommencement?

'Moses led the Hebrews from Egypt much as it is described in the Bible - but, before proceeding, I must rectify certain errors, since we know that many people on Earth are greatly interested in this famous Exodus.

'First of all, the Pharaoh at the time was Ramses II, who was successor to Seti I. Next, the Hebrews numbered 375 000 and, when they arrived at the Sea of Reeds, and *not* the Red Sea, our spaceships, numbering three, opened the waters, which were quite shallow, by means of our force field. We allowed the waters to close again, but not a single Egyptian soldier drowned - simply because they hadn't followed the Hebrews into the water. The Pharaoh, in spite of enormous pressure from the priests, did not retract his promise and let the Hebrews leave.

'The manna, distributed every day, came from our spacecraft. I must explain to you that manna is not only very nourishing, as you know, but also very compactable, which is why many spaceships carry it on board. However, if you leave manna too long exposed to the air, it becomes soft and rots within eighteen hours.

'That's why we recommended that the Hebrews take only as much as they needed for each day; and those who took more, soon saw they had made a mistake and that they should have followed the advice of 'the Lord God', who was actually us.

'The Hebrews did not take forty years to reach Canaan, but only three and a half years. Lastly, the story of Mount Sinai is almost true.

'We landed on the mountain so as not to be seen by the people. It was preferable at the time, for these simple people to believe in a God, rather than in extra-terrestrials who watched over them and helped them.

'So that is the explanation of the Hebrew people, Michel, but it isn't finished. In our eyes, these were the only people who followed the right direction, that is, the direction of spirituality. Among them, and, later, among their great priests, there were some who rumoured that a Messiah was going to come and save them. They should not have told the people that, for they were reporting a part of the conversation we had with Moses on Mount Sinai. Since then, the Hebrews have been waiting for the arrival of the Messiah - and yet, he has already come.

'Let's now jump in time. The Hebrews, back again in the land they had originally settled, were now better organised. They established a civilisation notable for great royal legislators such as Solomon and David, to name but two.

'We observed that these people, following Solomon's death, were heading towards anarchy and allowing themselves to be influenced by evil priests. Alexander the Great invaded Egypt but, in the end, did nothing constructive for the world. The Romans succeeded him, building an immense empire that was oriented more towards materialism than spirituality.

'The great peoples, such as the Romans, were technologically advanced for their time - relatively speaking, of course. But they brought with them a smattering of gods and beliefs - just enough to cause spiritual confusion, and, certainly, not enough to lead the people to Universal Truth.

'This time, we decided to give a 'big hand'. Rather than give it in a spiritually sterile land like Rome, we did it in Israel, thinking that the Hebrews were very intelligent, having ancestors who were spiritually highly advanced. We considered them adequate to propagate universal Truth.

'The Hebrew people were unanimously elected by the great Thaori. On Earth, they were referred to as the 'Chosen People' and the name could not be more appropriate - they were indeed 'chosen'.

'Our plan was to capture public imagination by sending a messenger of peace. The story of the birth of Jesus, as you know it, with the Virgin Mary as mother, is quite true. The appearance of an angel at the Annunciation is correct in every detail. We sent a spaceship and one of us appeared before the virgin, who was *indeed* a virgin, telling her she was going to become pregnant. The embryo was implanted in her while she was under hypnosis.

'I see, Michel, you are having enormous difficulty believing what I have been saying. Never forget that we have THE *knowledge* - you have not seen one-tenth of what we can do. Attend carefully and I will give you a few examples to help you understand what I'm going to tell you.'

Thao stopped talking and appeared to be concentrating. As I watched, her face became a blur and, instinctively, I rubbed my eyes. Of course, this did not help and, in fact, she became progressively transparent until I could see right through her. Finally, she was no longer there - she had completely disappeared.

'Thao,' I called, slightly concerned, 'where are you?'

'Here, Michel.'

I jumped, for the voice came as a whisper, quite close to my ear. 'But you are completely invisible!'

'Now, yes - but you are going to see me again. Look!'

'My goodness, what has happened to you?'

Several feet in front of me, I saw the silhouette of Thao, completely golden yet radiant, as though inside her there burned a fire, its flames brief but intense. As for her face, it was recognisable but her eyes seemed to send forth little rays each time she spoke.

She began to rise a few feet above the ground, without having moved a muscle of her 'body'; then she started to circle the room, so fast I had trouble keeping my eyes on her.

She stopped, eventually, above her seat and sat her ghostly form down. It was as though she were made of a shining mist - she was still recognisable as Thao and yet, quite transparent. The next instant she was gone. I looked around, but she had completely vanished.

'Look no further, Michel, I am back.' Indeed, there she was, in flesh and bone again, sitting on her seat.

'How do you *do* that?'

'As I was just explaining to you, we have THE *knowledge*. We can revive the dead; cure the deaf and the blind; make people walk who are paralysed; we can cure any malady you care to name. We are masters, not f Nature, but *in* Nature, and we can do the thing most difficult of all - we can generate life spontaneously.

'Out of the release of cosmic ray, we can create any type of living creature, including man.'

'You mean that you have mastered the 'test-tube baby'?'

'Not at all, Michel. You reason like an Earthling. We can create a human body, but that is done only by the great Thaori, taking infinite care, for the human body must be inhabited by several bodies, as you are aware - the physiological, the astral etc. If not, it would merely be a robot. Perfect knowledge is therefore required for such an undertaking.'

'So, how much time do you need to create a baby?'

'You have not quite grasped what I am saying, Michel. I am

speaking, not of a baby but, in this case, of an adult human being. A man of twenty or thirty years- of-age can be created by the Thaori in approximately twenty-four of your Earth hours.'

As one might expect, I was completely stunned by this disclosure. I had travelled in a spaceship at a speed several times that of light and had found myself billions of kilometres from my home. I had met extra-terrestrials, travelled in Astral body, journeyed in time to witness scenes that occurred thousands of years ago. I could now see Auras and understand languages I'd never heard before. I had even visited, briefly, Earth's parallel universe. I thought I knew what there was to be known, by an Earthling, of these people and their capabilities, thanks to the explanations given to me. Now - it seemed I was being told that what I'd been presented with was like an hors d'oeuvre. My hosts could *create* a living human being in *twenty-four hours!*

Thao was watching me, reading me like an open book.

'Now that you follow my meaning, Michel, I'll finish the story which is going to interest so many of your fellow men, in so far as the Bible has distorted it a little.

'So, our 'angel' implanted an embryo, so that Mary, a virgin, found herself pregnant. By acting in this way, we hoped to attract the attention of the people and emphasise that the coming of Jesus was really a remarkable event. On the birth of the child, we appeared before the shepherds in the same way that I demonstrated a few moments ago. We didn't send the three famous 'wise men' - they are part of the legend that has been grafted on to real events. However, we did guide the shepherds and a group of the people towards the spot where Jesus was born. This was accomplished by sending forth one of our spheres and rendering it luminous. The optical effect thereby created, made it, indeed, resemble a star over Bethlehem. Nowadays, if we were to do such a thing, people would be crying, 'UFO'!

Eventually the priests, and those who the priests named 'prophets', learned of the birth. In view of the phenomena of the star and the 'angels', the prophets announced to the people, the birth of the Messiah, referring to him as the King of the Jews.

'King Herod however, had spies in all quarters, as most leaders do. When they reported these remarkable events to him, he found it all difficult to understand and became frightened. In those times, the lives of the people were worth little to their leaders, and Herod had no qualms about ordering the deaths of 2606 babies in the region.

'While these deaths were being carried out, we evacuated, under hypnosis, Mary, Joseph and the baby Jesus, as well as two donkeys, in our spaceship, depositing them in a spot quite close to Egypt. Do you see how the facts have been distorted?

'Now, there are other details which were reported conscientiously, but they are inaccurate due to lack of information. Let me explain. The baby Jesus, born in Bethlehem, proved, by the miracles pertaining to his birth, that he was quite special and was, in fact, the Messiah. So, we had captured the imagination of the people but, when a baby is born, its Astral body cannot 'know all' in regards to its previous knowledge. This was the case of Moses too, and yet he was a great person.

'We required a messenger who would be able to persuade humanity that there was another life beyond this one, through reincarnation of the Astral body, etc. This was no longer commonly accepted since civilisation on Earth had become more and more degraded following the disappearance of Atlantis.

'You know that, when you want to explain something that is not a material fact, even to your closest friends, you are confronted by scepticism. People seek material proof and, if they don't see it with their own eyes, they won't believe.

'In order to transmit our message, we needed someone who behaved like an extraordinary being - like someone coming from 'the heavens', who performed what would appear to be 'miracles'. Such a person would be believed and his teachings would be listened to.

'As you know, an Astral body being reincarnated as a baby, passes through 'The River of Oblivion' and his earlier material knowledge is effaced. Therefore, the child born in Bethlehem would not have been able to perform 'miracles' even if he lived to 100 years of age. However, he was a superior being, like Moses. This is proven, by the way he astonished temple doctors at the age of twelve. Like the very young people now on Earth, who are called geniuses because they seem to have a calculation in their heads, Jesus was a human being inhabited by a highly evolved Astral body. And yet, even if he had studied in the very advanced schools on Earth, amongst the Nagas, for example, he never could have acquired the knowledge to revive the dead or cure the sick.

'I know that, on Earth, there are people who believe that, from the age of twelve, until his return to Judea, Jesus studied in the monasteries of India and Tibet. This is how they try to explain the gap that exists in the Bible, when Jesus simply disappeared from Bethlehem.

'He left his parents' home at the age of fourteen, accompanied by his twelve- year-old brother Ouriki. He travelled to Burma, India, China and Japan. His brother accompanied Jesus everywhere, until Ouriki was accidentally killed in China. Jesus took a lock of Ouriki's hair with him, for he loved him very much.

'Jesus was fifty years of age when he arrived in Japan, where he married and had three daughters. Finally, he died in the Japanese village of Shingo, where he had lived for forty-five years. He was buried in Shingo, which is on the main island of Japan - Honshu, and beside his tomb is another, containing the little box holding Ouriki's lock of hair.

'Those of your fellow men who like evidence can go to Shingo, formerly known as Herai, in the district of Aomori.

'But, let's go back to our precise mission in this regard... The only messenger we could send to Earth had to be one of us. The 'Christ' who died on the cross in Jerusalem, was called Aarioc. He was brought, by us, to the desert of Judea, having volunteered to change his physical body. Thus, he abandoned his hermaphrodite body, which had lived some considerable time on Thiaoouba, and took on the body of Christ, created for him by our Thaori. By so doing, he maintained totally, the knowledge he possessed on Thiaoouba.'

'Why couldn't he have remained in his body and simply reduced it in size, as Latoli and Biastra did, in front of me? Couldn't he have stayed long enough in a 'shrunken' body?'

'There was another problem, Michel, he had to resemble a human being from Earth in all respects, and, since we are hermaphrodites, we couldn't risk the Hebrews noticing that this messenger from God was half female.

'We can regenerate a body at will, which is why you have seen so few children on Thiaoouba. We can also create a body, as I have just explained, and we can reduce it in size. Don't look at me like that, Michel. I realise that it is difficult for you to assimilate all this and to believe what I tell you, but we have already revealed enough for you to know that we are capable of mastering most natural phenomena.

'Jesus, who came from Thiaoouba, was taken by us into the desert, and you know what followed. He knew that he would come up against numerous difficulties and that he was going to be crucified. He knew all, for he had 'previewed' his life with us, but he had done so as an Astral body in a physical body.

'He remembered, just as you will remember and will always remember your journey to Mu and the glimpses of your previous lives.

'The visions, I repeat, seen by Astral bodies in physical bodies are not erased in the way that visions seen by Astral bodies with the Higher-selves are. Thus, he knew all and knew exactly what to do. Of course, he had the power to resuscitate the dead, cure the blind and the deaf, and, when he was crucified and dead, we were there to take him away and revive him. We rolled the stone from the tomb, quickly took him to our spacecraft which was positioned nearby and, there, revived him. At the right moment, he appeared again, thereby providing his immortality, showing that there was, indeed, life after death, and regenerating hope among the people by persuading them that they did belong to the Creator and that *each of us* possesses a spark of *His divinity*.'

'So, all his miracles were performed in order to prove that what he preached was true?'

'Yes, because the Hebrews and the Romans would never have believed him if he hadn't proven himself. There was a very good example of the strength of scepticism among people on Earth regarding the Shroud of Turin. Although millions believe in the coming of Jesus and practise, more or less, Christian religions, they were anxious to hear the results of research by experts, into whether or not the Shroud covered

Christ after his 'death'. You now know the answer to this. However, people seek proof and more proof, and still more proof, for doubt still exists in their minds. Buddha, an Earthling, who acquired his understanding through his own study, did not say, as your fellow men do: 'I believe', but rather, *'I know'*. Faith is never perfect but knowledge is.

'When you return to Earth and tell your story, the first thing you will be asked is for evidence. If we were to give you, for example, a piece of metal which doesn't exist on Earth, there would always be one, among the experts who analyse it, who would insist that you prove the metal was not created by a clever alchemist of your acquaintance - or some such thing.'

'Will you give me something as proof?'

'Michel, don't disappoint me. You will have no material proof, for precisely the reasons I have just outlined - there *would be no point*.

'Faith is nothing in comparison with knowledge. Buddha 'knew' and when you return to Earth, you too, will be able to say *'I know'*.

'There is a well-known story of doubting Thomas who wanted to touch Christ's wounds, for, seeing them with his own eyes did not convince him enough; and yet, when he touched them, he was still doubtful. He suspected some kind of magic trick. You know nothing of Nature on your planet, Michel, and, as soon as something occurs which is a little beyond your understanding, everyone claims it is magic. Levitation = magic; invisibility = magic - and yet we are only applying natural laws. Rather, you should say, levitation = knowledge and invisibility = knowledge.

'So, Christ was sent to Earth to preach love and spirituality. He had to contend with people who were not highly evolved, speaking to them in parables. When he tipped over the merchants' tables at the temple, angry for the first and only time, he was making a statement against money.

'His mission was to impart a message of love and goodness - *'love one another'* and also to enlighten the people in regard to the reincarnation of astral bodies and immortality. This was all distorted by priests in the time that followed and numerous disagreements led to the rise of the many sects which claim to follow the teachings of Christ.

'Christians, throughout the centuries, have even killed in the name of God. The Inquisition was a good example, and the Spanish Catholics in Mexico behaved worse than the most savage tribes, all in the name of God and Christ.

'Religions are a veritable curse on your planet - as I have said, and as I have proved. As for the new sects that are springing up and flourishing all over the world, they are based on control by brainwashing. It is terrifying to see young people, healthy in body and spirit, throw themselves at the feet of charlatans claiming to be Gurus and great masters, when the latter are masters of only two things - talking and collecting fabulous sums of money. This, of course, gives them power and enormous pride to see themselves dominating entire crowds of people who submit to them, body and soul. Not long ago, there was even one leader who asked his followers to commit suicide, and they obeyed. Since on Earth they love 'proof, there is an excellent one to give them: Universal Law forbids suicide - if this 'master' had been genuine, he would have *known* this. In demanding this sacrifice from them, he presented the *greatest proof* of his ignorance.

'Sects and religions are a curse on Earth and when you see that the Pope sets aside millions of francs or dollars for his travel, when he could make do with much less, and use what money is available to help countries suffering from famine, you can not persuade me that it is the word of Christ which directs such actions.

'There is a passage in your Bible that says: 'It is easier for a camel to pass through the eye of a needle than for a rich man to enter Paradise.'

'The Vatican is certainly the wealthiest church on your planet, and yet the priests have made vows of poverty. They have no fear of being damned, (yet they believe in damnation), because they say it is the Church which is rich, not them. This is really just a play on words since they make up the Church. It's like the son of a multi-billionaire claiming that he is not rich - only his father is.

'The Church has not distorted the passage in the Bible relating to wealth. They have used it to their advantage, for isn't it preferable that the rich grow poorer at the profit of the Church?

'The young generations on Earth are in the process of self-examination. They have come to a turning point - events have led them to it and I know that they feel alone, more than any younger generation has before them. It isn't by joining sects or religious groups that they are going to be free of their solitude.

'First if you want to 'elevate' yourself, you must meditate and then concentrate, which is different, although often the two are confused. You do not need to go to a special place, for the greatest and most beautiful temple of man is *inside* himself. There, he can enter into communication with his Higher-self, by concentration; asking his higher-self to help him surmount his Earthly, material difficulties. But certain people need to communicate with other human beings, like themselves, and they can meet together for this purpose. Those of them who are more experienced, will be able to give advice, but no one should ever adopt a position as *master*.

'The Master came 2000 years ago - or, rather, I should say 'one of the masters', but men crucified him. However, for approximately 300 of your years, the message he brought with him was followed. After that, it was distorted and now, on Earth, you have returned to a point that is worse than that of 2 000 years ago.

'The young generation of whom I have just spoken, are rising up on your planet and realising, little by little, the truth of many of the things I have been talking about. But they must learn to look *inside* themselves for their answers. They should *not* wait for help to come to them from elsewhere, or they will be *disappointed*.'

Extraordinary journey meeting extraordinary 'people'

When Thao finished speaking, I could clearly see that her Aura had become dull. Outside, the rain had stopped; the sun shone on huge white clouds, tinting them blue and pink. The trees, whose branches swayed in a gentle breeze, looked refreshed and a thousand rainbows danced in the droplets of water, which clung to their leaves. The sweet songs of birds, welcoming the sun's return, blended with the soft musical sound of the insects and the light. That moment was the most magical I had yet encountered. Neither of us felt like talking and we allowed our souls to drink their fill of the beauty around us.

It was the sound of laughter and happy voices that roused us from our peaceful state. Turning around, we saw Biastra, Latoli and Lationusi approaching, each flying with her own Tara.

They landed just in front of the dokos and entered without fuss, large smiles illuminating their faces. We stood up to welcome them and greetings were exchanged in the language of Thiaoouba. I was still able to understand all that was said although I was unable to speak the language. This didn't seem to matter though, since I had little to say, and, in any case, if I spoke French, those who couldn't understand my words, understood my message telepathically.

Once refreshed with drinks of hydromel, everyone was ready to leave again. I put my mask on and followed them all outside, where Latoli approached me and attached a Tara around my waist. Then, in my right hand, she placed a Litiolac. I was quite excited at the thought that I was going to be able to fly like a bird. Since the first day I had landed on this planet and seen people fly by this means, I had dreamt of doing the same, but, so much was happening so quickly that, I must say, I didn't expect the opportunity to arise.

'Latoli,' I asked, 'why is it that you use a Tara and Litiolac to fly, when almost all of you are able to levitate?'

'Levitation requires great concentration and quite an expenditure of energy, Michel, even for us, and it only allows us to travel at seven kilometres per hour. Levitation is used during certain psychic exercises, but it is a poor means of transport. These apparatus are based on the same principle as levitation in so far as they neutralise what we might call 'the cold magnetic force' of the planet. It's the same force that you call 'gravity' and which holds all bodies on the ground.

'Man, like a piece of rock, is made of matter, but, by neutralising the cold magnetic force by raising certain high frequency vibrations, we become 'weightless'. Then, in order to move and direct our movement, we introduce vibrations of a different frequency. As you can see, the apparatus that accomplishes this is for us quite simple. This same principle was used by the builders of the pyramids of Mu, Atlantis and Egypt. Thao has already spoken to you of it, but now you will experience for yourself the effect of anti-gravitation.'

'What speed can be attained with these apparatus?'

'With this particular one, you can travel at around 300 kilometres per hour and at whatever altitude you choose, but it's time to get going - the others are waiting.'

'Do you think I'll be able to use it properly?'

'Of course. I will teach you how, and you must pay careful attention when you start. You could have a serious accident if you don't follow my instructions to the letter.'

Everyone was watching me, however it was Lationusi who seemed most amused by my anxiety. I held my Litiolac firmly in my hand, it's safety strap attached to my forearm. This meant that if I let go of the Litiolac, it would remain with me.

My throat was dry. I must say, I was not feeling very confident, but Latoli came over to me and put an arm around my waist, assuring me that she would not let go before I had familiarised myself with the apparatus.

She also explained I didn't need to concern myself with the Tara attached to my waist, but that the Litiolac was to be held firmly. First, one had to pull quite firmly on a large button, which rendered the apparatus useable - a little like turning the ignition key in a car. A tiny light appeared indicating readiness. The Litiolac was rather like a pear in shape. It was held with the base downwards, and its top ended in a mushroom-shaped 'hat', no doubt meant to prevent fingers from slipping. The 'pear' was grasped around its 'collar'.

Latoli explained that this Litiolac had been specially made for me, since my hands were about half the size of theirs and I wouldn't have been able to use a standard model. Besides, it is important that the size of the 'pear' be exactly suited to the hand that holds it. It was slightly soft, as though made of rubber, and filled with water.

Instructions received, I gripped the Litiolac so strongly that Latoli had just enough time to grab hold of me before we rose into the air.

We had made a leap of three good metres. The others were around us, stationary in the air at a height of about two metres from the ground and they all burst into laughter at Latoli's surprise.

'Careful', Thao said to her, 'Michel is a man of action. If you put an apparatus in his hand, he will use it immediately!'

'If you press the Litiolac as you just did, with a general, even pressure, you will rise vertically. If the pressure is slightly greater with your fingers, you will go left; with your thumb, you will go right. If you want to go down, either release the pressure or, to descend more quickly, you can press on the base with your left hand.'

As she spoke, Latoli had me practise the movements and we had climbed to an altitude of about fifty metres when we heard Thao's voice.

'Well done, Michel. You should let him do it alone now, Latoli. He has the idea.'

I would have liked her to keep her thoughts to herself. I didn't share her opinion at all and I felt much more confident under the protective 'wing' of Latoli - and I mean no play on words! She did release me, however, but remained close by and at the same height.

Gently, I released my grip on the Litiolac and ceased climbing. Releasing the pressure further, I began to descend; reassured, I pressed evenly around the 'collar' and shot upwards like an arrow - so far, that my fingers froze and I continued to rise.

'Relax your hand, Michel. Relax your hand,' shouted Latoli who, in the wink of an eye, had joined me.

Oh! I stopped - or almost, at approximately 200 metres' altitude, over the ocean, for I had inadvertently pressed more strongly on my 'frozen' thumb. The others joined us at our 200 metre high rendezvous. I must have been wearing a strange expression on my face, for even Lationusi burst into laughter, and that was the first time I had seen him do that.

'Gently, Michel. This apparatus is very sensitive to touch. I think we can go on our way now. We'll show you the way.'

They moved off slowly, Latoli remaining by my side. We maintained the same altitude. By pressing with the palm of my hand, I advanced smoothly and soon noticed that I was able to accelerate at will, merely by regulating this pressure on the Litiolac. Finger pressure regulated height and direction.

I still made some unexpected swerves, especially when my attention was distracted by three imposing characters who crossed our path. In passing, they threw me a glance, obviously quite astonished at the sight of me.

After a time I judged to be about half an hour, I began to master the machine - at least enough to fly successfully over the ocean. With no obstacles to negotiate, we gradually picked up speed and I was even able to fly in formation beside my companions without straying too often.

It was so exhilarating - I could never have imagined such a sensation. Because the equipment created a kind of force field around me, making me weightless, there was no sensation of being suspended, as there is in a balloon; nor was there the sensation of being carried by wings. Further, being completely surrounded by the force field, I couldn't even feel wind whipping at my face. I had the impression of being an integral part of the environment, and the more I exercised control over the apparatus, the more pleasure I gained from this new means of locomotion. I wanted to test my control and, so, descended slightly, only to climb again. This I did several times, choosing to gain or lose altitude on the others. Finally, I moved nearer to Thao and telepathically communicated my euphoria, letting her in on my intention of skimming the ocean that stretched, below us, as far as the eye could see.

She agreed and the whole group followed me at water level.

It was absolutely fantastic to be able to skim over the crests of the waves at a speed of approximately 100 kilometres per hour, as if we were all powerful gods, conquerors of gravity. From time to time, silvery flashes indicated that we were flying over schools of fish.

In my excitement, I was not aware of time, but it seemed that the voyage lasted three karses.

No matter which way I turned my head, I saw only the line of the horizon. Then, suddenly, Thao telepathised: 'Look over there, Michel.' Far away, on the surface of the water, I was able to make out a speck that grew rapidly to reveal itself as a mountainous island of reasonable size.

We could soon make out enormous rocks, bluish-black in colour, which plunged sharply into the blue-green waters of the ocean. By increasing altitude, we gained a bird's-eye view of the whole island. There was no beach to be seen, the enormous black rocks prohibiting access from the ocean. The waves crashing into the base of their imposing masses, were iridescent under the sun's rays, reflecting shimmering colours which contrasted with the uniform black of the basalt.

Half-way up the slopes which faced inland, grew forests of gigantic trees, their foliage strangely dark-blue and gold; their trunks blood-red. These trees covered steep inclines right to the edge of an emerald-green lake. In places, the surface of the lake was obscured by wisps of golden mist.

In the middle of the lake, as though floating on the water, we could make out an enormous doko, its point upwards. I later learned its diameter was about 560 metres.

Its exceptional size was not its only peculiarity however; its colour was another. All the dokos I had seen to date on Thiaoouba were of a whitish colour - even those at the city of the Nine dokos. This one, though, seemed to be made of pure gold. There it was, shining in the sun and, in spite of its very ordinary egg shape, its colour and size rendered it majestic. Something else surprised me greatly: *there was no reflection of the doko in the waters of the lake.*

My companions led me towards the dome of the gold doko. We flew slowly, at water level and, from this perspective, it was even more impressive. Unlike other dokos, this one had no point of reference to indicate an entrance. I followed Thao and Latoli who soon disappeared inside.

The other two were at my side, each having caught hold of me under an arm so that I wouldn't fall into the water, for, in my surprise, I had let go of my Litiolac. I was literally stunned by what I saw.

Here is what I discovered inside the doko:

I could see about two hundred people floating in the air with no help from any apparatus. The bodies seemed to be asleep or in deep meditation. The one closest to us floated about six metres above the water, for inside the doko, there was no floor. The bottom section of the 'egg' was actually in the water. As I have already explained, once inside a doko you can see outside, as though there were nothing between you and the world outside. So, in this case, I had a panoramic view of the lake, the hills and the forest in the background and, near me in the middle of this 'landscape', floated two hundred or so bodies. It was completely astonishing, as you would expect.

My companions were watching me in silence and, unlike other times when my wonder had made them laugh, they remained serious.

Looking more closely at the bodies, I began to notice they were generally smaller than my hosts and some had quite extraordinary - and sometimes monstrous - forms.

'What are they doing? Are they meditating?' I whispered to Thao who was at my side.

'Take your Litiolac, Michel. It's hanging on your arm.'

I obeyed, and she then, answered my questions. 'They are dead. These are corpses.'

'Dead? Since when? Did they all die together? Was there an accident?'

'Some of them have been here for thousands of years and the most recent, I believe, has been here for sixty years. I think (that), in your current state of surprise, you are not going to be able to operate your Litiolac effectively. Latoli and I will guide you.' Each of them took hold of me under an arm and we began to wander among the bodies. Without exception, they were entirely naked.

Among others, I saw a man sitting in the lotus position. His hair was long and of a red-blond colour. He would have been two metres tall when standing. He had golden skin and his features were remarkably fine for a man - and he was, indeed, a man rather than a hermaphrodite.

A little further away lay a woman, whose skin was coarse like that of a snake, or the bark of a tree. She appeared to be young, although her strange aspect made it difficult to judge her age. Her skin was orange coloured and her short, curly hair was green.

Most surprising though, were her breasts. They were quite large, but each one had two nipples, separated from each other by about ten centimetres. She would have been close to 180 centimetres in height. Her thighs were thin and muscular, and her calves quite short. On each foot were three enormous toes, but her hands were exactly like ours.

We passed from one to another, sometimes stopping, sometimes moving on - as one does among wax figures in a museum.

The eyes and mouths of all these people were closed, and they all occupied one of two positions - either sitting in the lotus position, or lying on their backs with their arms by their sides.

'Where do they come from?', I whispered.

'Various planets.'

We spent some time before the body of a man, apparently in the prime of his 'life'. He had bright chestnut hair that was long and curly.

His hands and feet were like mine. His skin was of a familiar complexion - that of someone from Earth. In height, he would have been around 180 centimetres. His face was smooth, with noble features and there was a soft goatee on his chin.

I turned to Thao whose eyes were fixed on mine. 'One would say that he came from Earth', I said.

'In one sense he did, but in another, he didn't. You know him well by having heard him spoken of.'

Intrigued, I examined his face more closely, until, telepathically, Thao said, 'Look at his hands and feet, as well as his side.'

Thao and Latoli brought me closer to the body and I could clearly see scars on his feet and his wrists, as well as a gash, approximately 20 centimetres long, in his side.

'What happened to him?'

'He was *crucified,* Michel. This is the *body* of *Christ* of whom we spoke this morning.'

Fortunately, my hosts had anticipated my reactions and supported me under the arms, for I am convinced that I'd have been unable to manoeuvre my Litiolac. There I was - staring at the body of Christ, worshiped and spoken of by so many on Earth - the man who had been the subject of so much controversy and so much research during the past 2000 years.

I reached out to touch the body, but was prevented from doing so by my companions, who drew me away.

'Your name is not Thomas. Why must you touch him? Is there doubt in your mind?' said Thao. 'You see, you confirm what I was saying this morning - you seek proof.'

I felt terribly ashamed for having initiated my gesture, and Thao understood my regret.

'I know, Michel that it was instinctive and I understand it. In any case, you can't touch these bodies - no one can, apart from one of the seven Thaori. In fact, it is the Thaori who install these bodies in a state of preservation and levitation, as you see them, and they alone, are capable of doing so.'

'These are the actual bodies they had during their lives?'

'Of course.'

'But how are they preserved? How many of them are there and why?'

'Do you remember me telling you, when we took you from your planet, that there were questions you would ask to which we would give no answers? I explained then, that you would learn with us all you needed to know, but that certain things would remain a 'mystery' because you must not document certain points. The question you have just asked cannot be answered for this very reason. However, I am able to tell you that there are 147 bodies in this doko.'

I knew that it would be futile to inquire further, but as we wandered among the bodies, I asked another burning question:

'Do you have Moses' body? And why are they all in levitation in this doko without a solid floor?'

'We have only the body of Christ from your planet. They are levitated in order to be perfectly preserved, and the properties peculiar to the waters of this lake assist this preservation.'

'Who are all the others?'

'They came from various planets where they have each had a very important role to play.'

One of the bodies I remember well. It was about fifty centimetres high and formed exactly like a being from Earth, except that it was dark yellow and had no eyes. Instead, it had a type of horn in the middle of its forehead. I asked how it was able to see and was told that there were two eyes at the end of the protuberance, multi-faceted like the eyes of a fly. I could see the closed eyelid with several splits.

'Nature is very strange,' I murmured.

'As I said, each body you see here, comes from a different planet, and it is the conditions in which they must live which determines the details of the physical bodies of the inhabitants.'

'I don't see anyone resembling Arki.'

'And neither will you.'

I didn't know why, but I 'felt' that I should not pursue this topic further.

Throughout this macabre visit, I saw bodies resembling North American Red Indians - but they weren't. I saw others like black Africans, but they weren't; nor was it the body of a Japanese that I saw floating in the air. As Thao had said, Christ's was the only body here that came, if one can say so, from Earth.

After an indeterminate time in this extraordinary and fascinating place, my guides led me outside. A lightly perfumed breeze carrying the scent of the forest caressed us and did me much good, for after such a visit, in spite of it being enormously interesting, I was feeling quite drained. Thao, of course, realised as much and said, in a lively voice, 'Are you ready, Michel? We are going home.'

These words, spoken intentionally in French and with an intonation distinctly 'Earthly', refreshed me at least as much as the evening breeze. Taking hold of my Litiolac, I rose in the air with the others.

We flew over the giant forest that climbed the rocky mountain slope. At its peak, we could, again, admire the ocean that stretched as far as the eye could see. Following a macabre afternoon, and in contrast to it, I found this planet even more beautiful. I remember it occurring to me again, momentarily, that perhaps this was all a dream or an illusion, or that, perhaps, my mind was failing me?

As usual though, Thao was on guard and intervened with a sharp order that resounded telepathically in my head like the crack of a whip, dispelling my vague doubts: 'If you don't press your Litiolac, Michel, you will end up taking a bath and, if we don't hurry, night will overtake us. That might be a little inconvenient for you, don't you think?'

Indeed, lost in my thoughts, I had descended and almost touched the waves. I pressed my Litiolac firmly and shot up like an arrow, joining Thao and the others who were high in the sky.

The sun was already quite low and the sky was totally clear. The ocean had taken on an orange colour, which was surprising. I never would have imagined water could appear such a shade. Inquiring about it, telepathically, it was explained to me that, sometimes, at this time of day, immense patches of orange coloured plankton would rise to the surface. These waters, it appeared, contained enormous quantities of plankton. What a sight it was: the sky was blue-green, the sea was orange, and everything was enveloped in the golden light which, on this planet, seemed to come from nowhere and everywhere.

Quite suddenly, my companions gained altitude and I followed them. We were about one thousand metres above the sea and accelerated in the direction we'd come from - I guessed north - to about 300 kilometres per hour.

Looking in the direction of the setting sun, I could make out a wide, black band on the water's surface. I didn't have to ask about it - the answer came quickly.

'It is *Nuroaka,* one of the continents. It's as big as the whole of Asia.'

'Are we going to visit it?' I asked.

Thao didn't reply, which quite surprised me. It was the first time she had ignored my question. I thought perhaps my telepathic powers had not been sufficient and, so, I asked the question again, in French, raising my voice as I did so.

'Look over there,' she said.

Turning my head, I saw a veritable cloud of birds of every colour, about to cross our path. Fearing a collision with them, I descended several hundred metres. They skimmed by me at an incredible speed - but was it they who travelled so fast, or us? I thought perhaps it was our combined speeds that made them disappear so quickly but, just then, something astonished me greatly.

Looking above me, I saw that Thao and the others had not changed their altitude. How was it they hadn't collided with this winged squadron? Glancing at Thao, I realised she had followed my thoughts - and it occurred to me that the birds had appeared at quite an opportune time - just when I had posed my question.

Accustomed to Thao, I knew that she would have her reasons for 'ignoring' me, and I let the matter drop. I decided, instead, to take advantage of this opportunity to fly without wings and I allowed myself to become intoxicated by the colours around me, which gradually changed as the sun sank towards the horizon.

The pastel shades that washed over the sky, were of a majesty quite indescribable with my pen. I thought I had already witnessed all the symphonies of colour possible on this planet and yet I was mistaken.

From our altitude, the effect of the colours of the sky, sometimes contrasting with those of the ocean and sometimes complementing them perfectly, was spectacular. How incredible it was that Nature could coordinate such a range of colours, always changing, always beautiful... I felt again, the beginning of the 'drunkenness' which had previously caused me to faint, and received the order, brief and clear: 'Close your eyes immediately, Michel.'

I obeyed, and the sensation of drunkenness dissipated. However, it is not easy to pilot a Litiolac and to remain in formation with closed eyes - especially when one is a novice in the area. Inevitably, I strayed left and right, up and down.

Another order was given, this time less urgent: 'Watch Lationusi's back, Michel. Don't take your eyes off him and watch his wings.'

I opened my eyes to see Lationusi in front of me. Strangely, it did not surprise me at all that he had sprouted black wings and I fixed all my concentration on them. After a time, Thao approached me, saying in French:

'We're nearly there, Michel, Follow us.'

I found it equally natural that Lationusi had now lost his wings. I followed the group down towards the ocean, where we could make out, like a jewel on a coloured tablecloth, the island where my doko was situated. We approached rapidly amidst a fantastic blaze of colour as the sun dived into the waves. I had to hurry to my doko. 'Drunkenness', caused by the beauty of the colours, threatened to overwhelm me again, and I was obliged to close my eyes partially. We flew now at sea level and, before long, crossed the beach and plunged into the foliage surrounding my doko. My landing, however, was unsuccessful and I found myself inside the doko astride the back of a seat.

Latoli was immediately at my side. She pushed in the button of my Litiolac, asking me if I was all right.

'Yes, but those colours!' I stammered.

No one laughed at my little accident and everyone seemed a little sad. It was so unusual for them that I was quite thrown by it. We all sat down and helped ourselves to hydromel and dishes of red and green food.

I was not feeling very hungry. I had taken off my mask and was beginning to feel more like myself again. Night fell quickly, as it does on Thiaoouba and we sat in darkness. I remember wondering over the fact that, while I could barely distinguish each of them, they could see me as easily as if it were daylight.

No one spoke; we sat in silence. Looking up, I could see the stars appearing one by one, shining colourfully as though a firework display had 'frozen' in the sky. On Thiaoouba, because their layers of gasses in the atmosphere differ from ours, the stars appear to be coloured and also much larger than they appear to us on Earth.

Suddenly, I broke the silence asking, quite naturally, 'Where is Earth?'

As if the group had simply been waiting for this question, they all rose together. Latoli took me in her arms like a child and we went outside. The others led the way and we followed a wide path that led to the beach. There, on the moist sand of the shore, Latoli set me down.

Minute by minute, the firmament was illuminated by more stars as though a giant hand was lighting a chandelier.

Thao approached me and almost whispered in a voice that was sad and one I could hardly recognise as hers: 'do you see those four stars, Michel, just above the horizon? They almost form a square. The one on the top right is green and shinier than the others.'

'Yes, I think that's it - yes, it forms a square - the green, yes.'

'Now go to the right of the square and slightly higher. You will see two red stars quite close together.'

'Yes.'

'Keep your eye on the one on the right and go a tiny bit higher. Can you see a tiny white star? It's barely visible.'

'I think so... yes.'

'And on its left a little higher is a tiny yellow one.'

'Yes, that's right.'

'The tiny white one is the sun which lights up the planet Earth.'

'So, where is Earth?'

'Invisible from here, Michel. We are too far away.'

I remained there, staring at that minuscule star which seemed so insignificant in a sky filled with large colourful jewels. That minuscule star, however, was perhaps at that very moment warming my family and my home, making plants germinate and grow...

'My family' - the words seemed so strange. 'Australia' - from this perspective I had trouble imagining it to be the largest island on my planet, especially when even Earth was invisible to the naked eye. Yet, I'd been told we belonged to the same galaxy, and the universe comprised thousands of galaxies.

What were we, poor human bodies? Hardly much more than an atom.

Coming back 'home'

The sheets of galvanised iron on the roof creak under the burning rays of the sun, and even on the verandah, the heat is almost unbearable. I watch the delightful play of light and shadow in the garden and hear the song of the birds as they chase each other across a pale blue sky - and, I am sad.

I have just put the final full stop at the end of the twelfth chapter of this book I was asked to write. The task was not always easy. Often details would escape me and I would spend hours trying to recall certain things which Thao had said, and particular things she wanted me to write. Then, at the moment when I was totally exasperated, it would all come back to me - every detail, as if a voice was dictating the words over my shoulder, and I would write so much I would develop cramps in my hand. For periods of about three hours, sometimes more, sometimes less, images would crowd into my head.

While writing the book, with words jostling each other in my mind, I often wished I had known shorthand - and now, again, the strange sensation is back.

'Are you there, Thao?' I would ask, never receiving a reply. 'Is it one of you? Thao? Biastra? Latoli? Lationusi? I beg you to give me a sign, a sound. Please respond!'

'You called me?'

I had spoken aloud and my wife had come running. She stood in front of me, watching me closely.

'No.'

'You are doing this periodically, aren't you - talking to yourself. I will be glad when this book is finished and you 'come back to Earth,' literally!'

She left. Poor Lina. She certainly has not had an easy time of it, these past months. How must it have been for her? She got up one morning to find me stretched out on the sofa, deathly pale, having difficulty breathing and desperately wanting to sleep. I asked her if she had found my note.

'Yes,' she said, 'but where did you get to?'

'I know you're going to find this hard to believe, but I was picked up by extraterrestrials and taken to their planet. I will tell you everything, but for now, please, just let me sleep for as long as possible. I'll go to bed now - I stretched out here so as not to wake you.'

'Your tiredness is not, I suppose, due to some other reason?' Her tone was bitter-sweet and I could sense her concern. However, she let me sleep and it was a good thirty-six hours before I opened an eye. I woke to find Lina bending over me, with the anxious air of a nurse watching someone gravely ill.

'How are you?' she asked. 'I very nearly called the doctor. I haven't known you to sleep for so long without once stirring - and yet you were dreaming and calling out in your sleep. Who is the 'Arki' or 'Aki' you mentioned? And 'Thao'? Are you going to tell me?'

I smiled at her and kissed her. 'I'm going to tell you everything.' It occurred to me then, that thousands of husbands and wives must say that very same sentence, having no intention whatsoever of explaining 'everything'. I wished I'd said something a little less vulgar and common.

'Yes, I'm listening.'

'Good, and you must listen carefully, for what I have to say is serious - *very* serious. But I don't want to tell the same story twice. Call our son in, so I can tell you both.'

Three hours later, I had largely finished my account of the extraordinary adventure I'd had. Lina, who is the least credulous member of the family when it comes to such matters, had detected, by certain expressions and certain intonations in my voice, that something really serious had happened to me. When one lives twenty-seven years with a person, some things cannot be misunderstood.

I was besieged with questions, especially from my son, for he has always believed in the existence of other planets inhabited by intelligent beings.

'Do you have proof?' asked Lina. I was reminded of Thao's words - 'They seek proof, Michel, and always more proof.' I was a little disappointed the question came from my own wife.

'No, none, but when you read the book that I must write, you will know that I tell the truth. You won't have to 'believe' - you will *know*.

'Can you imagine me telling my friends: 'My husband has just come back from the planet Thiaoouba?'

I asked her to speak of the matter to no one, since my orders were not to speak, but first to write. I felt it was better that way, in any case, because words can be lost in the breeze whereas what is written, remains.

The days and months passed by and now the book is finished. All that remains to be done is to publish it. On this subject, Thao had assured me there would be few problems. This was in response to a question I had asked in the spacecraft on our return to Earth.

The 'spacecraft' - how many things that word brings to mind...

That last evening, on the beach, Thao had pointed out the minuscule star that is the sun that now made me perspire. We had then taken the flying platform and headed for the space base - quickly and without a word being spoken. A spaceship, prepared for immediate departure, awaited us. During our brief journey to the base, I had observed in the darkness, that the Auras of my companions were not shining as brilliantly as usual. The colours were more subdued and stayed closer to their bodies. This surprised me, but I said nothing.

When we boarded the spacecraft, I assumed we were going on a trip, perhaps with a specific mission, to a nearby planet. Thao had told me nothing.

Our take off went according to normal procedures and was uneventful. I watched as the golden planet became rapidly smaller, presuming that I'd be returning in a few hours time - or perhaps the next day. Several hours had elapsed before Thao finally addressed me again.

'Michel, I know you have noticed our sadness. It is very real, for there are certain partings that are sadder than others. My companions and I have become very attached to you and, if we are sad, it is because, at the end of this journey, we must part. We are taking you back to your planet.'

Again, I felt a twinge in the side of my stomach.

'I hope you won't hold it against us that we left so quickly. We did so to spare you the regrets one always has when one leaves a place one is fond of - and I know you are enormously fond of our planet, and our company. It's hard not to think, 'this is my last night' or 'this is the last time I will see this or that.'

I looked down and had absolutely nothing to say. We sat together in silence for some time. I felt heavy, as though my limbs and organs were weighted. I turned my head slowly towards Thao, looking at her surreptitiously. She seemed even sadder and something different was missing. Suddenly, I knew - it was her Aura.

'Thao, what's happening to me? I can't see your Aura any more.'

'It's normal, Michel. The great Thaori gave you your two gifts - the ability to see Auras and understand languages, to serve as tools in your learning, but only for a limited time.

'This time has just elapsed, but don't be saddened by the fact; after all, these are gifts you didn't have when you first joined us. What you do take back is knowledge that you and millions of your fellow beings can profit from.

'Isn't that more important than understanding languages or being able to see Auras when you aren't able to read them? It is the reading of Auras that counts, after all - not the perceiving of them.'

I accepted her reasoning, but was disappointed nonetheless, for I had soon become accustomed to the radiance around these people.

'Don't be sorry, Michel,' said Thao, reading my thoughts. 'On your planet, most people don't have radiant Auras - far from it. The thoughts and concerns of millions of Earthlings are so closely related to material matters, that their Auras are quite dull; you'd have been disappointed.'

I looked at her closely; very conscious of the fact that soon I would see her no more. In spite of her large size, she was so well proportioned; her pleasant pretty face was without a wrinkle; her mouth, her nose, her eyebrows - all were perfect. Suddenly, the question that had been brewing in my subconscious mind for so long sprung to mind almost involuntarily.

'Thao, is there a reason for you all being hermaphrodites?'

'Yes, and it is important, Michel. I was surprised you didn't ask that question sooner.

'You see, as we exist on a superior planet, all we have that is material, is also superior, as you have seen for yourself. Our various bodies, including the physical body, must also be superior, and in this domain, we have progressed as far as it is possible to progress. We can regenerate our bodies, prevent them from dying, resuscitate them and even, sometimes, create them. But in a physical body, there are other bodies, such as the astral - indeed, there are nine altogether. Those which interest us at the moment, are the fluidic body and the physiological body. The fluidic body influences the physiological body which, in turn, influences the physical body.

'In the fluidic body, you possess six principal points which we call Karolas and which the yogis on your planet call Chakras. The first Chakra is the one situated between your two eyes, just a centimetre and a half above your nose. It's the 'brain' of your fluidic body, if you like; it corresponds to the pineal gland, which is placed much further back in your physical brain but on exactly the same level. It was by placing a finger on this Chakra that one of the Thaori was able to liberate in you the gift of understanding languages.

'Now, at the bottom of the fluidic body and just above the sex organs, is found a very important Chakra, which we call the Mouladhara, and which your yogis call Sacred. Above this Chakra, and meeting the spinal column, is the Palantius.

'It is in the form of a coiled spring and only reaches the base of the spinal column when it is relaxed.

'For it to become relaxed, it requires the accomplishment of the sexual act between two partners who must not only love one another, but also have a spiritual affinity between them. Only at that moment and under these conditions will the Palantius extend to the spinal column, transferring an energy and special gifts to the physiological body which then affects the physical body. The person concerned will experience happiness in sexual enjoyment that is far greater than normal.

'When, on your planet, you hear such expressions among people very much in love as: 'we were in seventh heaven', 'we felt light', or 'we were floating on air', you can be sure the couples were in physical and spiritual accord and 'made for one another' - at least for a while.

'Certain Tantrists on Earth have attained this point, but it isn't common among them, for still their religions, with ridiculous rituals and prohibitions, create a real obstacle to attaining this goal. When they look at the forest, they don't see the trees.

'Let's go back to our loving couple: The man has experienced great pleasure transformed into beneficial vibrations for the Palantius, thanks to a love which is genuine, and absolute compatibility. All these sensations of happiness were released by the accomplishment of the sexual act. The sensations of happiness are not the same with the female, but the process is the same with her.

'Now, to answer your question. On our planet, with bodies that are both male and female, we can achieve, at will, the sensations, both male and female. Of course, this brings us a much greater range of sexual pleasure than if we were mono-sexual. Further, our fluidic body can be at its best. Our appearance is, needless to say, more feminine than masculine -at least where our faces and breasts are concerned. Don't you agree, Michel, that, as a general rule, a woman has a prettier face than a man? Well, we prefer to have faces that are pretty, rather than unattractive.'

'What do you think of homosexuality?'

'The homosexual, female as well as male, is a neurotic (when it is not a matter of hormones) and neurotics can't be condemned but, like all neurotics, they should seek treatment. In all things, Michel, consider what Nature has decreed and you will have the answers to your questions.

'Nature gave every living thing the possibility of reproduction, (so) that various species might continue. According to the Creator's will, males and females have been created in all species. With human beings, however, and for the reasons we have already explained, he added features not given to other species. For example, a woman can bloom in sexual fulfilment, achieving a range of sexual sensations that can release the Palantius and bring about vast improvements in her physical body by way of the fluidic body.

That can happen over numerous days of the month without her becoming pregnant. A cow, on the other hand, will accept the bull only during a certain few hours of the month and, then, it is motivated only by the drive to procreate. When in calf she is no longer receptive to a bull's 'advances'. There you have a comparison between two of Nature's creations. The first is quite a special being, possessing nine bodies, whereas the second possesses only three bodies. Evidently, the Creator has taken special care to place, within us, much more than a physical body. Sometimes, on your planet, these special things are referred to as 'divine sparks' - and it is an appropriate comparison.'

'What do you think of deliberate abortion?'

'Is it a natural act?'

'No, of course not.'

'Then why do you ask - you already know the answer.'

I recall that Thao remained as though lost in thought for quite some time - looking at me without speaking; then she resumed:

'For approximately one hundred and forty years on your planet, man has been accelerating the destruction of Nature and the pollution of the environment. This has happened since the discovery of steam power and the combustion engine. You have but a few years left in which to arrest the pollution before the situation becomes irreversible. One of the principal pollutants on Earth is the petrol- driven engine and this could be replaced immediately with a hydrogen engine that would cause no pollution, so to speak. On certain planets, this is called the 'clean motor'. Prototypes for such an engine have been constructed by various engineers on your planet but they *must* be industrially manufactured in order to replace petrol engines. Not only would this measure mean a seventy per cent reduction in current levels of pollution by combustion waste, but it would also be more economical for consumers.

'The big petrol corporations had been terrified at the idea of this motor being popularised for it would mean loss of sales for their oil and subsequent financial ruin.

'Governments, too, who impose enormous taxes on these oils, would suffer equally. You see, Michel, it always comes back to money. Because of it, you have a whole economic and financial context that opposes progress towards radical change in the interest of all human life on Earth.

'The people on Earth allow themselves to be pushed around, bullied, exploited and led to the abattoirs by political and financial cartels which are sometimes even associated with well-known sects and religions.

'When these cartels fail to win the people with clever advertising campaigns intended to brainwash them, they try to succeed through political channels, and next through religion or through a clever blend of the lot.

'Great men wanting to do something for mankind have simply been done away with. Martin Luther King is one example; Ghandi is another.

'But the people of Earth can no longer allow themselves to be treated as fools and led to the abattoirs like flocks of sheep by leaders that they, themselves, have democratically elected. The people form the vast majority. In a nation of one hundred million inhabitants, it is absurd that a group of financiers comprising perhaps a thousand individuals can decide the fate of the others - like the butcher does at the abattoir.

'Such a group has well and truly stifled the business of the hydrogen motor so that it is no longer mentioned.

'These people couldn't care less what might happen to your planet in years to come. Selfishly, they seek their gains, expecting to be dead before 'whatever is going to happen' happens. If the Earth disappears, as a result of horrific cataclysms, they assume they will already be dead.

'There, they are making a big mistake, for the source of the coming disasters is the pollution which is growing daily on your planet, and its consequences will be felt very soon - much sooner than you can imagine. The people of Earth must not do as the child forbidden to play with fire; the child is without experience and, in spite of the prohibition, he disobeys and burns himself. Once burnt, he 'knows' that the adults were right. He won't play with fire again but he will pay for his disobedience by suffering for several days afterwards.

'Unfortunately, in the case that concerns us, the consequences are much more serious than the burn of a child. It's the destruction of your entire planet that is at risk - with *no second chance* if you don't place your trust in those who want to help you.

'It interests us to see that recently established ecological movements are gaining in momentum and power; and that the young people of Earth are 'carrying' other sensible people along with them in their fight against pollution.

'There is only one solution, as Arki told you - the grouping of individuals. A group is only as powerful as it is large. Those whom you call the conservationists are becoming stronger and stronger and will continue to do so. But it is *vital* that people forget their hatred, their resentment, and especially their political and racial differences. This group must be internationally united - and don't tell me that is so difficult - for already on Earth there exists a non-violent and very large international organisation - the International Red Cross, which has been functioning effectively for quite some time.

'It is essential that this conservationist group include in its programs not only the conservation of the environment from direct damage but from indirect damage as well, such as that which results from smoke: exhaust fumes from vehicles, smoke from factories, and so on.

'The waste water from large towns and factories, which is chemically treated, is also harmful and empties into *river systems* and *oceans.* Smoke from the USA has already caused more than forty lakes in Canada to become sterile by means of the acid rains it provoked. The same thing is occurring in Northern Europe due to pollution from French factories and the German Rhur.

'Now we come to another kind of pollution that is of no small concern, though people might readily dismiss it. As the great Thaora told you, *noise* is one of the most noxious pollutants for it upsets your electrons and unbalances your physical compartment. I haven't yet mentioned these electrons to you and I see that you are not following me very well.

'A normal human Astral body contains approximately four billion, trillion electrons. These electrons have a life span of approximately ten billion, trillion of your years. They were created at the moment of creation. Your Astral body contains them and, when you die, nineteen per cent rejoin the electrons of the universe until required by Nature to form a new body or a new tree or animal, and the eighty one per cent rejoin your Higher-self.'

'I don't quite follow you,' I interrupted.

'I know, but I intend helping you to understand. An Astral body is not quite what you would call a pure spirit. On Earth, there is a belief that the spirit is made of nothing. This is false. The Astral body is composed of billions of electrons, exactly marrying your physical shape. Each of these electrons has a 'memory' and each is capable of retaining as much information as is contained in all the books that fill the shelves of an average town library.

'I see you are staring wide-eyed at me, but it is as I say. This information is coded, like a microfilm containing all the plans of an industrial installation that a spy would be able to pass in a cufflink, though much more miniaturised than that. Certain physicists on Earth are now aware of this fact but the public, at large, hasn't been informed of it. Your Astral body transmits and receives messages, by means of these electrons, through the channel of your brain, to, and from your Higher-self. Information is being transmitted without you being aware of it, thanks to a weak electric current from your brain in harmony with your electrons.

'Since it is the Higher-self which sent this Astral body into your physical body, it is in the natural order of things that your Higher-self should receive information from your Astral body.

'Like all things electronic, the Astral body — tool of the Higher-self — is quite a delicate tool. During your waking hours it is capable of sending messages of extreme urgency to the Higher-self but the Higher-self seeks much more than that.

So, during sleep, your Astral body leaves your physical body to rejoin the Higher-self, either passing on required information or receiving information or orders. You have an old saying in French that: 'the night brings counsel'. This saying emerged from common experience. Over the course of years, people noticed that, on waking in the mornings, they often had the solutions to their problems.

'Sometimes this is so and sometimes it isn't. If the 'solution' will be profitable to the Higher-self you can be sure that it will be presented to you - if not, you will wait in vain.

'Now, those people who, through very advanced and special exercises, are able to detach their astral bodies from their physical bodies, will be able to see a light, silvery-blue thread, such as you saw yourself, linking their physical and astral bodies. Their Astral bodies, likewise, are visible during the time that the separation lasts. It is these same electrons which form your Astral body and which create the visible effect of the thread.

'I see that you follow what I am saying and that you have grasped my point. Let me finish by explaining the dangers of noise. Noise directly attacks the electrons of your Astral body creating parasites, to use a radio and television term. If you are watching a television screen and notice several white spots, this is an indication that a small 'parasite' is at work. Similarly, if someone is operating an electric tool next door to your house, such large parasites will be produced on your screen that the image will distort completely.

'The same thing occurs with the Astral body, but unfortunately you won't be aware of it in the same way that you are with a television screen; and, it's much worse, since noise *damages* your electrons. And yet people say: 'Oh, we get used to it.' Your brain 'tenses', so to speak and your psyche initiates self-defence mechanisms, but not so the Astral body; a parasite invades its electrons - which, of course, has disastrous repercussions for your Higher-self

'The sounds that reach your ears are clearly very important. A particular piece of music can elevate you to a state of euphoria, while another piece, although very pretty, will have no effect on you or, perhaps, irritate you. Try an experiment: take a piece of soft violin, piano or flute music that you like and play it as loudly as you can. The suffering of your eardrums will not be as great as the discomfort you'll feel within. Most of your fellow human beings on Earth consider noise pollution to be of negligible concern, but the noise of the exhaust pipe of a motor bike is three to four times worse than the noxious fumes that it discharges. While the fumes affect your throat and your lungs, the noise affects your Astral body.

'However, no one has ever been able to take a photograph of your Astral body and, so, people don't concern themselves with it!

'Since your fellow earthlings like proof, let them consider this: there are people on Earth who are sincere and who claim to have seen ghosts - I don't refer to charlatans.

'What they have seen is actually the nineteen per cent of electrons that don't comprise the Astral body. These electrons detach themselves from the physical body three days after its death. Indeed, as a result of certain effects of static electricity, these electrons can be seen having the same form as the physical body. Sometimes, before being re-utilised by Nature, they are 'vacant', but they, too, have memories and return to 'haunt' places they knew - places they loved or hated.'

'Or *hated*?

'Yes, but you'd need to write not one, but two books, if we were to concern ourselves with this subject.'

'Can you see into my future? Surely you can, since you are able to do things which are much more difficult.'

'You are correct. We have 'pre-viewed' your whole life - right up to the death of your present physical body.'

'When will I die?'

'You know very well that I won't tell you, so why do you ask? It is very bad to know the future and those who have their fortunes told commit a double error. First, the fortune teller might be a charlatan, and second, it is contrary to Nature to know what the future holds, for otherwise, the knowledge would not be effaced in the 'river of oblivion'.'

'Many people believe in the influence of the stars, and follow the signs of the Zodiac. What do you think of that?'

To this, Thao didn't reply but she smiled...

The entire return journey was like the first trip had been. We made no stops, but I was able, again, to admire the suns, the comets, the planets and the colours.

When I asked Thao if I would be taken back by way of the parallel universe again, she replied in the affirmative. I wondered why and she explained that it was the best way since it meant that they didn't have to contend with the reactions of witnesses.

I was re-deposited in my garden exactly *nine days* after leaving it and, once again, in the middle of the night.

Postscript

I am adding this postscript to my manuscript having completed my writing three years ago. During those three years, I tried unsuccessfully to have it published, until I met Arafura Publishing, who had the courage to publish such an extraordinary, unique story.

It was a difficult time for me, as contrary to my expectations, Thao didn't leave me any signs. I didn't have any contact, either telepathic or physical, apart from a strange apparition one day in Cairns, which was no doubt intended to prove that I was still being watched over, but there was no message. I now realise that the delay with the publisher was premeditated. Therefore, through a natural chain of events, Thao then took only two months to bring my book to the attention of the most suitable publisher.

They — Thao and her people — intended it to be that way, because three years ago the world wasn't ready to receive the message, whereas *now,* it is. That may seem strange at first, but not to me. Knowing them as I do, I know that they are capable of timing events down to the *very second,* if they think that they'll have the best impact a few seconds later.

During those three years, I allowed a few friends and acquaintances to read the manuscript and *that* is when I fully understood why they wanted me to write this book and why they 'physically' transported me to their planet. I insist on the word 'physically' because the most frequent response is, 'you must have been dreaming, you must have had a series of dreams'.

Whatever their reaction, everybody who has read the manuscript, has been fascinated by its contents. There are three types of readers:

• The first, who form the majority, have said they still don't believe I went to another planet, but have admitted they were moved by the book. In any case, they have said, it doesn't really matter whether or not it happened, what matters is the *powerful underlying message.*

• The second, is the former sceptic who, having read the book three times in a row, is convinced that my story *is* factual, and this reader *is right.*

• The third, is already more evolved from the outset, and *knows* from the outset that this is a true story.

I am, however, compelled to give the reader a word of advice. This book must be read and reread at least *three* times. Of the fifteen or so people who have read it, each has had something pertinent to say and has questioned me at length about it. A friend of mine is a psychology professor at a French university. Apparently, she has already read it three times, and keeps it on her bedside table. I can relate to that!

Nonetheless, I've had one reaction (fortunately only the one) from a friend, which upset me. He asked me, for example, whether the spacecraft was assembled with bolts or rivets and whether there were telegraph poles on Thiaoouba. I strongly recommended that he reread the manuscript. Another of his 'remarks' was that the book should contain more battles between spacecraft or planets, with missiles and deadly weapons. 'That's what people really like', he said. I had to remind him that this *was not* a science-fiction novel. In this case I don't think my friend is really *capable* of understanding this book, so he would be better off reading something else: he isn't ready for it yet, but unfortunately, he isn't alone. If you, the reader, were expecting to be aroused by space battles, blood, sex and violence, planets exploding and spitting out monsters, I'm sorry, you have wasted your time and money: you should have bought a science-fiction novel instead. You were warned in the preface. I urge you, now that you know this is *not* a science-fiction story, to reread it in a different frame of mind, that is, objectively and positively, in which case you won't have wasted your time. On the contrary, for the money you have spent, you will receive the greatest reward of your life - a spiritual rather than material reward - isn't that the most important kind?

From the people who have already read my manuscript, I have had a variety of feedback concerning religion, and in particular Christianity. I feel obliged to respond on that issue. If you are religious, and in particular Christian, and have been shocked by the 'Biblical rectifications', especially in the passage on the true identity of Christ who died on the cross, I am sorry; however I must *stress* that this book was not written with the intention of criticising *any religion whatsoever,* and that these are *not* my personal observations, but rather, the words of the Master of the Thaori, with the details *'dictated'* to me by Thao.

They recommended that I record *precisely* those things that were explained to me, and that I change *nothing.* I have followed their instructions.

I have had many other conversations with Thao which do not appear in this book. Believe me, these Beings are superior to us in their evolution, in *every* regard. I have learned things which are more incredible than those revealed in this volume, but I am not permitted to discuss them, as we are still far from understanding them. I will, however, take the opportunity in this postscript to voice my personal opinion.

I must warn the reader on some very important points.

I have already heard some remarks concerning this book that haven't impressed me at all: 'He thinks he's the new Christ'. 'He's a great Guru. We should follow his doctrine' or 'You should set up an Ashram, that would go down well', or yet still, 'You should found a new religion', and so on.

I must say in their defence that many of these people have only *heard* about my adventure. They haven't actually read the book. I cannot emphasise enough that it must be read *several* times. Why are people so eager to *hear* about something as important as God and the creation of the Universe, when they could be quietly reading about it, away from the noisy congregations? Remember, 'the spoken word vanishes, but the written word remains'.

Why do they want to form a *new* sect or religion with the contents of this book? The hundreds of religions we already have on this planet haven't done much good, have they?

The Moslems fought against the Roman Catholics during the Crusades, in the name of God and religion.

The Spanish Catholics plundered, raped and pillaged the Aztecs (whose civilisation was very advanced for the time) because the Aztecs did not practise Catholicism. In fact, the Aztecs had their own religion, which was no better since they sacrificed humans to their gods by the thousands, as did, if you recall, the Bakaratinians during the secession in North Africa, over one million years ago.

These religions had been carefully studied by the priests who wanted to keep the people under their rule, so that they could maintain power and wealth.

Any religion is like politics - with its leaders' arrogance and thirst for power. Christ mounted a donkey, he died on the cross, a religion was born, the donkey transformed into a Rolls-Royce...the Vatican is one of the wealthiest powers on this planet.

In politics, the insincere politician, and there are many of them, is puffed up with pride. He wants to be admired, along with his wealth and power and only then is he satisfied.

And what about the thousands or millions of people cheated by him, are they satisfied..?

Thao told me that this book is not only intended to enlighten the inhabitants of this planet, but also to open their eyes - wake them up to what is happening around them. Thao and her people are very concerned about the ways in which we allow ourselves to be led by a handful of rotten politicians, who skilfully make us believe we are free and democratic, when, in relation to the Universal Law, we are no freer than a flock of sheep. We may occasionally stray from the path and *think* we are free, but that's an illusion, because we end up in the meatworks without even realising it.

The politicians use the word democracy like a smoke screen. The majority of politicians have three gods - power, glory and *money*. They are, nonetheless, afraid of the masses because as Arki (See Chapter 10) demonstrated, groups of people who really get on well can achieve exactly what they want. Even the Communist party in Russia has now collapsed, and the world knows, the KGB was a vicious and powerful organisation, but I must admit, my - or rather *our* friends - avoided a huge amount of bloodshed by giving the 'go-ahead'. I've known this for a long time, and they may have deliberately delayed the publication of this book

157

so that I could include this in the postscript.

Remember that mankind was created with freedom of choice. All totalitarian regimes deny this, and they will collapse one day. I advise you to turn your attention to China...

The leaders of many countries, who have been elected in a so-called democratic fashion, just do as they like, once they're in power. A typical example is the French government, which is still carrying out nuclear testing in the Pacific and polluting with radiation the last great resource we have left, namely the *ocean*. I already know from a reliable source that the French scientists in Mururoa are very concerned about the 'gigantism' that affects some species of fish, particularly the parrot-fish, which has been subjected to atomic radiation in the area around Mururoa. These fish have grown to *three times* their natural size. Let's hope the same doesn't happen to the great white shark, which is found in our waters!

Furthermore, if you carefully follow the dates of the underwater explosions at Mururoa, you will notice that in the hours later (but more commonly two to four days after the event) there is *always* a large-scale earthquake somewhere on the planet, following the explosion, of course...

French politicians have thus been committing a crime on a planetary scale for several decades. I am sorry and ashamed to have been born French.

Sadam Hussein also committed a crime against the planet when he set light to hundreds of oil wells. He should *also* be tried for the atrocities he committed in Kuwait. What is the United Nations doing about it?

In Brazil, the governments that are systematically destroying the Amazon rainforests, *and* their own next generation, are also committing a crime on a planetary scale.

The people who say that the *system* must change are doing nothing about it. Everybody is grumbling about the bad penal system we have. Of course it is bad, the laws appear to have been made in favour of crooks. So *do* something about it!

Remember the penal system of the Bakaratinians? It wasn't unlike the Aztec system, which was excellent because of its efficiency.

It isn't enough to say 'the system is bad, they should change it'. *They* - whom do we mean by They? The parliamentarians, the heads of state, all those elected by the people, by *you*. In order to change the system, the laws must change, along with their leaders. *You* must force the politicians who represent *you* to change the inefficient laws, the inefficient *system,* once and for all. The politicians are generally too idle to undertake the task on their own. Each law requires a great deal of work and responsibility, and that's often too much to ask, because, as I've said, most of them are there for the prestige and big salary. Incidentally, if you want to attract good politicians, start by cutting their salary to that of a suburban bank manager and you will find that there are fewer applicants, but those who remain will be sincere human beings and *genuinely* want to do something for the people.

You are the people who voted for these politicians and most of you have had enough - they *haven't* done what you expected them to do for our country. Some day, the time will come when the citizens must force them to do their jobs: to fulfil the promises they made to the majority who elected them, before the election.

When there is no other solution, ordinary citizens can force politicians to do their duty - they *must*.

Careful - we are *not* talking about anarchy here, just discipline. In a country you need the discipline, not of a totalitarian regime, but of a democracy in which *promises are kept*. If promises are broken, it is up to you to act because it is abhorrent that politicians disappoint millions of people when they're in power and fool people until the *next* election.

These eminent politicians would be better off doing their jobs rather than spending 80 per cent of their time arguing among themselves over internal party politics.

People say to you, 'What can we do? There's nothing *we* can do', and that is *exactly* where they are wrong!

Ordinary people can and *must* force the government elected by the people and by referendum, to carry out the tasks for which they were elected.

Ordinary people possess enormous power. As Arki said *(See* Chapter 10) one of the greatest weapons that humans possess - thanks to their intelligence - is the power of inertia. It is a *non-violent* force and that is best, as violence breeds more violence. Christ said, 'He who lives by the sword will die by the sword'.

In Beijing, China, a man on his own *and* unarmed was able to stop a tank with his presence alone. How did he achieve that? Because the soldiers in the tank didn't DARE run him over, they were enthralled by the self-sacrificing act of the unarmed man.

Millions of people witnessed it on television.

Ghandi managed, on his own, to prevent terrible bloodshed. Lord Mountbatten himself realised that if he'd sent 50 000 troops to Calcutta, they would have been massacred and yet, Gandhi, *one man,* averted a massacre through non-violent means.

Once, in Arki's planet, they blocked the roads with so-called 'broken down' vehicles: there were 10 000 of them. The police contingent knew it was done on purpose, but they couldn't do anything about it. When the fire brigade or an ambulance had to pass, the people arranged to let them through by pushing their vehicles out of the way. They then pushed them back to where they were. *That is* the power of inertia. They didn't move; didn't eat; didn't scream. They were silent - confronting the forces of law and order. Obviously, they said, they would be more than happy to clear the road - but how could they, without mechanics..? The country was paralysed. They had no banners, no slogans, there was no shouting or yelling; just quiet defiance.

They waited to hear from their adversary, who was sinking deeper and deeper into his lies and deceitfulness. A letter had already been sent to the government, which was well aware of their demands and *knew* why they were there. The name of the person who sent the letter was Mr Citizen...

As Arki said, when 100 000 people calmly lie down on a tarmac, a railway line or in the streets and say to the police, 'I want to go home, please take me home, I am ill, I beg you to take me home', the police couldn't possibly hurl tear-gas into a crowd of sick people, for no reason, could they?

With the power of inertia, the people brought the entire nation to a standstill, *without violence.*

The outcome was quick to follow. The 'fat financiers', who carried much financial control in the business world (the stock market crash, the rise and fall of gold prices) and were in cahoots with the corrupt politicians, started to panic because they stood to lose millions of dollars in the market.

For every coin the people in the street lost by not working, they were losing hundreds of thousands. So, in the name of their sacred money, they had to do something - and the *people* won.

Little by little, you're being conditioned. That's what our extra-terrestrial friends are concerned about. You're a human being, not a robot. WAKE UP NOW.

Have you ever wondered, just to give you an example, what would happen if the electricity went out in a supermarket with the new cash registers and the new barcode system of recording prices? The check-out assistants wouldn't even be able to add up the goods - the codes on most articles would make it an impossible task. Has it ever crossed your minds that the encoding stops you, *the consumer* from knowing the price of a tin of baked beans, unless you go through the list you're given? But that's an arduous task. So you are less and less aware of how much you're spending and, *imperceptibly,* the financiers take control of *your* own money.

I knew a charming little shopkeeper who had a problem with his cash register. I arrived while it was being repaired. He sold me two articles at one dollar thirty eight cents each. It took him about three minutes to work out the total on a piece of paper, and he ended up giving me two dollars thirty four change from the five dollars I had handed him, simply because he'd lost the habit of making such a simple addition, even on paper. He trusts the machine, as do thousands of others like him. People put their trust in credit cards and computers, they're wrong because, imperceptibly, they're no longer thinking for themselves, they're letting the financiers add up for them. Imperceptibly, they're no longer 'in control'.

Let's do a little experiment together, and you'll see what I'm talking about.

Are you ready? Right, a few lines up, I did an addition for you and explained that I'd bought two dollars seventy six worth of goods, and that the shopkeeper handed me two dollars thirty four in change from five dollars. Fortunately, you weren't the shopkeeper, as I would have made you lose ten cents. I did that deliberately to catch you out. If, however, you are among those who stopped when reading the paragraph to check the sum, then that indicates that you're not easily led. If you fall into the second category, of those who didn't check, you'd better change your attitude *now*. You're a human being, containing a Divine fragment, be proud of it, and stop behaving like a sheep.

You've already read this book to the end, that's wonderful in itself. Wonderful? Yes, because that shows that you are interested in more than just your steak and chips, hamburger, sauerkraut or a glass of beer. So there you go!

What I have to say next is directly aimed at the millions of young people around the world. Everything Thao asked me to write, and, of course, everything I've just added, apply equally to young people, but I want to add a message *specially* for them.

My friends, the great number of you who have lost hope, are unemployed, bored or packed into towns, why don't you radically change your lifestyle? Instead of stagnating in unhealthy environments, you can organise yourselves along a completely different path.

Here, I'm talking about Australia in particular, as I don't exactly know what sorts of resources other countries have; however, the fundamentals could undoubtedly apply to all countries.

Get together, organise yourselves and ask the government to lease cultivatable land to you on a 99-year contract (there *is* such land available, believe me). That way you can create communal farms where you'll be self-sufficient. You'll have the satisfaction and pride of proving to those around you that you're not 'bludgers', that you are doing even better than a nation. You could even set up a 'county' with your own rules and internal disciplines, while *still respecting* those of the country you live in.

I'm convinced that a good government would happily give you a 'push in the right direction'. (It wastes so much money anyway, that for once, it would be giving out money for a great cause.)

Of course, you'll have to act responsibly because all the disparagers will be ready to pounce on you, since they're convinced you're 'no hopers'. Personally, I have complete faith in you, faith - that *you,* the young generation, will build a *better world,* cleaner and more spiritual. Is the message of the Thaori not addressed to you?

Hence, you must prove to be responsible and create your own rules. No drugs for a start, because as you know, drugs are disturbing your astral body which is your real self, and you don't need them at all. Those of you whose friends have fallen into that trap, will find a way out with your help - if they want. You have a huge job ahead of you, not only in helping your peers, but also in reorganising your lives along the new path. You will thereby discover untold joys. From a material perspective, you will make a 'return to nature' and you will be the first to do this seriously. What do you need for your survival? Air, water, bread, vegetables and meat.

You can achieve all those things on your own, and without using chemical products again. The Israeli 'kibbutz' functions perfectly. You may function even better because, in Australia, you are multi-cultural. Still it's not a question of outdoing others; it's a question of living well, and with self-respect. Then, on the spiritual and entertainment side, you'll have your own discos. A disco is just as much fun in the open countryside as in a town, you know! Your own libraries, your own theatres where you'll be able to create and perform your own plays. There'll be chess, table tennis, tennis, bowls, billiards, soccer, netball, archery, fencing, sail boarding, horse riding surfing, fishing, the list goes on... Some may prefer classical dancing, others, martial arts. You'll avoid violent games that engender too much animosity.

You can see that there are countless things you can do in nature, *many more than on some street corner, in any town.*

Your physical and spiritual well-being will benefit greatly from yoga. I'd like to insist on this discipline, and especially on the breathing through the chakras. Thirty minutes of yoga every morning and night would be perfect.

You are the new generation and most of you have understood that you must go WITH nature and the environment, and not AGAINST it.

Most of the idiots who go against nature will criticise you when you demonstrate, with good cause, for the preservation of trees. They pejoratively call you a 'greenie' or a 'hippy'. Prove to the whole world and mainly to yourselves that you can practise what you preach, because when you start working on your communal farm, you'll be able to do even more to preserve the environment; you'll even be able to create forests. Choose from among your groups some responsible people, not *bosses* or *masters,* but responsible people, *advisers,* who will be elected democratically. I'm convinced that you'll be able to show the whole world that you can do a better job than nations led by shady politicians, and in the name of the UNIVERSE, I thank you.

Thao told you *(See* Chapter 9) that religion and politics are two of the worst banes of society.

Therefore, if you intend to inundate my publisher with letters, that you want me to answer or with the suggestion that I become your guru or create a religion, think again. You'll be going against my will as well as the will of the Thaori and Thao, and you won't get anywhere.

Thao told you, 'The greatest temple of man is *inside* him; it is there that he can communicate at any time with the creator, his creator, using meditation and concentration through the intermediary of his

Higher-self.'

Don't speak to me about building temples, churches, cathedrals, ashrams or anything else.

Look *inside* yourself and you'll notice that you possess everything you need to communicate with Him, simply because it is HE who placed it there.

Finally, I'd like to finish by saying this: as the humble servant of Thao and the Thaori, who requested that I write this work, I want to remind you, for the last time, that whatever religion there is and whether you believe in one thing or another, that will *in no way* change what has been established by the great SPIRIT, GOD THE CREATOR - You can call HIM what you like.

No religion, no belief and no book, not even this one, will affect the truth and the order established by HIM in the universe.

Rivers will *always* flow from their source towards the ocean, even if a religion, a sect or billions of people want to *believe* the opposite.

The only TRUE, IMMUTABLE thing is the law of the CREATOR, the one He WANTED in the beginning, the UNIVERSAL Law, HIS LAW, and absolutely NOBODY will EVER be able to change that.

M. J. P. Desmarquet.

Cairns, Australia, April 1993

Printed in Great Britain
by Amazon

81254279R00098